Mrs. M. W. Martin.

from her pupils

Max + Charley.

BUREAU OF ILLUSTRATION.BUFFALO.

PRAYER

AND ITS

Remarkable Answers:

BEING A STATEMENT OF FACTS IN THE LIGHT
OF REASON AND REVELATION.

BY

WILLIAM W. PATTON, D. D.,

LATE EDITOR-IN-CHIEF OF THE ADVANCE, AUTHOR OF "THE YOUNG MAN," "CONSCIENCE AND LAW," "SPIRITUAL VICTORY," ETC.

CHICAGO:
J. S. GOODMAN.
CINCINNATI: C. F. VENT. SAN FRANCISCO: F. DEWING & Co.
1876.

MARDER, LUSE & CO.
ELECTROTYPERS AND STEREOTYPERS,
CHICAGO.

PREFACE.

AND is there room for another book on Prayer, after the treatises upon this fruitful theme, from the time of the Christian Fathers to the present day? In answering this inquiry, one must remember, that each age of the world must have its own literature. There must then be books to meet present phases of religious experience, even if the truths discussed made part of the most ancient faith. Prayer has had its interest, as a doctrine and as a practice, in all the centuries, and it is still the strength of the believer, and the scoff of the infidel. An attempt is made in this volume to give, in a popular form, the facts and the philosophy of the subject. It is written for the people; yet it assumes that they are neither children nor fools, and will welcome an intelligent discussion of a fundamental question. The first seven chapters aim, therefore, to elucidate the nature, characteristics, methods and conditions of Prayer; to show its true place in the system of the universe; and to answer the specious objections of the skeptics. The argument is designed to be thorough, without being dry and abstruse.

But the chief aim of the book is to furnish authentic facts, so grouped and explained, in the light of the principles set forth in the early chapters, as to dispel doubt, and encourage a rational and Scriptural faith. The answers to prayer have been drawn from a wide region of investigation. A few from the olden time have been inserted, but, for obvious reasons, preference has been given to those of recent date. These have been furnished by Christian brethren to an extent which compelled the author to use only a selection; but his hearty thanks are equally returned to all who have thus aided his researches, whether he has had space to insert their communications, or not. A few Christians, who deny the practical value of such testimony to the power of Prayer, will find their ideas curiously represented, and, it is trusted, satisfactorily discussed, in the concluding chapter.

These answers to prayer are styled "Remarkable," not because it is at all strange in itself, that such things should take place, under the divine government, but only that they appear so to the incredulity of the world, and to the weak faith of the church. If there were more real prayer, the striking answers would be everyday occurrences. The facts cited are made the subject of discriminating comment, to preserve the reader from unwarrantable inferences, and the embrace of theories which work delusion instead of faith. The desire of the author has been to produce a volume which should be welcomed by every pastor, as helpful to the progress of piety in his church, and which should encourage the Christian to ask and expect great blessings for himself and for others.

CHICAGO, ILL., Dec. 1st, 1875.

CONTENTS.

CHAPTER I.

PRAYER CHARACTERISTIC OF PIETY.

The cloud of incense ever rising—Thoughtful heathen and Mohammedans pray—A proof of conversion—The history of piety, the history of prayer—The Old Testament worthies—Also New Testament saints—Jesus and his disciples—Later history of the church—Martin Luther, quotations and Anecdotes—John Calvin—John Knox—Anecdotes—Melanchthon—Gustavus Adolphus—Philip Henry—Samuel Rutherford—Jonathan Edwards—David Brainerd—R. M. McCheyne—Thomas Arnold—Henry Martyn—James B. Taylor—Harlan Page—Normand Smith, Jr.—Montgomery's "Call to Prayer." 17-32

CHAPTER II.

WHAT TRUE PRAYER IS.

Importance of definite ideas—Christians who explain away Prayer—Accept God's explanation—Bible treats largely of this topic—F. W. Robertson's view; prayer is simply an act of submission to the Divine will—Prayer more than religious meditation—Is a direct address to God—Includes adoration, confession, thanksgiving and petition—Adoration, its idea and use—Illustrated by Daniel and Jesus—Confession, its necessity and effect—Cases of Abraham and Daniel—Thanksgiving, its propriety—Language of the Psalms, of Jesus, and of Paul—Petition, the object and heart of prayer

—Robertson's theory further stated—Similar views of a Western minister—Also of an Eastern minister—The Instincts of nature, and the words of Scripture contradict it—Ludicrous absurdity—The commands opposed to it—Also the promises—Also the form of reported prayers, of Jesus, David, Hannah, Daniel, the Church of Jerusalem, and a host of others—Also the specific answers recorded for Instruction and encouragement—Lines of Trench on value of prayer..33–48

CHAPTER III.

WHY PRAYER PREVAILS.

Inquiry for the principle that underlies prayer—Does God need human permission; or an increase of knowledge; or an improvement of disposition; or an amendment of plan?—The inquiries natural and proper—Crude ideas to be disowned—Bible condemns them—Priests of Baal and Elijah—Vain repetitions of the Heathen—Also of the Romanists—Doctrine of Jesus—God's moral government; its ends and means—Parental government, and its methods—Its wise use of prayer—Transfer of the conception to the Divine government—Prayer a simple but potent device to secure the chief thing at which God aims—Prayer prevails because it fulfills the necessary moral condition—Prayer deliberately inserted by God in the plan of his universe; as truly so as any natural law recognized by the physicists—God will adhere to his plan—Tennyson's tribute to prayer..................49–56

CHAPTER IV.

THE METHOD OF THE ANSWER.

Are answers to prayer natural or supernatural?—Is the supposition of a miracle necessary?—F. W. Robertson's theory—Mental reaction—Quotations—Physical philosophers admit a liturgical value—Their theory stated—The theory fails to cover the facts—Erroneously limits the effect to the petitioner and to spiritual results - Robertson's assertion incorrect—

Contradicted by the case of Jacob; of David; of Hezekiah; of Daniel; of Peter — These effects not reflex, nor spiritual — Spiritual answers also involve a supernatural power — The promised Comforter — The reflex theory suicidal — Men will not resort to prayer as a mere self-magnetism — Revert to the original inquiry, after the method — The fact alone important — God not shut up to one method — May answer directly, or mediately — Through natural causes; by men; or by angelic agency — Examples of each of these methods — Letter from a Massachusetts minister — Reasons for ordinarily using human agency — Striking fact in the experience of Dr. Judson — Professor Stowe's illustration and supposition — Lines by Adelaide A. Proctor 57–72

CHAPTER V.

CONDITIONS OF SUCCESS IN PRAYER.

Importance of the subject — The conditions to be learned from the nature of the case, and from express assertions of Scripture — 1. A sense of want — Need of God and the value of prayer realized — 2. Reverence — God must guard his own honor — 3. Filial spirit — God responds to his children — 4. Gratitude — Future blessings not to be expected, if ungrateful for past good — 5. Humility — Prayer to be based on the truth — Our demerits to be recognized — 6. Faith — Implied in the idea of Prayer — Positively required in Scripture — 7 Obedience — Only the loyal may petition — Only those in sympathy with God can prevail in prayer — 8. Forgiveness of injuries — Those who ask to be forgiven, must forgive — 9. Approved objects — God does not abdicate — Exercises his perfect wisdom — By his Spirit teaches us true wants and the meaning of his promises — 10. Importunate perseverance — Is much insisted on in the Bible — 11. Ask in the name of Christ — He the appointed Mediator — 12. Appropriate effort — Prayer no substitute for work, but its aid — 13. Union with others — Each prayer a power — United prayer an augmented power — All the conditions reducible to one — A right state of heart — The conditions real, and must be observed — Lines by Robert Southwell.....73–88

CHAPTER VI.

THE PRAYER OF FAITH.

The subject misunderstood — The deluded misjudge and distress others — Fall into difficulties themselves — A reported instance — Material for skepticism — The erroneous theory; anything to be had, by believing that it will be given — Supposed proof texts — Objections to the theory — 1. Makes God abdicate his throne — 2. Badly adapted to moral training — 3. Would ruin us and those for whom we pray — 4. Involves self-contradiction — 6. Fails to furnish evidence — Singular letter from "Father Nash" — His death from over-excitement, and a false sense of responsibility — Testimony of Rev. Asa Mahan, D D. — 6. Bible lends no support to the theory — Interpretation of the texts referred to — The correct theory; that in prayer one must believe that God will be true to all he has promised — What ground has faith to stand on? — 1. The general pledge that prayer shall be answered, in some way — 2. Specific promises, numerous and minute — Not to be interpreted imaginatively — The Bible not a conjuring-book — Unhappy delusions and mistakes from such a use — Facts in proof — Yet Holy Spirit may suggest and use particular passages — Case of Augustine — 3. Indications of Divine providence, revealing God's will — 4. Leadings of the Holy Spirit — These promised as aid in prayer — These show us our true wants — These explain Scripture — These interpret providences — Mr. Finney's anecdote — Professor Upham's view — Catherine Adorna — Lines by John Newton.....89–111

CHAPTER VII.

SKEPTICAL ASSAULTS ON PRAYER.

Opposition of skeptics to prayer — This natural, and ancient — Physical philosophers take the lead — The dilemma they propose — A brief counter-view — Explanation of the skepticism — Logical necessities — Prayer implies the whole of supernatural religion — Shyness of skeptics — Quotation from Rousseau — Comment — Prayer founded on reason — 1. A universal instinct — Guizot's beautiful tribute — Instinct pre-supposes a want and a supply — The parental analogy — Acknowledged by Professor Tyndall, as plausible — 2. Historic evidence of prayer as answered — In all ages men have so believed — Those who pray most, most certain — Prayer to be tested; but as a moral force — Not on merely physical conditions — The famous Hospital-test of Sir William Thompson and Professor Tyndall — Proposes to test the prayer-theory, yet violates the conditions — Makes an impossible demand — Encounters a moral difficulty — Ignores submission — Furnishes no assurance of good result — 3. Prayer based on moral necessity — In no other way can man be educated — Why skeptics object — From total misapprehension — Professor Tyndall's admission as to spiritual effect of prayer — Its greater difficulties — How prayer uses natural law — Illustration from man's use of it — Evolution furnishes an illustration of a possible explanation of prayer — The position of the mathematician Euler — A. A. Waring's lines..112–136

CHAPTER VIII.

BIBLE-ANSWERS TO PRAYER — OLD TESTAMENT.

The Bible teaches by example, as well as precept — Biography and History illustrate Doctrine — Numerous declarations of David — Select instances only given, to mark classes of cases — 1. Prayers for personal deliverance from danger — Jacob's prayer at Peniel — Charles Wesley's famous hymn — 2. Prayers for others — Moses as an intercessor — A type of Christ — Another poem of Charles Wesley — 3. Parental prayers — Hannah's petition — Samuel's character — 4. Prayer for reviving of religion — Elijah — Contest with the priests of Baal — 5. Prayer tested by its enemies — Daniel and the Persian Princes — Triumphant result — 6. Patriotic prayers —

The invasion of Judea — Danger of Jerusalem — Insulting letter — Hezekiah's prayer — Isaiah's prophecy — The overwhelming result — Byron's tribute to the sublime fact..137–154

CHAPTER IX.

BIBLE-ANSWERS TO PRAYER — NEW TESTAMENT.

A still clearer light with the advent of Christ — He the connecting link of earth and heaven — His ministry a series of answers to prayer — The New Testament motto is, "Pray without ceasing" — Facts selected, to illustrate four states of mind essential to success — 1. The prayer of Faith — The Roman Centurion and his sick servant — Confidence in the power of Jesus — Humility aids faith — 2. The prayer of importunity — The Syro-Phenician mother and her daughter — Another Gentile — Discouraging action of Jesus — The mother's perseverance and victory — 3. The prayer of union — Peter in prison, under sentence of death — A whole church prays for him — The last night comes, and the deliverance also — 4. The prayer of fervent spiritual desire — This for the gift of the Holy Spirit — A specific promise laid a foundation for faith — The ten days of prayer — The day of Pentecost — The incidental and the permanent — Review of the cases cited from the Bible — The facts confirm the theory — George Herbert's poem on Prayer..............................155–167

CHAPTER X.

PRAYER FOR THE SUPPLY OF TEMPORAL WANTS — (Commenced.)

Manna in the desert — Elijah's ravens — Is there such experience now? — Let facts answer — Mother of Dorothea Trudel — Her faith and its reward — Case of Henry Young Stilling — How he went to the University — How he was supported — A California experience related by Dr. Horace Bushnell — Deliverance at sea; the only survivor of the Albion — Direction in an emergency; Mr. Blair's experience — A result in Parliament; Sir Fowell Buxton's prayers — How the policy of Oberlin College was decided; Mrs. Shipherd's letter — Prayer for rain — Dr. E. Pond's account — Professor Cowle's statement — Mr. Finney's narrative — William Huntington's "Bank of Faith" — A college student supported — Mrs. Jane C. Pithey's daily life of faith; Poor Caleb; Prayer brings supply from an unknown source — John Logan's application of Jacob's prayer at Bethel.....168–189

CHAPTER XI.

PRAYER FOR THE SUPPLY OF TEMPORAL WANTS — (Concluded.)

Miss Lucy R. Drake's experience — Desire to be a foreign missionary — The hindrance — Engagement at the Consumptive's Home — Faith increased — Relinquishes salary — Gives away savings — Relies on God only — Money comes as needed — About to go to India — No society pledged for her support — Remarks of the author on this narrative — Miss Drake's practice not a law for others — Billy Bray's pulpit — Newport Gardener; a slave prays himself into freedom — Escape from a bear — A lady missionary testifies — A Will; an anticipative answer to prayer — Another case — Prayer a part of God's plan — Delivery from unjust wrath — Reconciliation — Another prayer for rain — Anna Shipton and the blind boy — Prayer in sundry exigencies — The smaller events of life — Lines by Paul Gerhardt.....190–211

CHAPTER XII.

PRAYER FOR PHYSICAL HEALING — (Commenced.)

Truth and error on this subject — James not to be misinterpreted — Various meanings suggested — Universal healing not intended — Healing may always be prayed for, with submission — Is often granted — Dorothea Trudel's experience — Her institution and methods — Classification of the facts — 1. Thorough consecration the basis — 2. The principal aim, spiritual results — 3. Natural auxiliaries not neglected — 4. No cures promised — Instantaneous relief not usually expected — 5. Like-minded helpers — Prayer availed at a distance — Case of Mrs. Jane C. Miller, the wife of a Congregational minister — Instantly healed of chronic rheumatism — Attestation by her husband and others — Case of Rev. A. Connett's daughter — Sciatic rheumatism, shrunken and shortened limb — Reads of Mrs. Miller's experience — Prayer of mother and daughter — The sudden cure — Healing of a Methodist minister's wife; case of Mrs. Ellen Clark Sherman — Numerous injuries — Bed-ridden condition — Spiritual exercises — A seeming vision or felt presence of Christ — Faith to be healed — Instant result — Permanent relief — A home missionary saved to the work — Testimony of Charles Cullis, M. D. — Cure of a tumor; of consumption; of cancer in cheek; of neuralgia — All cases not healed — Remarks by author — A visit to Männedorf — Further report of cases — Lines by Whittier. 212–242

CHAPTER XIII.

PRAYER FOR PHYSICAL HEALING — (Concluded.)

Luther's prayer for dying Melanchthon — Case of Rev. S. H. Platt, a Methodist minister — Statements by Rev. Horace Bushnell, D. D. — An English gentleman — Comment — Insanity cured — Another case — A young lady healed — Her letter — Bishop Simpson's life saved — Deafness of twenty years cured — Miss Lucy R. Drake's account; cured of consumption — Testimony of Mrs. C. S. Whitney — Two cases of children — A freedman cured of consumption — A girl cured — A case in New York city — Cure of Bright's disease and paralysis — Remarks upon cases cited — 1. Large proportion of cures gradual — 2. Vary as to use of medicine — 3. Many of the cures naturally explicable — 4. Connection of physical and spiritual — 5. The law of a specific faith — Views of Rev. C. B. Boynton, D. D. — Medical explanation of H. M. Lyman, M. D. — Lines in sickness, by Heinrich Puchta. 243–275

CHAPTER XIV.

PRAYER FOR SANCTIFYING GRACE.

The connection of inward and outward bestowments — Instances in the New Testament — Christ's double ministry — Spiritual victory possible — Only half-believed in — Power of prayer — How Paul obtained grace — His "thorn in the flesh" — An English lady's experience; transition-case from last chapter to this — Delivered from all fear and anxiety — Another lady; Victory over irritability; "Jesus, help me!" — Prayer the key to "Higher Life" experience — Remarks by the author — A student's victory — Full salvation by faith — "My richer experience," by Mrs. Whitney — The process — Desire, prayer, trials, and faith — Narratives of R. Pearsall Smith — Testimony of a physician — Of a Presbyterian minister — Lines of Horatius Bonar.................................276–293

CHAPTER XV.

PRAYER TO OVERCOME PHYSICAL HABIT.

Certain cases of sin call for special grace — Effect of sin on the body and mind — Failure of philosophy — Legal efforts unsuccessful — A gospel needed — Augustine's defeat and victory — Extract from his "Confessions" — Victory over tobacco and opium — Rev. W. H. Boole's facts — A church officer — Thirty years of bondage — An aged lady — A carpenter in Brooklyn, N. Y. — Cases reported by Mrs. C. S. Whitney — Triumph over tobacco — Prayer subdues the alcohol-appetite — The saved man now a minister — Testimonies collected by Rev. S. H. Platt — Victory over tobacco and alcohol — Lines by Charles Wesley.................................294–306

CHAPTER XVI.

PRAYER FOR INDIVIDUAL CONVERSIONS.

Startling language of the Bible — Can one man convert another? — Prayer a power — A Bible-class teacher's experience; immediate results; a late result — Illustration from pen of Prof. Austin Phelps, D. D. — A very difficult case at a distance — A circle of prayer — Power of united petition — Experience of Catherine Adorna — Prayer for soul of a sick man — The conversion of an infidel — A prompt answer — Conversion of a husband; a touching narrative — Effect of habitual prayer — Experience of Normand Smith, Jr. — Success in an unpromising case of a pupil — A praying acquaintance of Rev. C. G. Finney — A fact communicated by Rev. Enoch Pond, D. D. — Testimony of Rev. P. Hagler — Conversion of an infidel major and his family — A triple success to prayer — A father converted, at a distance — A case on missionary ground — A Brahman saved — A female skeptic converted — D. L. Moody and the Scotch infidel — Prayer opens a house and saves souls — A sister's prayers — How an Emperor of Russia was converted — Several children brought to Christ — A dreaded duty performed; the blessed results — Extract from "The Two Dreams." 307–337

CHAPTER XVII.

PARENTAL PRAYERS.

Parental prayer noted through the ages — Has a basis in the divine institution of the family — Also in special covenants and promises — Augustine and Monnica — Her anxiety and perpetual supplication — Long delay, but final success — His own account — Source of parental faith in prayer — Mr. Finney's remarks and illustration — Views of Rev. Howard Crosby, D. D., LL. D. — Illustrative cases — Two praying mothers — A son's account; Rev. C. B. Crane, D. D. — His father's petition — Narrative of Rev. A. S. Kedzie — A mother's faith and its reward — Two mothers — A praying father in Scotland; what came of it — A mother's confidence — A North American Indian mother — A burden rolled off — Heard at last — A son at school — Unsubmissive prayers; Warnings — Lines by Mrs. Hyde........ 338–357

CHAPTER XVIII.

PRAYER FOR MINISTERS, CHURCHES AND REVIVALS.

Prayer sweeps a wide circle — Praying to obtain a pastor — Dr. Wolcott's experience — Spiritual baptism of a pastor — How a church can better itself — Another case — The meeting at the red school house — Dr. Wisner's account of a revival — Revivals under Rev. Charles G. Finney — His revival lectures — A praying soul and a succession of revivals — A Scotch revival, two and a half centuries since — Recent revivals — In America — In Ireland — In Scotland — In Wales — The "week of prayer" as a sign of the times — Day of prayer for colleges — D. L. Moody's work — Prof. Upham's conception — Bonar's version of Psalm cxxvi.......................... 358–384

CHAPTER XIX.

PRAYER FOR CHARITABLE INSTITUTIONS.

These spring from the very heart of Christianity — Prayer naturally connects itself with them — Franke and the Orphan House at Halle — Succession of deliverances — Louis Harms and his missions — George Müller and his Orphan Houses — The Boston Consumptives' Home and Dr. Cullis — Chicago Foundling's Home and Dr. Shipman — Remarks of the author on the theory of non-solicitation — Its claim to be the faith-method — Three objections — No support from the reason of the case — None from Scripture — None from history — What its seeming success really means and teaches — Lines by Charlotte Elliot.. 385–400

CHAPTER XX

REVIEW OF FACTS IN CONCLUSION.

Is such a book properly helpful to Christian faith — Letter of a minister, in the negative — His argument — His agricultural illustration — His disgust with the constant citing of Müller's success — His idea of the use of prayer — Reply — His mistakes as to facts and principles — How cited facts on this subject may be appropriate — Right and wrong farming — Right and wrong praying — Why Daniel was tested, and the fact recorded — Why prayers seem to be unanswered explained by James — Lines by George Herbert.................... 401–408

PRAYER,

AND ITS

REMARKABLE ANSWERS.

CHAPTER I.

PRAYER CHARACTERISTIC OF PIETY.

It will prepare one to believe in the moral certainty of the prevalence of prayer, if he will consider how characteristic prayer has ever been of piety, and consequently what a cloud of incense has been rising before God, from the time of Adam's first petition, to the last ejaculation which has anywhere escaped the lips of a sorely distressed soul. The instinct is so universal, that there never has been a form of religion which did not include this as an essential duty; for, dark as the human mind may be, if once it conceives of God and man as in any kind of relationship, the idea of prayer springs up as the connecting link. Thus, the heathen pray; the Mohammedans pray; all sects of Christians pray; and even some of the skeptics have a vague faith in the exercise.

For piety is emphatically godliness — the constant recognition of God. It implies faith in his being, personality, character, providence and moral government. And such faith leads directly to him in conscious communion and worship. Prayer is this intercourse in its most pure, direct and natural form. Nothing else brings God so nigh to the soul; that is, nothing else so fills it with the sense of his presence. And we translate, as it were, into the language of prayer, all our thoughts of God, all the doctrines of religion, all the impressions made upon the mind by reading the Scriptures, or by laying to heart the lessons of providence.

This is the reason that prayer is enumerated among the evidences of conversion. "Behold he prayeth!" is as sure an indication of a new life in man now, as it was in the case of the converted Saul of Tarsus. It is as truly the natural act of a new-born soul, feeling its dependence upon God, as suckling is the instinctive act of the new-born infant. It must adore; it must confess; it must give thanks; it must petition. How else can it live?

"Prayer is the Christian's vital breath,
The Christian's native air;
His watchword at the gate of death:
He enters heaven with prayer.

"Prayer is the contrite sinner's voice,
Returning from his ways;
While angels in their songs rejoice,
And cry, 'Behold he prays!'"

Thus it may be said that the history of piety is the history of prayer. It evidently accompanied the accepted sacrifice of Abel, as he stood by his slain lamb, confessed his sin, and implored divine mercy. It must have been the breath of the spiritual life of the holy Enoch, during those three hundred years in which he "walked with God." For surely it was no silent walk; but a sweet, loving converse. It was the constant characteristic of Abraham, "the friend of God," who carried to his divine Friend all thoughts and plans for himself and for those he loved. Isaac and Jacob were praying men; and it was from this fact that the latter gained his immortal name of Israel — Prince of God; because by his urgent prayer he gained a victory, as one possessed of power like a prince. Moses had special power in this direction, and prevailed wonderfully in intercession for others. Samuel was noted for the same trait, and when he resigned his judgeship, the people made it their parting request, that he would not cease to pray for them. David was always on his knees, if we may judge from his psalms; which are as much prayers as praises, and in one of which he describes his own habit as follows: "Evening and morning and at noon will I pray, and cry aloud, and He shall hear my voice." His faith in this for all men, as well as for himself, led him to say: "O Thou that hearest prayer, unto thee shall all flesh come." Elijah, the petitioner, is as famous as Elijah, the reprover and reformer; so that in the far away time of the New Testament church, he could be held up as an example and encouragement in prayer, by James, who, in illustration of his assertion, "that the effectual fervent prayer of a righteous man availeth much," said: "Elias was a man subject to like passions as we are, and he prayed earnestly that it might not rain, and it rained not on the earth (the land where he lived) for the space of three years and six months; and he prayed again, and the heavens gave rain, and the earth brought forth her fruit." To name no other Old Testament saints, Daniel will stand forever associated with a willing martyrdom, so to speak, in behalf of this duty and privilege, as will his deliverance ever be a monument of its power.

The New Testament saints kept the same characteristic. One of the earliest personages in the history is the aged Anna, of whom it is said that "she departed not from the temple, but served God with fastings and prayers, night and day." The "devout" Simeon was of kindred spirit, as were Zacharias and Elizabeth, and Joseph and Mary. Jesus not only taught his disciples to pray, and himself offered petitions publicly, on various recorded occasions, but sometimes he spent whole nights in prayer, alone upon the mountain tops, or in the wilderness; and it was with praying breath that he expired upon the cross. The testimony borne concerning the thousands of converts made on the day of Pentecost is: "They continued steadfastly in the apostle's doctrine and fellowship, and in breaking of bread, and in prayers." The apostles themselves prayed for ten days, steadily, prior to that scene of wonders; and in every new trial or difficulty which occurred, we read of their uniting in solemn petition for divine aid. Paul, the last and greatest of the apostles, was full of the spirit of supplication; and not only does the book of Acts contain references to striking occasions on which he prayed, as for instance in the prison at Philippi, and the parting scene at Miletus, but his epistles constantly allude to the earnestness and frequency of his prayers for individuals and churches in whom he felt a special interest, and abound in commands and exhortations to Christians to pray in turn for him, and to maintain the habit of prayer "without ceasing."

The history of the Church since the apostolic period has presented a similar aspect. Prayer has held a prominent place in public worship, and has been inculcated and practiced as a private duty. Although it may be asserted, with some truth, that, at times, and with many individuals, this has been a mere form; yet it may be replied, that even the preservation of the form shows the importance attached to the duty theoretically, while to the spiritually-minded in every age it has been a precious reality. Hence we find, that in proportion to the devout character and spiritual earnestness of men, has been their reliance on prayer for advancement in holiness, and for success in their plans of life. This could hardly be otherwise when even the devout heathen had a right idea and practice on a point so fundamental; for Plutarch wrote: "If we traverse the world, it is possible to find cities without walls, without letters, without kings, without wealth, without coin, without schools and theaters; but a city without a temple, or that practiceth not worship, prayers and the like, no one ever saw." Christians have naturally made prayer the breath of their lives.

Martin Luther, speaking of his own delighted use of the Lord's Prayer, wrote: "For to this day, I suck still at the *Pater Noster*, like a child; I eat and drink thereof like a full grown man, and can never have enough." His custom in private was, to take its separate petitions, one by one, and to enlarge upon them; and he says: "And so I have often learned more in one prayer, than I could have got from much reading and composing." It was said of him, that "he could have what he would of God." And, as we shall have occasion to see, it seemed literally so. One who had overheard Luther at prayer on a certain occasion, spoke with wonder of the deep earnestness with which he pleaded with God. His tones were reverent, as if he felt he was talking to his Maker; and yet he manifested the confidence of one who is conversing with a sympathizing friend. There was at one time, a crisis in the affairs of the reformation, when only faith could see cause for hope. Persecution had broken out with such power as to threaten to carry all before it. Friends were few and feeble; enemies were many, strong and exultant. But Luther did not waver. He remembered his own sublime hymn:

"Ein feste burg ist unser Gott,"

(A strong fortress is our God) and sank upon his knees, that Omnipotence might come to the help of weakness. He wrestled alone with God in his closet, till, like Jacob, he had prevailed. Then he went into the room where his family were assembled, with joyous heart and shining face, and raising both hands, and lifting his eyes heavenward, exclaimed: "We have overcome! we have overcome!" It afterwards proved that just at that time, the Emperor Charles V., issued his proclamation of religious toleration in Germany. No doubt Luther had pleaded, in his prayer, the declaration of Scripture: "The king's heart is in the hand of the Lord, as the rivers of water: he turneth it whithersoever he will." Proverbs xxi: 1.

As to John Calvin, Dr. Paul Henry, his biographer, says: "To characterize Calvin's holy disposition in a few words, I will direct attention to one of its most remarkable signs, viz., his child-like trust in God, and his invincible faith in prayer, which was his strength and daily resource. In the perilous circumstances of his life, and in his last hours, he constantly expressed the desire that his friends should pray for him and for every good thing."

John Knox was famous for his earnest prayers. He was heard at the great crisis to plead: "Give me Scotland or I die;" and Queen Mary said that she feared his prayers more than she did all the armies of Europe. And this seemed a curious presentiment; for one night, in the bloody times of persecution, as he and several friends were praying together, Knox spoke out and declared that deliverance had come, though he could not tell how. The next news was that "Bloody Mary" was dead.

Zuinglius, the Swiss reformer, was also a man mighty in prayer, and he laid the heavy burden which he was trying to bear, upon the Head of the Church, in these words: "O Jesus, thou seest how the wicked and the blasphemous stun thy people's ears with their clamors. Thou knowest how, from my youth up, I have abhorred controversy, and yet, against my will, thou hast never ceased to impel me to the conflict. Therefore do I call upon thee with confidence to finish what thou hast begun! If in anything I have builded unwisely, let thy hand of power cast it down. If I have laid any other foundation beside thee, let thy mighty arm overturn it. O thou vine, full of sweetness, to whom the Father is the husbandman, and we are the branches, abandon not thy tendrils. Hast thou not promised to be with us unto the end of the world?"

Melanchthon so prized prayer, that he feared to lose anxieties, lest he should lose the blessed relief of prayer. He said: "If I had no anxieties, I should lose a powerful incentive to prayer; but when the cares of life impel to devotion, the best means of consolation, a religious mind cannot do without them. Thus trouble impels me to prayer, and prayer drives away trouble."

In Gustavus Adolphus we have not only a sagacious king and successful general, but a man of prayer.

When he was in camp before Werben, on one occasion, he had remained alone in his private apartment for some hours, and at such seasons his attendants were not allowed to disturb him. At length, however, a favorite, who had something important to communicate, presumed to look in the door, softly, and found the king on his knees. Gustavus called him in, and said: "Thou wonderest to see me in this posture, who have so many thousands of subjects to pray for me; but I tell thee that no man has more need to pray for himself than he who, having to render an account of his actions to none but God, is, for that reason, more closely assaulted by the Devil, than all other men besides."

The venerated Rev. Philip Henry, the father of Matthew Henry, the commentator, was a specially godly man. In his life it is said: "He and his wife constantly prayed together, morning and evening." We are told, also, that he made a conscience of family worship, and abounded in it. He said to his children and friends: "Be sure you look to your secret duty; keep that up, whatever you do; the soul cannot prosper in the neglect of it. Apostacy generally begins at the closet door." As to family worship he would say: "If the worship of God be not in the home, write, 'Lord, have mercy on us' on the door, for there is a plague, a curse in it."

Rev. Samuel Rutherford, the pious Scotch minister, in the days of persecution for the sake of the "Covenant," was said to be "always praying, always preaching, always visiting the sick, always catechising, always writing and studying." When settled at Answorth, he was constantly praying as well as laboring for his people; so that he says: "There I wrestled with the angel and prevailed. Woods, trees, meadows and hills are my witnesses that I drew on a fair match betwixt Christ and Answorth."

President Jonathan Edwards, at the beginning of his Christian life, adopted this resolution: "*Resolved*, Very much to exercise myself in this all my life long; viz., with the greatest openness of which I am capable, to declare my ways to God, and lay open my soul to him; all my sins, temptations, difficulties, sorrows, fears, hopes, desires, and everything and every circumstance." "He made a secret of his private devotions," observes Dr. Hopkins, one of his biographers, "and therefore they cannot be particularly known; though there is much evidence that he was punctual, constant and frequent in secret prayer, and often kept days of fasting and prayer in secret, and set apart times for serious, devout meditations on spiritual and eternal things as part of his religious exercises in secret. It appears from his diary that his *stated* seasons of secret prayer were, from his youth, three times a day, in his journeys as well as at home. He was, as far as can be known, much on his knees in secret, and in devout reading of God's word and meditation upon it. And his constant, solemn converse with God in these exercises of secret religion, made his face to shine, as it were, before others."

The Rev. David Brainerd has, for more than a century, been a model of Christian earnestness and missionary devotion. In the memoir written by President Edwards, it is said: "Though he was of a very sociable temper, and loved the company of saints, and delighted very much in religious conversation, and in social worship, yet his warmest affections, and their greatest effects on his animal nature, and his sweetest joys, were in his closet devotions and solitary transactions between God and his own soul; as is very observable through his whole course, from his conversion to his death. He delighted greatly in secret retirements, and loved to get quite away from all the world, to converse with God alone in secret duties." Again it is said: "How sensible was he of his own insufficiency for this work, and how great was his dependence on God's sufficiency! How solicitous that he might be fitted for it; and to that end, how much time did he spend in prayer and fasting, as well as reading and meditation; *giving himself to these things!*" Again: "Among all the many days he spent in secret fasting and prayer, of which he gives an account in his diary, there is scarcely an instance of one which was not either attended or soon followed with apparent success, and a remarkable blessing, in special influences and consolations of God's Spirit; and very often before the day was ended. But it must be observed that, when he set about this duty, he did it in good earnest, 'stirring up himself to take hold of God,' and 'continuing instant in prayer,' with much of the spirit of Jacob, who said to the angel, 'I will not let thee go, except thou bless me.' "

Rev. R. M. McCheyne was so deeply impressed with this subject, that, as he made advance in piety, he drew up a paper to embody his improved purposes, in which he says: "I am persuaded that I ought never to do anything without prayer, and, if possible, special secret prayer. * * * I ought to pray far more for our church, for our leading ministers by name, and for my own clear guidance in the right way, that I may not be led aside, or driven aside from following Christ. * * * I should pray much more in peaceful days, that I may be guided rightly when days of trial come. I ought to spend the best hours of the day in communion with God. It is my noblest and most fruitful employment, and is not to be thrust into any corner. The morning hours from six to eight are the most uninterrupted, and should be thus employed, if I can prevent drowsiness. A little time after breakfast might be given to intercession. After tea is my best hour, and that should be solemly dedicated to God, if possible."

Rev. Thomas Arnold, D. D., who accomplished so noble a Christian, as well as literary work, at Rugby, showed his appreciation of prayer as one of the most important instrumentalities, by introducing a special prayer before the class which he taught, in addition to the general prayers of the whole school. His biographer says: "On the morning on which he first used it, he said that he had been much troubled to find, that the change from attendance on the death-bed of one of the boys in his house to the school-work, had been very great; he thought that there ought not to be such a contrast, and that it was probably owing to the school-work not being sufficiently sanctified to God's glory; that if it was made really a *religious* work, the transition to it from a death-bed would be slight; he therefore intended for the future to offer a prayer before the first lesson, that the day's work might be undertaken and carried on solely to the glory of God and their improvement—that he might be the better enabled to do his work."

Among the heroes as well as the saints of the church must be counted Henry Martyn, whose ripe scholarship and many personal attractions adorned his arduous missionary life, whose fervent piety has kindled the devotion of thousands, and whose lamented and lonely death has stirred the sympathies of every reader of his memoir. The church of England has never produced a more beautiful character. His biographer bears this testimony of his habit of drawing near to God: "As these extraordinary and seemingly contradictory qualities were not imparted to him but by the Spirit of God, so they were not strengthened and matured, but in the diligent use of the ordinary means of grace. Prayer and the Holy Scriptures were those wells of salvation out of which he drew daily the living water. Truly did he 'pray always, with all prayer and supplication in the Spirit, and watch thereunto with all perseverance.' "

Multitudes will thank God for the impetus given to their Christian lives by the memoir of James Brainerd Taylor, whose early death deprived the church of one who gave unusual promise of becoming a successful minister. His biographer says: "The attentive reader has doubtless already observed that the great means by which Mr. Taylor made such distinguished attainments in piety were the Bible, as noticed before, and the *throne of grace*. He was remarkably a man of prayer. In secret devotions he had his consecrated place and fixed time; nor would he allow anything to interfere with this arrangement. And as he did himself, so he exhorted others to do, 'have a fixed place and time for devotion.'"

Harlan Page was a plain man, of humble, rural origin, and of only ordinary education; but his success in winning souls to Christ has made him an example and an encouragement to multitudes. He relied on prayer as the grand instrumentality of power in religious effort, and in his memoirs we read: "He expected success from God through the blessing of the Holy Spirit in answer to prayer. * * * HE LOVED PRAYER. Besides prayers at social meetings, with the families and individuals he visited, and on special occasions frequently recurring, he regularly not only conducted family worship, accompanied by singing, but every morning and evening prayed with his companion, as they retired and rose, and also poured out his heart to God alone in the closet."

Another layman, Normand Smith, Jr., a sketch of

whose life, written by Rev. Dr. Joel Hawes, has been published by the American Tract Society, and whose piety and generosity are consequently widely known, is thus described: "The frequency with which he observed days of fasting and prayer has already been noticed. He was eminently a man of prayer. He aimed every day, and in all things, to maintain a close and humble walk with God. It has been said by one who had the best means of knowing, that prayer seemed to be his meat and drink. It was his constant practice to rise before the family, and spend one or two hours by himself, before attending family duties. At noon, he had a season of prayer, and no company would prevent his retiring; as he would always excuse himself for a little while, that he might enjoy his accustomed converse with God. He usually attended some meeting in the evening, but always prayed before he went. He had a room expressly set apart for private devotion, and would never be disturbed in his retirement. * * * He had a place for prayer also in his store, and would often invite his brethren, when they came in, to unite with him in prayer."

Here let us pause, as one might write the biography of every Christian, were he to tell of all the men of prayer. Piety is prayer.

"Come to the morning-prayer;
Come, let us kneel and pray:
Prayer is the Christian pilgrim's staff,
To walk with God all day.

At noon, beneath the Rock
Of Ages, rest and pray;
Sweet is that shelter from the heat,
When the sun smites by day.

At evening, shut thy door;
Round the home-altar pray;
And, finding there the house of God,
At Heaven's gate close the day.

When midnight veils our eyes,
Oh, it is sweet to say,
I sleep, but my heart waketh, Lord,
With thee to watch and pray."

—*James Montgomery.*

CHAPTER II.

WHAT TRUE PRAYER IS.

IF one is to consider the question, whether God really answers prayer, he must have before his mind a definite idea of what prayer is. Disputes arise from ignorance and mental confusion. Men differ about words, when they agree in the things. They also differ about things, when they agree in the words. There has been a great deal said about prayer, which lacked discrimination; and so the arguments for and against it have failed to convince. We should then define our ground distinctly, so that friend and foe may know precisely what we mean to cover by our assertions and our proofs.

There are antagonists who will concede the value of prayer, if allowed so to define the act as to leave it a mere religious meditation. We never knew anybody who thought it worth his while to oppose religious meditation; perhaps, because men are not likely to take very much of it, pure and simple. And so there are philosophizing Christians, and even ministers, who timidly explain away prayer, till its substance is gone, and then think that they have accomplished wonders in behalf of religion, by showing that no objections can be raised against so rational a theory. As little can any advantages be gained by it for practical piety. There is an equation; but it is 0=0!

There would seem to be but one sure way of deciding what the true nature of prayer is, as an antecedent to ascertaining its value. It is vain to try to settle it by abstract speculation alone. Doubtless something is to be learned from "the nature of things," of which philosophers and theologians have so much to say. But in this particular case we shall make more progress by studying the nature of God, as He has revealed it to us in his Word. Prayer has to do with God. On that all are agreed. How much it has to do with him, and why, and how, are the disputed questions. He can tell us better than the philosophers can; for He knows Himself, his creatures and his plans. He can tell, therefore, whether He has fitted prayer into his plans; and, if so, in what sense. And if He certifies us of the fact, He can take care of the philosophy, whether we can or not. No human philosophy can destroy a fact. This is just as true in the moral world, as is the famous assertion of the physicists in their realm, that every atom of matter is indestructible, or that force is persistent. Let us therefore rely principally upon the Scriptures to tell us what prayer is. Fortunately that is a favorite topic with the inspired writers; for prayer enters largely into the divine promises and manifestations, and also into human experiences. And consequently prophecy and history are equally full of it. Commands and thanksgivings are fellow-witnesses to its nature. It will aid our object to consider the true idea of prayer as related to its nature, its source of power, and its method of answer. The first topic will alone occupy us in the present chapter.

What is the proper conception of prayer, as to the nature of the act? Is it a dealing with one's self, or with God; or, possibly, with both? Is it simply a devout contemplation of the divine character and works, though clothed in the garb of an address to God? Is it, as Rev. F. W. Robertson asserts, only a submission of the human to the divine will; a saying merely, "Not my will, but thine be done"? Or is it substantially and principally a cry of want, a petition for aid, a direct asking of God, for the purpose of receiving? If the latter be the authentic view, there is something to be said, for or against it, in the matter of answers: otherwise the subject of answers is an impertinence, and its discussion a waste of breath.

The word prayer, both in scriptural and in popular usage, denotes a somewhat comprehensive exercise, throughout which there is a personal approach of the soul to God. It may be in connection with others, in public or family worship; or it may be as an individual and private act only. In either case, and whether the words be audibly repeated or silently thought, the man speaks with God, mind with mind, heart with heart. It is not mere meditation upon God, but a direct address to him. Man talks with God. So Abraham felt, when he said: "Behold now I have taken upon me to speak unto the Lord, who am but dust and ashes." Gen. xviii:27. When a man comes thus to God he is in a complex state of mind; that is, numerous thoughts crowd in, and various emotions are felt. Hence prayer divides itself naturally into parts, which give expression to these struggling exercises. Sometimes these occur in consecutive order, especially in the case of cultured minds and of public exercises; but more commonly they are intermingled, as one or another idea comes uppermost. These parts have been named Adoration, Confession, Thanksgiving, and Petition.

With *Adoration* we usually commence our prayers, and express our sense of the divine majesty and glory. Thus Daniel began his prayer: "O Lord, the great and dreadful (or awe-inspiring) God, keeping the covenant and mercy to them that love him and to them that keep his commandments." Dan. ix:4. When the persecuted apostles made their appeal, their first words were: "Lord, thou art God, which hath made heaven and earth and the sea, and all that in them is." Acts, iv:24. The Lord's Prayer also opens: "Our Father, which art in heaven." By thus dwelling, for a moment, on God's presence, power, wisdom, holiness, condescension and love, and on his works of creation and providence, we pay him a due tribute of worship, fill our minds with a suitable reverence, and bring to thought precisely those considerations which prepare the mind for what is to follow in the prayer. In other words, we are made to realize with what kind of a being we have to do; how infinitely above us He is, in position and character, and how able and ready to meet our wants.

Confession is naturally the next utterance. We pass from a thought of God to a remembrance of our own insignificance and vileness. His greatness reminds us of our littleness, while his purity stands in contrast with our sin. As we exalt him, so we abase ourselves. Truth demands it. It is the fit introduction to what further we have to say; for it shows what has been our dependence upon divine aid and mercy in the past, and what it must be in the future. Abraham called himself "dust and ashes," as we have seen; Job said, (vi : 5); "Behold, I am vile, what shall I answer thee" Isaiah exclaimed (vi: 5); "Woe is me! for I am undone; because I am a man of unclean lips, and I dwell in the midst of a people of unclean lips;" and Daniel added to the words before cited, "We have sinned, and have committed iniquity, and have done wickedly, and have rebelled, even by departing from thy precepts; " and he continued thus to speak for some time. Confession is especially necessary, when the soul is burdened with a sense of guilt, and the main object of the prayer is to apply to God for forgiveness. Then the application for pardon is to be preceded by the frank, humble and penitent acknowledgment of the sins. One comes to God in such a matter, as he would to an injured or offended fellow man. No one would approach a person whom he had wronged, to ask a favor, without acknowledging his unworthiness, confessing his misdeed, and imploring reconciliation. We can do no less in drawing near to God.

The soul is then prepared for *Thanksgiving.* How can it forget, or omit to remember, what God has already done for it; especially in view of the multitude of his mercies to one richly deserving his wrath? Hence we often notice, in perusing the Psalms — which are in large part prayers — that they begin with ascriptions of praise, which occupy many verses before we reach the expression of want and the requests for aid. Thus the ninth begins: "I will praise thee, O Lord, with my whole heart: I will show forth all thy marvelous works." The seventy-third opens: "Truly God is good to Israel;" the eighty-fifth: "Lord, thou hast been favorable unto thy land;" the one hundred and third: "Bless the Lord, O my soul, and all that is within me bless his holy name;" and not a few are wholly occupied with thanks. So in David's prayer on the occasion of associating Solomon with him in the government, and the setting apart of treasures with which to build the temple, he broke out in this preliminary utterance of mingled thanksgiving and adoration: "Blessed be thou, Lord God of Israel, our father, for ever and ever. Thine, O Lord, is the greatness and the power and the glory and the victory and the majesty: for all that is in the heavens and in the earth is thine; thine is the kingdom, O Lord, and thou art exalted as head above all. Both riches and honor come of thee, and thou reignest over all, and in thy hand is power and might; and in thy hand it is to make great, and to give strength unto all. Now, therefore, our God, we thank thee, and praise thy glorious name." 1 Chron. xxix: 10–13. It will also be remembered that Jesus began one of the brief recorded prayers thus: "I thank thee, O Father, Lord of heaven and earth" (Mat. xi: 25); and that his prayer at the grave of Lazarus commenced, "Father, I thank thee that thou hast heard me" (John xi: 41); and that Paul wrote to the Philippians (iv: 6): "Be careful for nothing; but in everything by prayer and supplication with thanksgiving let your requests be made known unto God." Probably one reason why our prayers are not more prevalent is, that we are not sufficiently thankful for what we have already received.

And now the soul is prepared for *Petition*, which includes the asking of favors for ourselves, and intercession for others. This is the very heart of prayer, which is prompted by a sense of want. The man goes to God, not only to adore and praise, but also to petition. Otherwise it would suffice for him to sing psalms and hymns. These have their delightful use and powerful influence, but do in no respect supersede prayer, which has the distinct office of asking aid for human weakness. No nation, however ignorant, has confounded two such distinct exercises, although the two acts may properly be associated. In prayer the adoration and praise are intended to prepare for the petition. They are the gateway to the edifice. They show us how to approach God, in order that we may draw near acceptably, and may state freely and fully all our wants. Such is the grand design of prayer as a divinely appointed means of securing needed aid.

Here is where Rev. F. W. Robertson, in his sermon on prayer, comes far short of the truth. Taking for his guide a single expression of Jesus, in the experience of agony in the garden, "Not as I will, but as Thou wilt," he resolves prayer into mere submission to the divine will, instead of simply recognizing submission as one condition of acceptable prayer. He says: "All prayer is to change the will human into submission to the will divine." "Prayer is one thing, petition quite another." "The divine wisdom has given us prayer, not as a means whereby to obtain the good things of earth, but as a means whereby we learn to do without them; not as a means whereby we escape evil, but as a means whereby we become strong to meet it." This is of the character of all half-truths; it is a view practically false and injurious. If generally accepted, it would lead to a fatalistic passivity, instead of a resolute activity, and would end in the total disuse of prayer. Indeed, he accepted that conclusion, for he remarks: "That life is most holy in which there is least of petition and desire, and most of waiting upon God." And in his misapprehension of the inference to be drawn from the exclamation of Jesus, before quoted, he says: "Practically, then, I say: Pray as He did, till prayer makes you cease to pray." This was said devoutly and earnestly, by a truly spiritual man; but by one, also, who looked at truths too exclusively in a subjective way, shrinking from their objective reality, and who also by temperament and disease inclined to the mystical side of religion.

Mr. Robertson is by no means alone in this conception of prayer. Apart from the magnetism of his influence over readers, and the speciousness of his quite too limited illustrations of petition to God, there is a disposition at present to concede too much to the objections of the philosophic skeptics, and to render prayer unobjectionable by making it almost objectless. Thus a valued ministerial friend, at the West, writes to the author: "My own mind looks more to prayer as a power for uplifting the spirit to divine communion, and so helping not so much to obtain what we may desire or want, as to bring us into perfect acquiescence with the order of Providence, and into obedience. Our Lord did not encourage those who sought for 'signs and wonders.' * * * I trust your book will be guarded against giving countenance to sensational religion, for I think that is one of our modern weak points." Another able but eccentric minister at the East, writes: "I do not dare preach to my people that men ought always to pray, because they will get what they ask for. My doctrine is, that 'men ought always to pray and not to faint,' *whether their prayers are answered or not.* And I deplore the tendency which would seem to exhort people to prayer as a short way of getting what they want. The true value of prayer is, that it stops people from wanting what they can't get." The wonder is, that such a theory is held by one who is a disciple of him who taught his followers to "ask," with the promise that they should "receive," and not that they should stop wanting; and who backed his instruction "always to pray and not to faint," with the parable of the widow who *obtained* from the judge what she so importunately asked for, and added: "And shall not God avenge his own elect, who cry day and night unto him, though he bear long with them?" Thus, as Dr. Bushnell says, "Prayer becomes a kind of dumb-bell exercise—good as exercise, but not to be answered." Let the Savior's words be carried out in the various figures used, on this theory, and its absurdity becomes at once apparent. He bids us "ask." Imagine a child asking for some favor, or for the relief of some want, and standing, hour after hour, repeating his requests, and being told by the father: "Go on asking, my child; it does you much good to ask. The longer you ask, the more good it will do you. Do not expect to receive anything, however, as the principal benefit of asking is that, by and by, you will not want anything, and will cease to make any request." Jesus bids us "seek." Imagine a mother seeking a lost child. She looks through the house and along the streets, then searches the fields and woods, and examines the river-banks. A wise neighbor meets her and says: "Seek on; look everywhere; search every accessible place. You will not find, indeed; but then seeking is a good thing. It puts the mind on the stretch; it fixes the attention; it aids observation; it makes the idea of the child very real. And then, after a while, you will cease to want your child." The words of Christ are "Knock." Imagine a man knocking at the door of a house, long and loud. After he has done this for an hour, a window opens, and the occupant of the house puts out his head, and says: "That is right, my friend; I shall not open the door, but then keep on knocking. It is excellent exercise, and you will be the healthier for it. Knock away till sundown, and then come again and knock all to-morrow. After some days thus spent, you will attain to a state of mind in which you will no longer care to come in." Is this what Jesus intended us to understand, when he said: "Ask, and ye shall receive; seek, and ye shall find; knock, and it shall be opened unto you"? No doubt one would thus soon cease to ask, to seek, and to knock; but would it not be from disgust?

To see the error of such a view, one need only study nature, and the pages of the Bible. Nature makes us feel the *need* of prayer, and the Bible teaches us *how* to pray. The fact is, that we are pressed on every side by imperious wants, the supply for which is only slightly within our own control. Often the exigency is great, and the relief must be speedy. In such an extremity, men have always betaken themselves to God, in every age of the world, under all forms of religion. It is a primal and ineradicable instinct of human nature, and cannot lead astray. What it prompts to is petition to God. In that it is supported by all the analogies of experience. The child is dependent on the parent, and goes daily and hourly to its parent with requests for things needed. The subject is in many things dependent upon the ruler, and offers his petitions for requisite aid or relief. God is felt to be the universal Father and Ruler, and to him, therefore, his children and subjects naturally go with prayers for assistance in life's necessities. If it be replied that God does not need to be informed of our wants, or urged to do us good, as do earthly parents and rulers; we answer, that to impart information and incline to compassion are not the only reasons for petition in these latter cases, and need not be any reason in the case of God. There may be abundant other ground why a parent should encourage a child to ask help, and why a ruler should be pleased when the people send in respectful petitions; as we shall see in the next chapter. And so, doubtless, it is in relation to God.

But why rest upon general reasoning and analogy, when the Bible makes the matter perfectly clear? No one not morbidly possessed by a theory which destroys his mental vision, can fail to see that in the Bible, from Genesis to Revelation, prayer means simply petition. It is not merely submitting in ignorance to whatever God may choose to send; but it is asking him, reverently and in a childlike way, to send specific things felt to be pressingly needed. This is plain from the commands, from the promises, from the prayers and from the answers; all of which are placed on record for our instruction.

Jesus commanded his disciples to pray for specific blessings, and not merely to submit themselves to the will of God in general; and the Lord's Prayer, which he gave as a model, contains seven distinct petitions. Again we read: "He spake a parable unto them, to this end, that men ought always to pray, and not to faint." Luke xviii : 7. And the parable was that of the importunate widow, who had a specific request which she urged, and urged, and urged, without ceasing, till it was granted. Similar is the command of Paul, already cited: "Be careful (or anxious) for nothing, but in every thing by prayer and supplication, with thanksgiving, let your requests be made known unto God." Phil. iv : 6. This directs us to make particular requests, as the precise thing which God wishes us to do.

The promises state the same truth, or carry the implication. Instead of reading: Submit, and all things shall be done for you, we read: "Ask and ye shall receive; seek and ye shall find; knock and it shall be opened unto you; for everyone that asketh receiveth, and he that seeketh findeth, and to him that knocketh it shall be opened." Then the analogy which nature suggests, Jesus positively endorses: "What man is there of you who, if his son ask bread, will give him a stone, or if he ask a fish, will give him a serpent?" Matt. vii : 7–11. No language could more plainly authorize specific requests. Take, further, such promises as these: "Call upon me in the day of trouble; I will deliver thee, and thou shalt glorify me." Ps.

1 : 15. "If I shut up heaven that there be no rain; or if I command the locusts to devour the land; or if I send pestilence among my people; if my people, which are called by my name, shall humble themselves and pray, and seek my face, and turn from their wicked ways, then will I hear from heaven, and will forgive their sin, and wilt heal their land." 2 Chron. vii : 13, 14. "And all things whatsoever ye shall ask in prayer, believing, ye shall receive." Matt. xxi : 22. "And if we know that he hears us, whatsoever we ask, we know that we have the petitions that we desired of him." 1 John v : 15. If prayer is submission, but not request, what do such words mean; words which encourage us to ask of God specific relief for the particular evils which at the time are distressing us?

Let us pass, then, to the prayers on record in Scripture, which were acceptably offered, and observe whether the good men only asked to be made submissive to the divine will, whatever that might prove to be; or whether they ventured to mention the things which they desired, not imagining that to ask for and expect them, was unsubmissive in spirit. And with these let us note also the answers which were returned. Take the case of Jesus himself, to whom Mr. Robertson makes particular reference. His prayer in the garden was conditionally made, with submission to the Father's will; but it was yet a specific request — "Let this cup pass from me." And so, at the grave of Lazarus, he asked for the one thing then desired, and said, "Father, I thank thee that thou hast heard me, and I know that thou hearest me always" — words which obviously mean that God was accustomed to grant him the particular requests which he made. Daniel tells us (chapter ix) of his anxiety to know of the divine purpose as to the return of the Jews from the captivity at Babylon, and that he made it the subject of special prayer and fasting; whereupon an angel was sent to give him the exact information desired. When he was cast into the den of lions, because of his faith in prayer to Jehovah, he made petition for safety, and God granted just what he asked, and shut the mouths of the lions. David prayed repeatedly for deliverance from the hands of King Saul, and afterwards from that of his parricidal son, Absolom, and received the very blessings for which he prayed. When Peter was cast into prison, and lay there under sentence of death, we are told that "prayer was made without ceasing of the church unto God for him." What they prayed for was, that, in some way, Peter might be saved; and God granted that very thing. And so it was in cases without number. What men wanted they asked for, and when they asked aright, and for things truly needed, God granted them. Prayer is thus seen to be in its nature petition, and not merely meditation or worship, or submission. The experience of all saints is like that of Hannah. She had in her heart one all absorbing desire, which she silently expressed to God, in the presence of Eli, who said, "Go in peace, and the God of Israel grant thee thy petition that thou hast asked of him;" and eventually she stood again before the venerable high priest, and said: "O my lord, as thy soul liveth, my lord, I am the woman that stood by thee here, praying unto the Lord. For this child I prayed, and the Lord hath given me my petition which I asked of him." 1 Sam. i: 17, 26, 27. Prayer is then an application to God to relieve human want.

"Lord, what a change within us one short hour
Spent in thy presence, will prevail to make!
What heavy burdens from our bosoms take,
What parched grounds refresh, as with a shower!
We kneel, and all around us seems to lower;
We rise, and all, the distant and the near,
Stands forth in sunny outline, brave and clear.

"We kneel how weak, we rise how full of power!
Why, therefore, should we do ourselves this wrong,
Or others, that we are not always strong;
That we are ever overborne with care;
That we should ever weak or heartless be,
Anxious or troubled; when with us is prayer,
And joy and strength and courage are with thee?"

—*R. C. Trench.*

CHAPTER III.

WHY PRAYER PREVAILS.

HAVING ascertained that as to its object, the nature of prayer is petition, and that it is therefore susceptible of an answer, it is important to inquire next for the principle upon which it produces its effect. Why does prayer prevail? To what is it indebted for its power? How can it possibly operate on God, to induce him to do that which otherwise he would not do? If his power is almighty, it will be said that he has tho ability to reach us, nor must ask our consent. If his knowledge is complete, then He needs no information from our prayers as to what are our necessities. If his character is perfect, his benevolence requires no prompting to undertake our relief. And if his plan is all-comprehending, he has already provided for our wants, and our petitions are useless. How is it possible, then, for prayer to prevail without arguing imperfection in God? What principle of explanation is suggested by reason and Scripture?

These are natural questions to an inquiring mind, and we are not left without a legitimate reply. We are to dismiss, at the outset, the crude idea of early ages and of heathen nations, in which God is not only conceived of in a human manner—which in a degree is necessary and appropriate—but is represented as having human limitations and imperfections. The Bible rebukes such a degradation of the Deity. Thus the worshipers of Baal thought that their prayers would attract the attention of their unheeding god, and so Elijah mocked their loud cries, ironically saying: "Cry aloud, for he is a god [and ought therefore to help you, if his attention can be gained]; either he is talking, or he is pursuing, or he is on a journey, or peradventure he sleepeth and must be awaked." 1 Kings, xviii: 27. Evidently the prophet meant to deny that such or any kindred hindrances characterized Jehovah, the true God. There are people who think that there is a merit in prayer, which in some manner brings God into our debt, and obliges him to grant that which we need; or at least that the act so pleases him that he is persuaded to be complaisant to our wishes. Hence great faith is placed in the number of prayers, and the heathen resort to a praying machine turned by wind or water, to the wheel of which written prayers are attached; while the Romanists repeat, with breathless haste, *Pater Nosters* and *Ave Marias*, keeping count upon the beads of a rosary! But the Bible denies human merit, and Jesus said: "When ye pray, use not vain repetitions as the heathen do; for they think that they shall be heard for their much speaking. Be not ye therefore like unto them, for your Father knoweth what things ye have need of before ye ask Him." Mat. vi : 7, 8.

The Bible emphasizes everywhere the divine omniscience, and will not allow that our prayers afford God the least information. Therefore, in the same discourse Jesus reaffirms this truth, saying: "Your heavenly Father knoweth that ye have need of all these things," (Mat. vi : 32,) and makes that fact the basis of his exhortation not to be anxious about food, or drink, or clothing. And equally explicit is the Bible as to the comprehensiveness of the divine plan; that it includes all things. "For of him and through him and to him are all things," writes Paul, who also affirms that "we know that all things work together for good to them that love God." Rom. x: 36, and viii : 28. And yet the writers of Scripture, while thus teaching, as strenuously as does any modern philosopher, the perfection of the divine power, knowledge, character and plans, urge with equal freedom and emphasis, the duty and privilege of prayer. Plainly they think that it is a provision required rather than excluded by his perfection, and therefore embraced in the scope of his plan; which is precisely the truth in the case.

To understand this, we must call to mind the circumstances in which God is acting. He is carrying forward a moral government; which involves the training and control of free, rational and sensitive beings, by the influence of perceived and appreciated truth. The principal truth which they need to know and appreciate, pertains to his own nature and character. In this respect he is situated as is the father of a family; and he has instituted the earthly family that in it we may gain those initial ideas and that preliminary training which will fit us to understand and trust him. What a human father needs is, to gain the confidence and love of his children, and to produce in them a sense of their dependence, and of his desire to promote their best welfare. Is it not, then, quite conceivable that he should take pains to use methods which will promote as free an intercourse as possible between him and the children? And would anything conduce more surely to this end than to encourage them to ask him for every needed supply, even when he already knew the state of the case, and was ready to bestow aid? For the thing to be gained is an impression upon their minds of his power, wisdom and love, so that they shall delight to obey him. This is even more important than the specific supply of their wants, which he could provide for otherwise. The mode of supply may thus transcend in value the fact of supply.

Transfer this simple conception, with which the whole world is familiar, to the relation of God and his human children, and the philosophy of prayer, as regards its moral principle, is at once explicable. We are God's children; but he is invisible, and our knowledge of him is small. Yet that which of all things is most important for our well being is to know him; for on him are we unspeakably more dependent than children are upon an earthly parent, and God has so made us, that the perfection of our being and of our happiness is to arise from knowing, loving, trusting and enjoying him. Hence the emphatic language of Jesus: "This is life eternal, that they might know thee, the only true God, and Jesus Christ, whom thou has sent." John xvii: 3. But how shall every human soul be brought into free, personal intercourse with the invisible Father, so that childlike faith and loving obedience shall be developed? How shall this be made a power so permanent and so available at all times, as to be a perpetual moral education? By instituting prayer, as the grand source of religious impression, and of needed comfort and help, and by making it, to a large extent, a condition of obtaining special divine aid. One cannot conceive of a device more simple, and yet more potent for gaining the great end of divine manifestation and human impression.

For, consider its necessary effect. It bases itself on a natural instinct to look for aid to some friendly superior power. And to what power should the dependent creature apply, if not to its Creator? It keeps before the mind the thought of his omnipresence, of his knowledge, and of his all-sufficiency. It implies his uninterrupted connection with earthly affairs; the universality and particularity of his providence; or, as Jesus phrased it, "Are not two sparrows sold for a farthing? and one of them shall not fall on the ground without your Father. But the very hairs of your head are all numbered." Mat. x: 29, 30. It presents God as a loving parent, who sympathizes with our sorrows; who understands, better than we ourselves do, our circumstances; who has power and wisdom to help our right endeavors and extricate us from peril; and who shows tender mercy to our many weaknesses and sins. In other words, he is the very helper we need, at all times. Now the soul that recognizes this fact, and acts upon the invitation to pray, is certain to live, as it were, in a divine atmosphere; to be kept continually in reverential, humble, trustful, grateful thought of God and realization of his presence. The act of prayer is more solemn and impressive than any other form of religious exercise; the approach to God is so personal and direct. One calls up the highest and grandest conceptions of the Deity in the words of adoration, the most abasing views of himself in those of confession, the most touching and endearing recollections in those of thanksgiving, and the profoundest sense of dependence in those of petition. Surely nothing else can make God stand forth with such reality before the mind, or can bring him into such intimate communion with our souls. And true prayer is an exercise which more than any other tends to its own reproduction, or repetition, as the soul increasingly feels its need, and has experience of the benefit of appeal to God. Thus, at length, it becomes a habit, a state of mind, an abiding rest in God; which is the very end which God seeks, and to which a created spirit must be brought for its highest good. And, as prayer is one of the simplest of acts, it is within the reach of children and of the most ignorant adults, and is thus adapted to a universal moral training.

It is thus evident that prayer may prevail with God

by reason of its fulfilling, on the part of man, a necessary moral condition, which God wisely requires. He needs no information; nor any coaxing or persuasion to rouse his benevolence and induce him to come to our aid. But he ought to see us in a proper position of humility, faith and love, before he gratifies our desires, and he appoints prayer as the means of bringing us into that position. This shows his wisdom as a moral ruler; and a very great defect would have been manifest in his scheme of training, had He omitted prayer, and left us to a bare use of the laws of nature according to our imperfect understanding of them. For, in that case, he would have withheld needed help and would have shut us up to mere mechanical influences, which would have been only slightly operative on character; whereas now we have larger hope and we come into vital, warm, personal contact, such as gives us an immediate impression of himself. Moreover, by annexing such a condition to his gifts, God not only brings us into a position honorable to him, and wise for us, as a condition precedent to the bestowal of desired favors, but he also secures in us such a state of mind as makes the blessings bestowed tenfold more valuable; their incidental effect being worth far more than the direct.

We are thus brought to the most rational conclusion, that God has deliberately, wisely, and from the beginning, made prayer a part of the plan of the universe. Far from contravening that plan, it simply fulfills it. Instead of changing the divine will, it thoroughly carries it out. Instead of violating law, it complies with that law which is highest, as having sweep in the highest or moral realm; only, according to universal analogy, subordinating the lower laws of lower realms. Thus we see chemical law overruling mechanical law, and vital law overruling both mechanical and chemical law, and the law of the moral universe overruling that of the physical universe. For when we talk of God's laws and plan, we must not pause at the bottom of his system, or busy ourselves merely with the scaffolding of his structure. Matter is made for the use of mind, and the material universe is only a platform and an agency for the spiritual. And thus, as God has made gravity a law in one realm, he has made prayer a law in a higher realm, and it is even greater folly to ignore the latter than the former. And so it is no more true that God is a Creator of worlds, than it is that he is a HEARER OF PRAYER.

"More things are wrought by prayer
Than this world dreams of. Wherefore let thy voice
Rise like a fountain for me night and day.
For what are men better than sheep or goats,
That nourish a blind life within the brain,
If, knowing God, they lift not hands of prayer,
Both for themselves and those who call them friend!
For so the whole round earth is every way
Bound by gold chains about the feet of God."

—*Tennyson.*

CHAPTER IV.

THE METHOD OF THE ANSWER.

VARIOUS have been the explanations given of the manner in which prayer receives its answer. How does God bestow the blessing desired? Is the answer to be regarded as supernatural, or natural? Are answers to prayers miracles? When a Christian asks something at the hand of God, does he virtually request God to work a miracle for his benefit? Or has God natural channels of communication with this world, through which he can secure for his people that which they need and for which they pray? One cannot avoid meeting these questions, when handling the subject of answers to prayer.

The simplest explanation offered is that of Rev. F. W. Robertson, who, with many others that stand in unwholesome fear of skeptical scientists, propounds the theory of mental reaction. This is a logical inference from his notion of the nature of prayer as only a meditation on God and a submission to his will. He asks, "Does prayer change the outward universe, or does it alter our inward being? Does it work on God, or does it work on us? He answers these questions in favor of the latter alternative; and how little he encourages the idea of our receiving any actual bestowment in answer to our petition, is seen from his remark, that, "it would be a strange family, where the child's will dictates; but it would be also strange where a child may not, as a child, express its foolish wish, if it be only to have the impossibility of gratifying it explained." He asks also, increduously, "Whether the good derived has been exactly this, that prayer brought them the very thing wished for?" His idea of the manner in which prayer is answered, is that the effect comes "in moderating our wish; in changing the passionate desire into still submission, the anxious, tumultuous expectation into silent surrender." He also states, "And so, in the expectation of impending danger, our prayer has won the victory, not when we have warded off the trial, but when like him (Jesus) we have learned to say, 'arise, let us go to meet the evil.'"

This is the view of some of the physical philosophers, who allow a certain value to prayer in the spiritual realm, though even there, wholly of a reflex action. The answer to prayer is but a self-answer. It has no divine element. The effect is only liturgical and amounts to a self-magnetising. The form of prayer being that of petition to God, they talk of an answer, yet strangely allow no agency of God in the matter. The manner of the answer, they say, is this: the soul comes before God with a burden of grief, or of desire, or of fear, and expresses itself freely, bringing to mind his greatness, wisdom and love, to which facts it constantly returns for comfort. Thus, after a time, having relieved itself by words, and having become reminded that God's will must be right, and will and ought to be done, it goes away in such a reverent, humble and trustful frame, as to acquire new strength for duties and trials. God has done nothing, and will do nothing, because of the prayer. The man has simply meditated aloud, throwing his thoughts into the form of petition, and his mind has received a reflex impression from the truths which were thus called up; much as if he had been reading or conversing upon similar topics. He has had a devotional exercise spiritually elevating.

The difficulty with the whole theory is, that it fails to cover the facts. It starts with an erroneous limitation to the petitioner and to spiritual results, denying effect on others and any physical effect on him, except as the body may share through the nervous system in the reaction of the mind. Yet nothing is more abundantly capable of proof, than that prayer works results beyond the individual himself, both in the physical and in the spiritual world, as the subsequent chapters of this volume will show. It is not true, as Mr. Robertson declares, that prayer never removes the trial, but only gives strength to bear it. There are, indeed, many cases in which God does not see fit to remove the trial — as in the case of Paul's thorn in the flesh — and then the submissive and conditional prayer is answered by the bestowment of gracious divine aid through the Holy Spirit, and not by mere natural reaction of the mind; as the apostle distinctly teaches. 2

Cor. xii: 7–9. But the Bible is full of prayers offered for specific deliverance of an outward character, and the answers came in outward effects wrought in nature and in men. Such was the answer to Jacob's prayer for deliverance from his angry brother, Esau; to David's many prayers to be saved from the hand of Saul; to Hezekiah's prayer after the insulting threats of Sennacherib; to the prayer of Daniel for preservation in the den of lions; and to the prayer of the Jerusalem Church for the escape of Peter. There was no answer in the mere reflex manner, in such cases. And if it should be said that those were exceptions, in the days of miracles; we reply that no miracles were wrought to prevent Esau and Saul from carrying out their murderous threats, while yet the prayed for event was secured according to promise; and that similar instances of success in prayer, and that too, in connection with other persons than the petitioners, occur daily at the present time.

Moreover, it is to be noticed, and Mr. Robertson as a Christian minister should have given great weight to the fact, that, even in spiritual results secured in the mind of the one who prays, there is a supernatural power involved, over and above the natural reflex action of the prayer as a devotional exercise. The promise of the Comforter is to that very end; and this gift is declared to be the one which God is specially willing to bestow for our enlightenment, comfort and sanctification. And at the day of Pentecost, the marvelous effects, on friends and foes, of a ten days' prayer meeting, are ascribed not to a reflex influence of the praying, on the apostles and others assembled with them, but to the descending power of the Holy Ghost. Paul also said that his ability to endure the thorn in the flesh was by "grace" received, and because "the power of Christ rested upon" him.

Furthermore, a fatal objection to the Robertsonian theory is, that it is suicidal. The moment it should come to be generally believed, prayer would cease! For the instinct to pray is connected with a conviction that God will in some way bestow the needed aid. Our necessities drive us to our knees, because we must have help out of ourselves, and we have faith that God hears prayer. Now prayer does beyond question react favorably upon our own minds; but even this is because we are expecting something far higher and more important, and are looking with reverence, penitence, gratitude and trust to a Heavenly Father, who actually listens to our petitions and sends the needed blessing. Destroy that conviction, persuade men that prayer has actually no influence on the divine will, and is not a condition of the divine action, and the chief motive to prayer is withdrawn. Tell them that they are only magnetizing themselves and going through a profitable devotional exercise, and they will conclude that meditating can as well be done in some other way; sitting as well as kneeling; reading as well as praying; silently as well as audibly. And, as we have seen, Mr. Robertson had a suspicion that such might be the final result, and hence we find him questioning whether prayer be a duty, and saying: "Prayer then is a necessity of our humanity, rather than a duty. To force it as a duty is dangerous. Christ did not; never commanded it, never taught it, till asked." He counts it only an initial thing in a Christian's experience: "Hints are given us, which make it seem that a time will come, when spirituality shall be so complete, and acquiescence in the will of God so entire, that petition shall be superseded." Not in this world will this be, we suspect, and possibly not in any world; though the command in the opposite direction to "pray without ceasing," may bring an abiding state of mind, which shall be itself a constant petition; by which God shall feel continually appealed to, to honor the faith placed in him and the request ever going up, by granting perpetual guardianship from evil, or perpetual grace to endure it.

Rejecting, then, this insufficient statement of the manner in which prayer is answered — a statement which substitutes the incidental for the main effect, and confounds a single reason for prayer with its chief agency — we come back to the original question: By what method or agency does prayer receive its answer? In reply to this it is to be said, that so long as we can claim the reality of the answer, and God as its author, it is of no consequence whether we can trace the method, or not. A true philosophy reasons about this as about other phenomena. It is chiefly anxious to make sure of its facts. The facts here are, that petitions offered to God are heard; and that, in some way, God arranges to bestow what is properly desired, or what will be its equivalent. If this is clearly taught in Scripture, and abundantly demonstrated by experience, faith needs nothing more for its intelligent support, and piety is furnished with every needed source of comfort and of courage. The curious may naturally ask by what methods God operates to secure the object for which prayer was offered, and it may add to knowledge, and thus to one's intellectual happiness, to learn something on that point: otherwise it is of no importance, and ignorance of the method cannot impugn the fact.

We do not know that God is shut up to any one method in this matter. He may work directly, or mediately. He may himself use the system of second causes which he has established, much as we use it, only with a perfect understanding of its forces and a complete ability to employ them; or he may put in motion angelic and human agency, by some secret inspiration. The Bible unhesitatingly places all instrumentalities at his disposal, and represents him as working back of visible agencies. There is truth as well as wit, in the oft repeated anecdote of the good man that, in his poverty, prayed for bread, and was overheard by a skeptic, who, as a joke, tossed in a loaf through the window. Thereupon the thankful receiver fell on his knees, and expressed his gratitude to God; and, when the skeptic laughed at him for this, and told him how the loaf came to be thrown in, shrewdly replied: "No matter; God sent it, even if the devil brought it!"

The Bible recognizes various modes of divine action in answering prayer. In the olden time, when God was founding the true religion, and attesting it by signs, evidently supernatural, and intended to manifest his immediate presence and power, prayer appeared to be answered, on many occasions, by direct act of God: at least no other agency seemed to be employed. It was so, when, at the prayer of Jesus, God raised Lazarus from the dead; when, at the request of the centurion, the servant was healed immediately and at a distance; and when, after the earnest entreaty of Elijah, fire came down and consumed the sacrifice on Carmel. But, in other cases, God put natural causes into motion, to secure the desired end. Thus, when Moses prayed in behalf of Pharaoh, that the plague of the locusts might be removed, we read: "And he went out from Pharaoh, and entreated the Lord. And the Lord turned a mighty strong west wind, which took away the locusts, and cast them into the Red Sea: there remained not one locust in all the coasts of Egypt." Ex. x: 18, 19. Subsequently, when the Israelites stood on the shore of the Red Sea, with the Egyptian army pressing up behind, and Moses prayed for deliverance, the record is: "The Lord said unto Moses, Wherefore criest thou unto me? Speak unto the children of Israel that they go forward. * * * And the Lord caused the sea to go back by a strong east wind, all that night, and made the sea dry land,

and the waters were divided." Ex. xiv: 15–21. And so, when Hezekiah was sick unto death, and prayed to be spared, the prophet Isaiah was sent to say: "Thus saith the Lord, the God of David, thy father; I have heard thy prayer, I have seen thy tears; behold I will add unto thy days fifteen years;" and afterwards we read: "For Isaiah had said, Let them take a lump of figs, and lay it for a plaster upon the boil, and he shall recover." Is. xxviii: 5–21.

In yet other instances prayers were answered through the ministry of angels. Thus, when in the deadly agony of the garden, Jesus offered his conditional and submissive prayer to the Father for needed aid, we read: "And there appeared an angel unto him from heaven, strengthening him." Luke xxii: 43. Similarly the record is, that when Daniel was preserved from the lions, in answer to prayer, he said to king Darius: "My God hath sent his angel, and hath shut the lions' mouths that they have not hurt me." Dan. vi: 22. And in like manner, when Peter was saved from imminent death at the hand of Herod, in answer to the prayers of the church, we read: "And behold an angel of the Lord came upon him, and a light shined in the prison; and he smote Peter on the side, and raised him up, saying, Arise up quickly. And his chains fell from off his hands. * * * And he went out and followed him. * * * And they went out and passed on through one street; and forthwith the angel departed from him." Acts xii: 7–10. So when Daniel prayed to be made to understand the prophecies about his people, his own account is: "And while I was speaking and praying, and confessing my sin and the sin of my people Israel, and presenting my supplication before the Lord, my God, for the holy mountain of my God; yea, while I was speaking in my prayer, even the man Gabriel, whom I had seen in the vision, in the beginning, being caused to fly swiftly, touched me about the time of the evening oblation. And he informed me, and talked with me, and said, O Daniel, I am now come forth to give thee skill and understanding." Dan. ix : 20–22.

Very commonly God has answered prayers through human agency. In ways past our present knowledge, he can touch the hearts of men, and incline their minds to do what is requisite for the good of his praying ones. As a general intimation of this it is written: "The king's heart is in the hand of the Lord; as the rivers of water; he turneth it whithersoever he will." Prov. xxi: 1. Beautiful illustrations of this occur in the books of Ezra and Nehemiah. Daniel and other pious Jews had been praying, as we have seen, for a return of God's people from their captivity at Babylon, and for the rebuilding of the holy city and the temple, and these writers tell us how the prayers were answered through Cyrus and other kings of Persia. Ezra opens with these words: "Now, in the first year of Cyrus, king of Persia, that the word of the Lord by the mouth of Jeremiah might be fulfilled, the Lord stirred up the spirit of Cyrus," etc. Ezra i: 1. And after reaching Jerusalem and rebuilding the house, amid many fears, and tears, and prayers, they dedicated it with joy; "for the Lord had made them joyful, and turned the heart of the king of Assyria unto them," (vi:22;) and Ezra wrote in his journal: "Blessed be the Lord God of our fathers, which hath put such a thing as this in the king's heart, to beautify the house of the Lord which is at Jerusalem." vii:28. Every one will recall the touching narrative of Nehemiah, as he tells (ii:1–8,) how he longed to leave the court of Persia, where he was high in favor as the king's cup-bearer, and to go to Jerusalem with authority to rebuild its prostrate walls; and how he told the king what was the occasion of his sad face. "Then the king said to me, For what dost thou make request? So I prayed to the God of heaven. * * * And the king granted me according to the good hand of my God upon me."

These Scriptural illustrations will show how varied were the divine methods of answering prayer, anciently. He operated directly, through his own natural laws, by angels, and by men. The method was comparatively nothing. The fact which it was important to remember, and to act upon, was, that God ordered events in harmony with the prayers of his people. Of what account is it to us how he does this? There is no reason to suppose that he is any more limited in his methods now than of old; or that prayer is any the less a power with God, because we can ordinarily trace the second causes which he is pleased to use in granting our petitions. Unbelief on such a ground would be as irrational as for a child, who had asked a gift of his father, to doubt, when it was received, whether it had really come from him, because it was actually placed in his hand by another person, through whom the father had sent it.

The reader will now appreciate the meaning and force of a letter which the author recently received from a minister of a church in Massachusetts, who wrote thus: "The Lord has answered my prayers as certainly and constantly as father or mother supplied my wants when a boy, at my request; and in such way that I could not fail to see the Lord's hand as the gifts came out of it. Yet he has always done it as naturally as father and mother did it, and I suppose always will. I could tell you of a way opened to the ministry, in answer to prayer; of a life-partner so given; of horse and carriage, and saddle, etc., sent to me (though I paid for them); of fitting places of work made ready for me through the Lord's planning of months, sometimes; of my present charge given me as directly as anything ever was given; of deliverance from sickness and pain; of help in hard places, etc. Yet none of it was ever supernatural [in form], but planned for and given me, as I plan for and give to my little girl the things she asks for. There is not a thing that I want, great or small, that I do not ask the Lord for, with the fullest assurance—begotten of experience as well as of faith—that he will give it to me, if it is wise and kind to do so; but I do not look for answers otherwise than in the most natural ways, or what would seem to others to be such ways."

This undoubtedly expresses the usual method which God adopts in answering prayer. Other methods, when they occur, are exceptions to what is wisely the ordinary rule; as God properly arranges to have all parts of his system work co-operatively. He can secure a double benefit, when, in relieving our wants, or fulfilling our desires, he can use the benevolent agency of others, and can give a blessing to well directed efforts of ourselves and our friends. And here may come in place the experience of Rev. Dr. Adoniram Judson, the missionary, as given in the second volume of his memoirs. It appears that Dr. Judson became intensely interested in behalf of the Jews, while he was laboring among the heathen of India. He not only prayed earnestly for their conversion, but awakened an interest in others also, so that he raised one thousand dollars towards a mission in Palestine, which he urged the Baptist Missionary Union to establish. But, to his great regret, the enterprise was not undertaken. Were his prayers, then, left unanswered? Let the facts speak. Many years subsequent, indeed only a fortnight before his death, Mrs. Judson read to him from Rev. Dr. Hague's journal of travels in the East, this extract: "There (at Mr. Goodell's house in Constantinople) we first learned the interesting fact, which was mentioned by Mr. Schauffler, that a tract has been published in Germany giving some account of Dr. Judson's labors in Ava; that it had fallen into the hands of some Jews, and *had been the means of their conversion;* that it had reached Trebizond, where a Jew had translated it for the Jews of that place; that it had awakened a deep interest among them; that a candid spirit of inquiry had been manifested; and that a request had been made for a missionary to be sent to them from Constantinople." Mrs. Judson adds: "His eyes were filled with tears, when I had done reading, but still he at first spoke playfully, and in a way that a little disappointed me. Then a look of almost unearthly solemnity came over him, and clinging fast to my hand, as though to assure himself of being really in the world, he said: 'Love, this frightens me; I do not know what to make of it.' 'What?' 'Why, what you have been just reading. I never was deeply interested in any object, I never prayed sincerely and earnestly for anything, but it came; at some time, no matter at how distant a day; somehow, in some shape, probably the last I should have desired, it came. And yet I have had so little faith! May God forgive me, and, while he condescends to use me as his instrument wipe the sin of unbelief from my heart.'"

As bearing both upon the *fact* and the *method* of God's answer to prayer, Prof. C. E. Stowe, D. D., has a pertinent argument and illustration in "Remarks on Prayer," published in the *Biblical Repository*, vol. viii of the second series. "Let us now suppose an example. A pious man in the city of Erfurt, in the reign of Maximilian, mourns over the corruptions of the church, and most earnestly longs for a reformation.

He prays, day and night, that the emperor may be converted, and feels that his prayer is accepted, and that his request will be granted. A charity student at law, in the University, the son of a poor miner in a neighboring village, is walking with a friend, that evening, when a sudden flash of lightning throws them both to the ground. He recovers, but finds that his friend is dead. This awful visitation is the means of his conversion to God, and he resolves, on the spot, to devote his whole life to the service of Christ, in the ministry of the gospel. Is this an answer to the good man's prayers? He is praying for the conversion of the emperor, as a means of reforming the church; but this young charity-student is Martin Luther, a man whom God has qualified to do more for the reformation of the church, than twenty such emperors as Maximilian could have done, had they been converted ever so thoroughly. We do not know, and we cannot always know, what are the best means which God can employ for the accomplishment of his work; but we do know the great ends he has to accomplish; and while we are praying sincerely, and acceptably, for him to set in motion a particular instrumentality towards the accomplishment of these purposes, he may, in answer to our prayers, set in motion another, which is a thousand times more efficient."

Methods are thus various and of minor account. God has his choice of many, and his own reasons for preferring now one and then another. The kind of answer is determined by his sovereign wisdom; and this, in a measure, adjusts the propriety of the instrumentalities, as direct or indirect.

> "Pray, though the gifts you ask for
> May never comfort your fears,
> May never repay your pleading:
> Yet pray, and with hopeful tears.
> An answer — not that you sought for,
> But diviner — will come one day:
> Your eyes are too dim to see it;
> Yet strive and wait and pray."
>
> — *Adelaide A. Procter.*

CHAPTER V.

CONDITIONS OF SUCCESS IN PRAYER.

As prayer is one of the essentials of a life spiritually successful; and as our continual dependence and oft recurring temptations and trials make it daily necessary, the subject of the conditions of its success, as an appeal to God, ought to be of the deepest interest to every Christian. What are these conditions? We learn them from the nature of the case, and from the express statements of Scripture. They stand related to the object which God has in view, in requiring us to pray; to-wit, the securing a state of mind which shall honor him, shall promote right character in us, and shall make his gifts, when received, most pleasant and profitable. The promises to hear prayer are not made to the mere form, but to the appropriate spirit. That spirit has regard to various particulars.

1. A Sense of Want. Those who use prayer as a mere form have no real sense of want. They follow a habit, or comply with a custom. Why should God hear them? They do not feel that they need him. They are not so burdened with their wants, as to be driven to prayer, as the only resource. It is reasonable that God should withhold a blessing, until we feel our need of it sufficiently. It is not enough that we

mention our supposed wants, in the way of petition. We must reflect upon our condition and circumstances until we are borne down with a sense of need, and fall upon our knees in earnest prayer, as having something really to ask.

2. Reverence. God must regard his own honor. It is for our good, as well as for his glory, that he should be approached with reverence. "Hallowed be thy name" is the first petition in the prayer which Jesus taught. This forbids the coming to God in a light and thoughtless manner, or in a way of indecorous familiarity. It should prevent, also, everything noisy, boisterous and confused, as being inconsistent with a true conception of God's presence and character. Cyprian, bishop of Carthage and martyr, well says in his treatise on the Lord's Prayer: "Let our speech and petition, when we pray, be under discipline, observing quietness and modesty. Let us consider that we are standing in God's sight. We must please the divine eyes both with the habit of body and with the measure of voice. For as it is characteristic of a shameless man to be noisy with his cries, so, on the other hand, it is fitting to the modest man to pray with moderate petitions." And Tertullian, in his treatise on Prayer, inculcating the same duty, said: "But we more commend our prayers to God, when we pray with modesty and humility. * * * The sounds of our voice likewise should be subdued; else, if we are to be heard for our noise, how large windpipes we should need!" The majesty of God should greatly impress

us. Every person of dignified station should be treated with due respect by inferiors, and should not grant favors to those who are irreverent.

3. A Filial Spirit. Reverence need not beget slavishness. God would have us realize that we are his children, and he invites us to come with the words "Abba, Father" upon our lips, and the filial spirit in our hearts. A parent is grieved, when his own child comes to him in a cold, distrustful way, as if approaching a stranger. Jesus taught his disciples to begin their prayer with, "Our Father," in order to cherish this childlike spirit, which God loves to reward. It is our special privilege as Christians to understand this. Faber beautifully expresses it:

"The light of love is round His feet,
His paths are never dim;
And He comes nigh to us, when we
Dare not come nigh to Him.

"Let us be simple with Him, then,
Not backward, stiff, or cold,
As though our Bethlehem could be
What Sinai was of old."

4. Gratitude. Can we expect future mercies, if we are not thankful for past blessings? If a spirit of discontent and murmur is in our hearts, as though God had not dealt kindly with us, are we in a frame to approach him, and implore his continued protection? Or if we accept his gifts so lightly, and as a matter of course, that we are not impressed with his goodness, have we not missed their principal benefit, and thus

disqualified ourselves to ask or to receive added favors? It is not by accident, that the Psalms of David are half petition and half thanksgiving. Let them be an example, while the needed precept is furnished by Paul, when he says: "In everything by prayer and supplication with thanksgiving let your requests be made known unto God." Phil. iv: 6. There is nothing like gratitude to secure renewed benefactions.

5. Humility. One must approach God in the spirit of truth; and humility is simply owning the truth as to our character and deserts. As a fact, we are infinitely beneath God in our powers, while our character is sinful, and our desert is that of evil only. Can we approach his mercy-seat, and forget this? And if we should, could he consistently accept us? Jesus taught his disciples to say, "Forgive us our debts"; and he related the parable of the Pharisee and the Publican to enforce the same idea. "God be merciful to me a sinner!" uttered with downcast eye and with the hand smiting the breast, was the sentence which God heard with delight. "Humble yourselves in the sight of the Lord, and he shall lift you up," is the language of James (iv: 10). Confession of sin, heartfelt and definite, is an important condition of acceptable prayer. Therefore the wise man said: "He that covereth his sins shall not prosper; but whoso confesseth and forsaketh them shall have mercy." Prov. xxviii: 13. Abraham declared himself to be but "dust and ashes," when he prevailed in prayer. Gen. xviii: 27. The Psalms also abound in penitent confessions of sin.

6. Faith. The very idea of prayer implies faith; for why come to God for aid, if there is doubt of his ability, or his willingness, to help us? To approach him in unbelief is to mock him, and to stultify ourselves. It makes prayer a self-contradiction. It is as though a man should come to us, saying, "I am in great trouble, and need your help, but I have no belief that you will render me assistance"! We should be quite likely to verify his unbelief. Faith is so essential to the divine honor, that uncommon stress is laid upon it as a condition. When salvation is asked, the grand condition is, faith in Christ as the divinely provided Savior. And similarly every other request must be accompanied by faith in God's willingness to grant it, if best, and to make good any promise which is connected with it. Jesus said to the afflicted father, who prayed that the demon might be cast out of his child: "If thou canst believe, all things are possible to him that believeth." Mark ix: 23. Of a certain city which he visited, it is said: "He did not many mighty works there, because of their unbelief." Mat. xiii: 58. To the healed woman he said: "Thy faith hath saved thee: go in peace." Luke vii: 50. And so it was in connection with all the miraculous aid which he dispensed: he required the applicant to have faith. And he laid down this general rule: "What things soever ye desire, when ye pray, believe that ye receive them, and ye shall have them." Mark xi: 24. The epistle to the Romans (iv: 19–21) commends Abraham, because, "being not weak in faith * * * he staggered not

at the promise of God, through unbelief; but was strong in faith, giving glory to God, and being fully persuaded, that what he had promised, he was able also to perform." Similarly James writes: "If any of you lack wisdom, let him ask of God, that giveth to every man liberally and upbraideth not, and it shall be given him. But let him ask in faith, nothing wavering. For he that wavereth, is like a wave of the sea driven with the wind and tossed. For let not that man think that he shall receive anything of the Lord." James i:5–7. A failure in this respect will explain the want of success of many in their prayers. They do not "lift up holy hands, without wrath and doubting." 1 Tim. ii:8.

7. Obedience. He who prays for divine help must not insult God by maintaining, at the same time, an attitude of opposition to him. The second and third petitions of the Lord's Prayer are: "Thy kingdom come; thy will be done in earth as it is in heaven." No prayer offered in a spirit inconsistent with this can hope to be accepted. Reason affirms this and the Bible is explicit. Only the prayers of one who is truly consecrated to God can have power with him. God is not a mere convenience, to be resorted to for selfish purposes, in time of trouble. He invites us to enter into his spirit and plans, to identify ourselves with his cause and kingdom, to carry out in our lives his will; and he promises, on this condition, to care for us, and to hear our appeals for aid and blessing. Therefore we read in his Word: "The Lord is far from the

wicked, but he heareth the prayer of the righteous." Prov. xv: 29. "He that turneth away his ear, from hearing the law, even his prayer shall be abomination." Prov. xxviii: 9. "If ye abide in me, and my words abide in you, ye shall ask what ye will, and it shall be done unto you." John xv: 7. "The eyes of the Lord are over the righteous, and his ears are open unto their prayers." 1 Peter iii : 12. "And whatsoever we ask, we receive of him, because we keep his commandments, and do those things that are pleasing in his sight." 1 John iii: 22. Thus it will be seen, that when the sinful feel their need of God, and begin to pray to him, a first step must be, "to lift up holy hands," as Paul expresses it; to forsake all that they know to be wrong; to repent of evil thoughts and evil ways; to dedicate themselves to his service; to accept his law as their rule of life; to implore forgiveness for the past, and to make a consecration of the future.

8. Forgiveness of Injuries. Acceptable prayer must imply that we are forgiven of God; for how can an unpardoned sinner hope to have influence with him? But of nothing are we more plainly assured in the New Testament, and by the Savior himself, than that our own forgiveness by God is conditional upon our forgiveness of those who have injured us. The fifth petition of the Lord's Prayer significantly implies this, when it says: "Forgive us our debts, as we forgive our debtors;" and, at the close of its record in Matthew, as if to enforce this particular thought more

than any other, these words of Jesus are added: "For if ye forgive men their trespasses, your heavenly Father will also forgive you: but if ye forgive not men their trespasses, neither will your Father forgive your trespasses." (vi: 14, 15.) As if to emphasize this further, on another occasion he directed this forgiveness to be repeated, if necessary, seventy times seven; uttered the instructive parable of the servant who, owing his lord ten thousand talents, and being forgiven, would not forgive his fellow servant, who owed him but a hundred pence, and was therefore handed over to "the tormentors;" and concluded with this application: "So likewise shall my heavenly Father do also unto you, if ye from your hearts forgive not every one his brother, their trespasses." Mat. xviii: 23–35. And that this truth is to be especially borne in mind in prayer, Mark reminds us (xi: 25): "When ye stand praying, forgive if ye have aught against any, that your Father also which is in heaven may forgive you your trespasses." And with this may be compared the words of Jesus about bringing a gift to the altar and there remembering that our brother has something against us, which should be settled. Mat. v: 23, 24. Many unanswered petitions may be thus explained.

9. Asking for Approved Objects.—God does not mean, in hearing prayer, to abdicate his throne, or to substitute our judgment for his own. Hence he requires us to ascertain, as far as possible, what his judgment is, and to conform our prayers to it. Therefore it

is written: "And this is the confidence that we have in him, that if we ask any thing according to his will, he heareth us." 1 John v : 14. When, with reference to any specific object, we cannot ascertain God's exact will, we are to offer our petitions conditionally, with submission to the perfect wisdom and love of our heavenly Father. Thus Jesus, in the agony of the garden, prayed: "O my Father, if it be possible, let this cup pass from me: nevertheless, not as I will, but as thou wilt." Mat. xxvi : 39. To aid us in understanding our true wants, and the application of the promises to them, we need the enlightening and sanctifying influence of the Holy Spirit, which is freely offered. Thus we are taught that it is our duty to be "praying in the Holy Ghost," (Jude xx,) and to be "praying always with all prayer and supplication in the Spirit," (Ep. vi : 18,) while Paul assures us, (Rom. viii : 26, 27,) that "likewise the Spirit also helpeth our infirmities; for we know not what we should pray for as we ought; but the Spirit itself maketh intercession for us with groanings which cannot be uttered; and he that searcheth the hearts knoweth what is the mind of the Spirit, because he maketh intercession for the saints according to the will of God." Thus we have divine aid in learning what objects are approved by God. Other light will be thrown on this condition of acceptable petition in the following chapter.

10. Importunate Perseverance.—This is a prerequisite to success in prayer, because it has an intimate connection with the preparation of a right spirit-

ual condition in us. We saw at the outset that one must have a sense of want. God desires to deepen this to the utmost, and at the same time to test our faith, and to bring it out clearly to ourselves and to others. And so he delays the answer to our prayers, till they assume a more and more earnest tone, become importunate, and show a spirit of perseverance, born not of blind presumption, or of unsubmissive desire, but of enlightened persuasion that the object is important, proper, and one that God will eventually grant. Thus Paul teaches us to pray "always, with all prayer and supplication in the Spirit, and watching thereunto with all perseverance and supplication for all saints." Ep. vi : 18. Jesus spake a parable "to this end, that men ought always to pray and not to faint;" and the parable was of the importunate widow, who, by her continual coming, gave the judge no rest till he redressed her wrongs; and he added: "Shall not God avenge his own elect, who cry day and night unto him, though he bear long with them?" Luke xviii : 1–8. In the Old Testament is the example of Jacob's prayer for deliverance from his brother Esau, and the wrestling with the divine angel, refusing to let him go, till assured of the needed blessing. In the New Testament is the illustrative case of the Syro-Phenician widow, who besought Jesus to heal her possessed daughter, and would be deterred neither by neglect, nor by seeming rebuff, and who was finally rewarded for her perseverance and faith by gaining the desired answer. Do not our prayers fail sometimes because through discouragement we cease to pray? In the case of not a few successful prayers importunity has risen to the height of agony. This does not warrant us in saying, with some, that agony is a condition of prevailing prayer; for agony is not a matter of will, but depends upon temperament and occasion; it is nowhere prescribed in the Bible, and it by no means always attends success in petition. Many an accepted petition has risen to God from the quietude of a complete faith. Yet the agony of spirit which a sense of the need of the divine aid sometimes develops, in great emergencies and previous to striking answers, shows the relation of persevering importunity to success. The same earnestness is also manifested by fasting; all strong desire tending to destroy appetite, and the voluntary laying aside of food, in connection with prayer, indicating a spirit of humility and earnestness. Hence Jesus said of certain very difficult cases of exorcism: "This kind (of demons) goeth not out but by prayer and fasting." Mat. xvii : 21.

11. Asking in the Name of Christ. — A sinner must needs have an intercessor. This idea was represented ritually in the Old Testament economy, by the priesthood and its sacrifices; an arrangement which prefigured the atoning death and living advocacy of the Lord Jesus Christ. The statement of the Epistle to the Hebrews is: "But this man, because he continueth ever, hath an unchangeable priesthood. Wherefore he is able also to save them to the uttermost that come unto God by him, seeing he ever liveth to make

intercession for them," vii : 25. This explains the meaning of Jesus, when he said, just before his betrayal, trial and death: "Whatsoever ye shall ask in my name, that will I do, that the Father may be glorified in the Son. If ye shall ask anything in my name, I will do it." John xiv : 13, 14. Again: "Whatsoever ye shall ask the Father in my name, he will give it you. Hitherto have ye asked nothing in my name; ask and ye shall receive, that your joy may be full," xvi : 23, 24. The idea is, that as sinners, we must come in the way which God has provided, even as Jesus had before said: "I am the way and the truth, and the life; no man cometh unto the Father but by me," xiv : 6. It were contempt for us to approach without using the advocate which God has provided; while to come through him is to make sure of a favorable hearing, if our spirit be otherwise appropriate. The famous hymn of Charles Wesley, "Arise, my soul arise!" is the very essence of the gospel in this respect, especially the lines:

"He ever lives above,
For me to intercede;
His all-redeeming love,
His precious blood to plead."

And also these:

"Five bleeding wounds he bears,
Received on Calvary;
They pour effectual prayers,
They strongly speak for me."

12. APPROPRIATE EFFORT. Prayer would be an injury, were it to supersede human action. For character depends not a little upon personal effort. The result would be weakness and not strength, if all our wants could be supplied through prayer, with no exertion of our own. We see the effect in the case of the children of rich parents, who are unduly indulged, and have all for which they ask, without necessity of work. They seldom develop into a true manhood. God trains his children in a better way. The heathen understand this. Hence the ancient fable ridiculing the wagoner who piteously called on Hercules, to extricate his wagon from the mud, without putting his own shoulder to the wheel. The Christian as well as the pagan motto is, that God helps those who help themselves. Prayer must never be made an excuse for idleness and sloth. Its design is to rouse us to effort, by the hope of a divine blessing. Not until we are shut up to a difficulty which we can in no way touch, may we rely on prayer alone. In the matter of personal sanctification, the exhortation is to watch *and* pray. A significant implication is found in Christ's words: "I have chosen you and ordained you that ye should go and bring forth fruit, and that your fruit should remain; that whatsoever ye shall ask the Father in my name, he may give it you." John xv: 16. Thus Jesus made labor a condition of acceptable prayer, as being a manifestation of sincerity, earnestness and self-denial, and as tending to the highest good of ourselves and of others. He himself labored and prayed, and taught

his disciples so to do. His instruction concerning daily bread was not simply to pray for it, but to work with faith that God would prosper industry, making his providence second our exertions. Thus Paul, in answer to his prayers, was assured that no life should be lost by the shipwreck at Melita; and yet he required the seamen to use the appropriate means for an escape, asserting that otherwise they could not be saved. Acts xxvii: 22–32. Probably some Christians fall into an error the reverse of that of men of the world: the one class substituting prayer for labor, and the other labor for prayer. But each was intended to aid the other, and progress was to be made by the use of both; as the body avails itself of two arms and two feet, and as a boat is propelled by the simultaneous stroke of both oars.

13. Union with Other Petitioners. If the prayer of one saint has power with God, as fulfilling the requisite moral condition of the bestowment of blessing, then the prayer of two saints may be said to have double the moral power; and in proportion as God's people unite in asking for a specific gift, must be the certainty of its bestowment. The way is thus opened more clearly and perfectly for the divine action. Therefore Jesus said: "If two of you shall agree on earth, as touching anything that they shall ask, it shall be done for them of my Father who is in heaven." Mat. xviii: 19. Hence the marvelous effect of the prayers of the disciples at Jerusalem, before the day of Pentecost, concerning which we read: "These all

continued with one accord in prayer and supplication, with the women, and Mary the mother of Jesus, and with his brethren." Acts i: 14. This was evidently one reason why Paul continually besought the Christians to whom he wrote, to join their prayers to his, to secure the objects which he mentions. "Now I beseech you, brethren, for the Lord Jesus Christ's sake, and for the love of the Spirit, that ye strive together with me, in your prayers to God for me." Rom. xv: 30. "Ye also helping together by prayer for us, that for the gift bestowed upon us by the means of many persons, thanks may be given by many in our behalf." 2 Cor. i: 11. It is thus evident, that we may strengthen our prayers by associating others with us in making common petition for the desired object.

These thirteen conditions are annexed to prevailing prayer; but they are really so many specifications of the one condition of a right state of heart — a heart unselfish, in sympathy with God, jealous for his honor, and desirous of carrying out his will and promoting the good of all. There is no mysterious or inexplicable condition, and none beyond the reach of the humblest petitioner. Yet as these conditions do reasonably and necessarily exist, they must be regarded by those who wish to prevail in prayer. And it would be both unchristian and unphilosophical, for one to think that he could test prayer in a manner inconsistent with any of these prerequisites to success. For moral experiments, equally with those in physical science, have their essential conditions, which arise from the very nature of the case. When God ordained the physical system, he did it with strict reference to the nature and laws of matter; and when he ordained the moral system, of which prayer is a force, he did it with equally strict reference to the nature and laws of mind. But of this further notice will be taken, when we come to consider skeptical objections to prayer.

"When thou dost talk with God — by prayer, I mean —
Lift up pure hands; lay down all lust's desires;
Fix thoughts on heaven; present a conscience clean:
Since holy blame to mercy's throne aspires,
Confess faults' guilt, crave pardon for thy sin,
Tread holy paths, call grace to guide therein.

"Even as Elias, mounting to the sky,
Did cast his mantle to the earth behind,
So, when the heart presents the prayer on high,
Exclude the world from traffic with the mind:
Lips near to God, and ranging heart within,
Is but vain babbling and converts to sin."

— *Robert Southwell.*

CHAPTER VI.

THE PRAYER OF FAITH.

A chapter is devoted to the Prayer of Faith, because the subject is of importance, and is often misunderstood. The misunderstanding, moreover, is not without evil effect. Error never is harmless. In this instance, it has served to perplex and distress some good people, and to delude others; while providing skeptics with a host of objections against the idea of all prayer. Those have been perplexed and distressed, who were wishing to pray acceptably, and were told that they were not exercising the required faith; while yet they were conscious of a readiness to credit God's word. Having read the Bible carefully, on the subject, and studied the particular proof-texts to which they were pointed, they were not certain as to the extent of their meaning. They were then charged with not being willing to believe the Scripture, and thus with defeating their own prayers, in connection with objects which they greatly desired to secure; such as the conversion of individuals in whom they were specially interested, or the occurrence of a revival in certain churches. Urged by persons in whose supposed superior piety and spiritual discernment they had confidence, they sought to increase their faith by a desperate will-work; but in vain. And so they remained in a state of bewilderment and discouragement; not knowing whether they were guilty of unbelief, or whether the Bible did not mean what it seemed to say.

The deluded class have also had an unpleasant experience. Persuaded that their theory of prevailing prayer was correct, they tried to reduce it to practice. In so doing, they had for a time seeming corroborations of their view, the facts coming out according to their desire and petition. This gradually emboldened them to enlarge their experiments, and to announce the result confidently before hand. When the case was plainly going against them, they endeavored to believe more firmly; insisting that their faith was being put to the test, and that, in the end, it would signally triumph. Quite possibly, also, they fell into criticism of those who doubted their assurances of a favorable result, and thus grieved true hearted brethren and sisters, and created coldness where there should have been warm sympathy. Finally, they were put to confusion by the disappointment of their hopes and the non-fulfillment of their predictions; which left them on the edge of a reaction into an actual and sad unbelief; and for a time paralyzed their spiritual influence.

A case was reported to the author, as having these characteristics. The "prayer of faith," technically but improperly so called, was brought to bear on a lady seriously ill with organic disease, and whose recovery was pronounced impossible by the attendant physicians; and she was assured not simply that God could and might heal her, but that, in answer to the petitions of a circle of prayer, she was to be fully restored to health. This assurance was repeated to the last, and it was said (but this may have been untrue) that some even expected that she would be raised from the dead, to save the credit of their theory and predictions. But the result was sorrowful in all respects. The lady was kept in a dubious and distracted state of mind, between the contradictory declarations of the physicians and her intimate Christian friends, so that her last days were robbed of much of the peace which might have characterized them, and the gospel of Christ failed to secure the triumphant dying testimony of victory to which it was entitled. The effect upon the unconverted was also unhappy, as it led them to doubt the confident assertions of Christians as to the teaching of the Scriptures. Of course that circle of prayer fell into disrepute, and its leaders lost no small part of the influence which they had previously possessed. It was a clear case of being misled by an erroneous theory.

It will be noticed, furthermore, that when skeptics assail the doctrine of prayer, they invariably state it in the form of this obnoxious theory; knowing that unanswerable objections can be brought against it. They thus succeed in rendering the idea of prayer ridiculous to the minds of those who have not sufficient knowledge of the Bible, to discriminate between the view presented by the inspired writers and this delusion.

This theory teaches, that we can receive, in answer to prayer, any gift which we really think to be desirable, if we believe, at the time of offering the prayer, that it will be granted. This is said to be "The Prayer of Faith," which always prevails; and the cause of failure to receive anything for which one prays is declared to be, a lack of the specific faith, that the exact thing petitioned for, will surely be given. As faith, to be reasonable, must rest upon evidence, we are referred to a pledge which God is said to have given to the effect named, in the texts of Scripture which, without naming any limitation, bid us ask, and assure us that we shall receive; to the texts which name faith as the necessary condition of prevailing prayer; to the words in Mark xi: 24: "What things soever ye desire when ye pray, believe that ye receive them, and ye shall have them;" and to the language in James v: 15, "The prayer of faith shall save the sick." God, it is argued, has thus placed himself at our disposal; so that whatever may be our felt want, a believing petition will secure its relief. But to this view many things may be objected.

1. It implies that God virtually abdicates his throne in our favor; for it represents him as pledging himself in advance to do whatever we ask him to do. That would be to make man ruler. God would even exceed the folly of Oriental monarchs, who, like Ahasuerus, were accustomed to assure their favorites, in a mood

of generosity, that they would give them their request "even to the half of the kingdom"; or, like Herod, to "promise with an oath to give whatsoever they would ask." It is impossible that God could intend to place the scepter in our hands, by assuring us that he would always conform his action to our petition. Such an unconditional pledge leaves no place for a divine plan. The Bible assures us, that God is operating upon a wise and minute plan, which is to be carried out for the general good and his own glory. But he must needs surrender such plan, if he is to hold himself bound to grant every petition which we present with faith — a faith, observe, not in his general wisdom, but in his readiness to give us such specific things as we may happen to think desirable.

The only possible reply to this objection would be, to claim that, in God's all-comprehending plan, he has from the beginning arranged, that no prayer shall ever be offered in the faith of a specific answer, but such as he shall inspire, and shall be determined to hear. But such a claim cannot be sustained; facts are against it. There have been numerous cases in which, under the influence of this theory, Christians have selected an object for prayer, and assumed that it would certainly be granted, and then have been disappointed. But a modification of this view has a great truth in it. Let us imagine a soul entirely consecrated to God, and habitually in union with him, which, not merely with reference to some selected object is full of prayer and of faith, but with reference to all objects; and it may be truly affirmed, that God will so regulate its desires, that they will fasten only upon such specific blessings as he is about to bestow; and that concurrently he will excite a corresponding expectation in the mind. But the naked, unqualified theory, as before stated, begins at the human instead of the divine end of the series of acts, and puts man's desire, petition and faith first, and God's operation second. This rules out a divine plan, and supposes that the one who prays can make no mistake in his judgment, can have no blindness in his desires.

2. This method would be badly adapted to our moral training, which is the end chiefly had in view in the introduction of prayer into the divine economy. It would breed presumption rather than faith, self-confidence rather than humility; and it would fail to develop the spirit of patience, submission, importunity, perseverance and labor. It would introduce into God's family the very evils which are to be deplored in human families where parental indulgence is the only rule.

3. It would ruin us and those we love and for whom we offer petitions. We should be certain to ask for gifts (as all children do) which would not be for our own good, or for the benefit of those for whom we might pray. Desire is ever blind. We think we need a multitude of things, which we are better without. In times past we have asked for that which, afterwards, we were glad not to have received; and we have prayed to have events prevented, which we now see to have

been for our good. God is too benevolent to put so dangerous a power into our hands.

4. The theory involves self-contradiction; for it would bind God to do opposite things, at the same time, if opposing prayers should chance to be offered by those who accept the supposed pledge. One man wishes dry weather, to-day, while another particularly desires to have it rain; and each could present an excellent reason for his prayer, so far as he himself is concerned. Christian people are attached to conflicting parties and interests in politics, in ecclesiastical matters, in business enterprises, in military struggles. Did any such invariable rule of answer to prayer exist, they would call upon God to do the most contradictory things, daily! Can it be that God has exposed himself to such embarrassment?

5. The theorists themselves either never venture to act upon their theory, or are unwilling witnesses of its failure. For plainly they do not secure a multitude of objects which they most desire to secure, and for which either they strangely do not pray, or else pray in vain. Their friends and relatives die; their enterprises fail; their troubles come and remain, as in the case of other men; and their spiritual undertakings are no broader, or more successful than those of Christians who pray on a different understanding of the conditions. The wonder is, if this absolute and specific faith is always rewarded, as they assert that it is, that they do not pray with the requisite faith for the conversion of all around them; for the removal of the

prevailing evils, which they observe and feel; and, in fact, for the salvation of the whole world. What could be more appropriate? Yet they have never succeeded in accomplishing such ends, and their efforts to come into the requisite state of mind, have brought about sad results. The following is an extract from a letter communicated to the author, when he was editor of *The Advance*, (see paper of March 26, 1868,) by the gentleman who had the original in his possession. It was written by "Father Nash," as he was familiarly called, who had special power in prayer, and was eminently useful, in that way, in the great revivals of the State of New York, forty-five years ago. But he carried his idea of the "Prayer of Faith" to an unscriptural extreme; which led him to a feeling of personal responsibility exaggerated and overwhelming, and by which his physical system was utterly broken down. The letter is dated, Verona, Oneida Co., N. Y., Nov. 7, 1831, and would occupy many pages, if given in full: the following extracts will show his theory:

"Since you were here I have been thinking of prayer—particularly of praying for the Holy Ghost, and its descent. It seems to me I have always limited God in this respect. * * * I have never felt, till since you left us, that I might rationally ask for the *whole* influence of the Spirit to come down; not only on individuals, but on a whole people, region, country and world. On Saturday I set myself to do this, and the devil was very angry with me, yesterday, for it. I am now convinced, it is my duty and privilege, and the duty of every other Christian, to pray for as much of the Holy Spirit as came down on the day of Pentecost, and a great deal more. I know not why we may not ask for the *entire and utmost* influence of the Spirit to come down, and, asking in faith, see the full answer. * * * I think I never did so freely ask the Holy Ghost for all mankind. My body is in pain, but I am happy in my God. * * * I have only just begun to understand what Jesus meant when he said, 'All things whatsoever ye shall ask in prayer, believing, ye shall receive.' I suppose millions have gone to hell, because I had no more faith to pray for them, and I do not see why I do not deserve to be damned for this. * * * I suppose I have done the world much more hurt than good. * * * Thus, by my unbelief, I have robbed God, robbed heaven, benefited hell, cheated sinners out of their souls, and cheated myself; so that my portion will be small in heaven; for it will be according to the service which I shall have done for God. I wonder he does not let me go to hell! Wretch that I am, I suppose, however, that I shall just escape, as Paul did, because I did it ignorantly, and in unbelief."

Now this was making himself personally responsible for the salvation of the world; as if it depended on his offering "the prayer of faith," as he understood that phrase. He could not endure the strain, and the next morning he added: "I have felt a little like praying that I might be overwhelmed with the Holy Ghost, die in the operation, and go to heaven thus;

but God knows." Need any one be surprised to learn that, a few days after "Father Nash" had penned these words, he was found dead, upon his knees! He reasoned too logically from his mistaken premises. He believed that, as God had promised to grant any thing which a Christian asked with specific faith, he was bound to secure by prayer the conversion of neighbors, countrymen, and mankind; and he therefore struggled, agonized, and snapped the cord of life, in a desperate attempt to work himself into a faith sufficient to save the land and the world. Rev. Asa Mahan, D. D., who lived and labored, at the time, in that region, states, in a communication to *The Advance* of May 21, 1868, that several died from a similar cause, while many others suffered from a physical prostration and a moral and spiritual paralysis, from which they never recovered. Yet the first effect of the preaching of this theory seemed remarkably good; for it had in it a partial truth.

6. Nor does the Bible lend support to this view. Some think that the Bible means a peculiar kind of prayer, by "*the* prayer of faith;" which differs from other acceptable prayer, in that it always secures its specific object by believing that it will receive the very thing desired; and that this can be offered only in certain cases, where special promises exist, or special indications are made of the divine will. But the words of James, "the prayer of faith shall save the sick," do not imply any such peculiarity; but only that the prayer so offered, with a faith appropriate to

the circumstances, would secure the desired result. He does not affirm that we ought not always to offer "the prayer of faith," whatever that may be. Plainly we should; for, as was proved in the last chapter, *faith is made a condition of all acceptable prayer.* No man has a right to expect any blessing from God, through prayer, without faith, any more than without reverence, or sense of want, or gratitude, or humility, or submission, or obedience. He must "lift up holy hands, without wrath or *doubting.*" All true prayer must be the prayer of faith.

But in interpreting Scripture, one must never forget that, usually, but a single topic is handled at a time, and the reader is expected to know, or to learn, what is elsewhere said. Because in one passage salvation is made to turn upon the fact of repentance, it must not be concluded that there is no other condition attached. Further inquiry shows that we must also believe on the Lord Jesus Christ. And so when we read a text which gives one condition of acceptable prayer, we must not think that this is to be taken alone, apart from the limitations and qualifications mentioned in other texts. Each must aid to define the others. Thus the familiarity of a filial spirit must be limited by reverence; and a spirit of importunity by a feeling of humility. A reliance on the name and merit of Christ must be accompanied by a full purpose of obedience; a faith that God will give, by a submission of the form and time to his superior wisdom.

Here is where a mistake is made by the theory

under condemnation. It finds a passage which reads, "What things soever ye desire, when ye pray, believe that ye receive them, and ye shall have them," and it fails to remember, that this presupposes that another condition, shaping the desire and the prayer, has already been complied with; to-wit, that we should ask only for the things which are according to the will of God. John says, "And this is the confidence that we have in him, that *if we ask anything according to his will*, he heareth us;" which certainly does not mean, that if we ask anything according to our own will, (provided only we ask believingly,) he will always hear us. But Jesus, assuming that we understand this, says, that, when we thus have an object of desire, which we have evidence is according to the divine will, then, if by a firm faith, we believe that we have it, we shall find it to be indeed so. This leaves us to submit unknown matters to the yet unrevealed divine will; making our prayer with respect to them conditional. Thus did Jesus in his prayer in the garden; and received that which was best. Similar was the spirit which Paul exercised with respect to "the thorn in the flesh;" for the removal of which he thrice prayed specifically, without obtaining the desired object; yet found his faith honored and his prayer answered, by a spiritual equivalent, even special grace which enabled him to gain a victory over the trial.

What, then, is the Scriptural doctrine of the prayer of faith? Simply this, that *when we pray, we must fully believe that God will be true to all that he has promised.* This implies that we are ready to learn what his promises are, and to make them the basis of a sure expectation. Less than this would not harmonize with the texts which require faith as a condition of prevailing prayer, or with that general principle so clearly announced in Heb. xi: 6; "But without faith it is impossible to please him; for he that cometh to God must believe that he is, and that he is a rewarder of those that diligently seek him." That it may be seen to what divine assurances faith gives credence, when it engages in prayer, attention should be paid to four points.

1. *The general pledge that Prayer shall be answered.* As we have already seen, the Bible abounds in declarations that God answers prayer; as when the Psalmist says: "O thou that hearest prayer, unto thee shall all flesh come;" and when Jesus says, "Ask and it shall be given unto you." This is, of course, subject to the natural and obvious limitation, that God will use his superior wisdom in deciding what to give and what to refuse, and also when and how to bestow his favors. Prayer does not set aside God's sovereignty; which is simply his love directed by his wisdom. But then these general pledges are an assurance of real aid. They mean that in human experience prayer will be found to be an actual help; that it will not prove a mockery of human hope. Faith will accept these pledges at their full value, and will so rest upon them, as habitually to carry all wants to God in child-

like petition, certain that he will do the very best for us that is possible, and taking the comfort of that fact. It will also have the spirit of expectation, and will watch for answers to its petitions, relying on the fatherly character of God and his invitations to his children to make known their desires with the utmost freedom.

2. We must notice the reason for faith, found in the *promises of the Bible on specific subjects.* God does more than to give general assurance of a willingness to hear prayer, and to relieve human want. He makes mention of specific blessings, which he is ready to bestow. These more minute pledges are in various forms of promise, prophecy, covenant and command. A promise is a direct engagement; a covenant is a still more formal and solemn act, usually accompanied by a seal; a prophecy is a statement of divine purpose, intended for our encouragement in prayer and labor; and a command always implies a result which God is willing to aid us in securing. It is only necessary, then, to ascertain that the desired favor is covered by some promise, covenant, prophecy, or command, to have a perfect warrant for faith that, in answer to prayer, God will bestow that very thing. One could not ask for a better ground of assurance.

> "How firm a foundation, ye saints of the Lord,
> Is laid for your faith in his excellent word!"

We are entitled to claim, at God's hand, whatever he has been pleased graciously to promise. And so our prayers may and should have the characteristic of perfect faith, that they will be literally answered according to the blessing asked.

Are these specific pledges numerous? Do they cover the ground of our usual necessities? Will they impart an element of certainty to our prayers, in the emergencies which men are often called to face? An affirmative reply to these questions is authorized by the language of Scripture. For we find, in the Bible, promises to the righteous of protection, deliverance, food, raiment, wisdom, guidance, sustaining grace, reward for industry and beneficence, and the presence and power of the Holy Spirit as a guaranty of peace, holiness and usefulness. The prayer of faith uses these divine assurances as a sufficient ground of conviction that God will aid in the emergency to which any of these promises applies, according to the exigency of the case. The man feels that he can pray with an accompanying certainty of being heard. It is not now so much an occasion of submission, as of grateful expectation. God here has made known his will, in advance. The true submission to it is, to take him at his word, and joyfully to claim what he has authorized us to ask. Not to do so, is a distrust of him, as well as a robbery of our own souls. It is as though a poor man should neglect to present a benefactor's check at the bank, fearing that it might not mean what it said on its face, or might for some cause not be paid. As such lack of confidence is grievous to our heavenly Father, so a firm faith is his delight.

In interpreting the specific promises, we must guard against a merely imaginative, or a fortuitous interpretation of them; in which some indulge without warrant from the Bible itself. There are those who, not content with a legitimate inference from Scriptural promises, treat the Bible as a conjuring book, or an instrument of fortune-telling. They wish to be divinely guided; and so, after prayer, they open the sacred volume, determined to take the first text which meets the eye, as an indication from God of what they are to do. Or they read the Bible devoutly, or engage in prayer, and meet with or suddenly think of a passage, the wording of which powerfully impresses their imagination as applicable to their case; especially if it harmonizes with their natural wishes. The difficulty is, that a rational faith has no ground on which to rest, in such a case; there being *no assurance in Scripture* that God will reveal his will in that way. And it often results in lamentable delusion; as when ignorant persons think they are converted and forgiven, because the words, "Thy sins are forgiven thee," have flashed into their minds, when they were in mental distress. It happens, sometimes, that a truly pious man, whose temperament is enthusiastic, being seriously out of health, is impressed in reading, or in thought, with some such words as those of the Psalmist: "I shall not die, but live and declare the works of the Lord." Perhaps he seizes upon this, as an assurance that he is to recover, and have the enlarged opportunities of usefulness which he earnestly desires.

This may be but imagination, and this mistaken confidence, though it imparts a joyous hope to the last months of his life, may also so far mislead him, in his plans and arrangements, as to prevent desirable things from being said and done, which would be said and done, were not the mind preoccupied with an expectation which is not to be realized. The effect upon others, also, is unfortunate, in that it persuades them that faith is but imagination.

It is not intended, by these remarks, to deny that the Holy Spirit often uses passages of Scripture unexpectedly seen, to lead the mind to needed spiritual results; nor yet to express doubt that God may be pleased to arrange in his providence that the eye, at times, shall meet appropriate texts, which fill the soul with needed comfort. The instances in proof of such a divine guidance are too numerous and striking to allow of denial. The conversion of Augustine seems to have been thus ordered; for, at the acme of his internal struggle, on the point whether he could forever renounce the pleasures of sinful indulgence, for Christ's sake, and when he was weeping alone, in agony of conflict, he heard a child in a neighboring house singing something in which occurred the words, "Take up and read." And so he rushed to where there was a volume of Scripture, and, to give his own words: "I seized, opened, and in silence read that passage on which mine eyes first fell — 'Not in rioting and drunkenness, not in chambering and wantonness, not in strife and envying: but put ye on the Lord Jesus Christ, and make not provision for the flesh to fulfill the lusts thereof.' No further would I read; nor needed I; for instantly, at the end of this sentence, by a light as it were of serenity infused into my heart, all the darkness of doubt vanished away." Here was appropriate instruction fitted to every such soul. But where does the Bible convey a warrant for us to turn it by prayer into an accidental prophet, in a way not very unlike fortune-telling by cards. The case of a minister of strong self-will could be mentioned, who in this way deluded himself into the idea that he was being divinely guided in a course which came near to a shipwreck of his character and usefulness. Only the persistent contradiction of facts drove him finally to a rational and genuinely Scriptural conduct. And this consideration prepares us for the next support of faith.

3. Another warrant for faith, in connection with prayer, may be found in the *indications of divine providence.* Jesus told the Pharisees, that if they had studied the signs of the times, as diligently as they had the signs of the weather, they would have understood the will of God. We might not be able to interpret these signs, were it not for the word of God, which pre-announces his purposes; but with the Bible in our hands, to assure us of the divine plans, we ought to be able to discern the evidence that they are in process of fulfillment in specific cases. When a friend has publicly stated, that he intends to build a house, and soon after we notice that sand, lime, brick and lumber are being drawn to land which he owns, we are war-

ranted in the inference, that he is now carrying out his intention, and will fulfill any promise which he may have made in connection with it. And so God's people find special ground for the exercise of faith as to the answer of their prayers, when they discern, in the events of the day, in the peculiar ordering of circumstances around them, evidence that God is preparing to accomplish a part of his work in the world in which they feel a special interest. For his will appears in his providence, as truly as in his Word; and they who make a study of divine providence (as all God's people should do) become quick to discern its meaning, and to foretell coming events of a moral and spiritual character. The prayers of such saints are full of confidence, and petition almost turns into anticipative thanksgiving.

4. There is still another warrant for a prayer of faith, found in *the leadings of the Holy Spirit.* That these are a reality, no devout Christian will be disposed to deny. The New Testament is filled with declarations on this point; and it was the chief theme of discourse of our Savior at the institution of the Lord's Supper. As the promised Comforter was to be the universal spiritual helper of Christ's followers, we are prepared to learn that his aid has a special relation to our supplications. We are therefore directed to "pray in the Spirit," and are assured that "the Spirit also helpeth our infirmities; for we know not what we should pray for as we ought; but the spirit itself maketh intercession for us with groanings which cannot

be uttered. And he that searcheth the hearts knoweth what is the mind of the Spirit; because he maketh intercession for the saints according to the will of God." Rom. viii: 26, 27. It will be seen from this statement, that the work of the Spirit pertains to the exact point requisite to faith; to-wit, an understanding of the proper objects of prayer, and of the actual will of God. The Spirit may then beget in the soul a strong faith, which shall be concurrent with the divine plans; a supposition which is in accord with the idea that prevailing prayers are inspired of God, as we read: "I will pour upon the house of David and upon the inhabitants of Jerusalem, the spirit of grace and of supplications." Zech. xii: 10.

In consequence of this bestowment of the Holy Spirit, the soul of the Christian is prepared to pray with faith. First of all, the Spirit awakens right desires and directs them to the proper objects; so that prayer goes straight to its mark. When not thus influenced, our desires are blind, being occasioned by mere natural impulse; and consequently they often long for objects which God cannot wisely bestow. But by the Spirit our desires are chastened, elevated, purified, and thus brought into sympathy with the divine plans, as respects ourselves and others. We are prepared to pray with a spiritual intelligence and intuition, and to have a corresponding confidence awakened that we shall be heard.

Moreover, the Spirit guides to a true interpretation of Scripture; so that we understand the promises, covenants, prophesies and commands, in their adaptation to our duties, temptations, trials and labors. When these are made clear to our apprehension, and we feel that in them we are come into contact with the heart of God, to learn the extent of his love, we exercise faith as the most natural of inward acts. What else does prayer signify, we say, than the use of the means appointed to obtain precisely what we need, and what God has promised?

In a similar manner, the Spirit aids us to interpret the divine providence. He who is in spiritual sympathy with God's aims, and is led to an understanding of his Word, has the key to the mystery of earthly events. He sees along the line of divine purposes, and thus with a longer and clearer vision than that of men of the world. During our late war, there were no citizens so persistently hopeful, so certain of success, even at the darkest periods, as those who saw in the struggle great moral issues; and who believed that the time had come for an answer to the prayers which had so long been offering for the overthrow of slavery. It is true also, that some Christians have a prevision of coming scenes of religious revival. Thy are "filled with the Spirit," and can see indications which others do not notice. They have a consciousness that their peculiarly strong spiritual desires have been kindled by the Comforter, to be gratified and not to be disappointed. Thus in his "Lectures on Revivals," Mr. Finney tells this anecdote: "There was a woman in the state of New Jersey, in a place where there had been a revival. She was very positive there was going to be another. She insisted upon it, that they had had the former rain, and were now going to have the latter rain. She wanted to have conference meetings appointed. But the minister and elders saw nothing to encourage it, and would do nothing. * * * She went forward, and got a carpenter to make seats for her; for she said she would have meetings in her own house: there was certainly going to be a revival. She had scarcely opened her doors for meetings, before the Spirit of God came down with great power." The history of almost any church will furnish similar facts, and the same truth holds true as to individual conversions.

We come, then, to this conclusion; that there is no prayer acceptable to God, but the prayer of faith; and that this simply means, that all prayer must be offered in full confidence that God will be true to his word. Perhaps the truth has been sufficiently expressed by Professor Thomas C. Upham, D. D., in his "Life and Experience of Catharine Adorna," of whom he makes these excellent remarks:

"She had faith in God's character, faith in his goodness and wisdom, faith in his providential arrangements, faith in his promises. And this faith she exercised constantly and practically, during the heavy trials of the earlier part of her life, and amid the weighty duties, which characterized its later periods. If she wanted wisdom, for instance, all she had to do was, to exercise, in sincere dependence upon God for his direction, those rational powers which God had given her, fully *believing* that he would guide her to all those results which were proper, and which were most beneficial. She did not regard it as necessary or desirable, that she should have full or absolute knowledge; but only that kind and degree of knowledge which God sees best. And in the same manner, if she desired to be delivered from the presence of any temporary evil, she laid the case before God; fully believing that God would grant all that relief which he saw to be beneficial; and she accepted the result, whatever it might be, as the true answer to her prayer, and with entire submission and gratitude. True faith, as it seems to us, is always exercised with the limitation implied in these remarks. It believes that God will give us whatever we ask in accordance with his wisdom and will. It neither goes, nor desires to go farther."

Behold the throne of grace!
  The promise calls me near:
There Jesus shows a smiling face,
  And waits to answer prayer.

That rich atoning blood,
  Which sprinkled round I see,
Provides for those who come to God,
  An all-prevailing plea.

My soul! ask what thou wilt;
  Thou canst not be too bold:
Since his own blood for thee he spilt,
  What else can he withhold?

—*John Newton.*

CHAPTER VII.

SKEPTICAL ASSAULTS ON PRAYER.

Modern skeptics have made multiplied assaults upon prayer. Plainly they deem the practice one of the worst forms of superstition, and the faith in it one of the most serious obstacles to the progress of unbelief. Undoubtedly the latter supposition is correct. The more cautious or complaisant of the number graciously allow, that prayer may have value as a liturgical exercise, by its reflex influence; but they all agree in ridiculing the unreasonableness of petition for divine aid with expectation of an agency to be put forth in answer to it. This is, indeed, no new development of unbelief; for scoffers were found in the days of Job, of whom he testifies, (xxi : 14, 15:) "They say unto God, Depart from us; for we desire not the knowledge of thy ways. What is the Almighty, that we should serve him? and what profit should we have, if we pray unto him?" But of late there has been a fresh outbreak of opposition to this universal religious rite; as though its absurdity and mischief had been set in a new light.

The physical philosophers have taken the lead in this latest assault. Professors Huxley and Tyndall follow their captivating popular lectures on science and their brilliant experiments, with articles in the reviews, which question the reality of answers to prayer. Their unbelief spreads like contagion, and those who have omitted prayer from moral distaste, not finding it congenial with the character of their lives, rejoice to be furnished, from respectable sources, with a philosophical reason for their neglect. They tell us that we must choose between the horns of a logical dilemma. Either God does, or he does not, intervene in the affairs of men: if he does, and is a being of infinite power, wisdom and goodness, prayer is unnecessary; since he already knows our wants, and is disposed to relieve them; if he does not intervene, but has framed a perfect system of natural laws, to whose working he leaves us, it is useless to ask him to depart from these wise methods to serve our individual convenience; it is even impious and insulting to request it. To this we answer promptly, that God does intervene in human affairs, and yet with no departure from a perfect plan; since the plan provides wisely for such action, on his part, while all natural laws are so constituted as to allow of the inter-play of supernatural forces. Moreover, his previous purpose to intervene does not in the least render unnecessary the appointed use of prayer, as an appropriate means of moral education for us; which is its true design.

But before we enter into the details of the argument, let us inquire why there should be this marked hostility to prayer — a rite which is not peculiar to

Christianity, but enters into all religions, and might therefore well claim to be a doctrine of natural or absolute religion. The assault would seem to be the more reckless, in view of the fact that men find in prayer such comfort in trial, such strength in weakness, such refuge from despair, and such a means of making spiritual ideas impressive. The explanation is, that unbelief must work out its necessary logical conclusions. Logic knows no compassion. It is a matter of reason, not of sensibility. It deals with consistency, not with feeling. It drives the skeptic from point to point in his negations, without mercy to him or to others. It necessitates his rejection of prayer, lest, in admitting that, he admit, in principle, nearly everything to which, as an unbeliever, he objects.

For the principle of prayer involves Christianity. It starts with the conception of a personal God, in opposition to atheism and pantheism. It involves the idea of a perpetual and minute divine providence, contrary to the assumptions of naturalism. It implies a direct intercourse of the soul with God, as of man with man, by reason of which there is a divine influence to impart wisdom, strength, courage, hope and purity, and a divine regulation of outward events to adapt them to the wants of petitioning individuals and communities. But to admit all this, is to admit the whole doctrine of supernaturalism upon which Christianity is based. For, if the love, sympathy and personal intervention of God, by inward and outward influences, be thus at the call of petitioners, at the present time; then what can be more natural and reasonable, than the Christian doctrine of interpositions in the early days, by inspired teachers, and even by an incarnation, should that be requisite to meet a great moral crisis? The question is no longer one of power and principle, but simply of wisdom and degree. Prayer thus sets wide open the gate into the realm of the supernatural; and once open, who shall close it? The divine Spirit in direct intercourse with the soul for purposes now needful, prepares one to believe that it may have been in direct intercourse with the soul of Moses, of David, of Isaiah, of Jesus, of Paul, for purposes needful in their days. A perpetual inter-play of supernatural forces with the natural, such as prayer pre-supposes, gives one also, a conception of a supernatural realm, and of a moral order, to which what we call nature must be subordinate. Thus reason suffers no shock, when miracles are announced in connection with a divine revelation and a process of redemption.

The temptation to a somewhat devout skeptic to admit prayer into his system is indeed great, and the old English Deists were disposed to yield the point, as the condition of having any system worthy of the name of religion. For to acknowledge a God, and then to put him out of connection with human affairs, was an unprofitable, if not an irrational procedure. But the modern skeptic has been taught caution. He sees that the concession will cost him dear, logically; that it will plant a germ of faith which may grow to an overshadowing tree, beneath which skepticism cannot thrive. The native shyness of the skeptic in this respect comes out curiously in the case of Rousseau (see Morley's Life of Rousseau, I, p. 75). He had a sentimental recognition of God in connection with natural scenery, and, at one time, used to begin the day, as he tells us, on a hilltop back of his residence, gazing at the sunrise, and engaged in a form of worship, which "did not consist in a vain moving of the lips, but in a sincere elevation of the heart to the author of the tender nature whose beauties lay spread out before my eyes." "This act," he observes, "passed rather in wonder and contemplation than in requests; and I always knew that with the Dispenser of true blessings the best means of obtaining those which are needful for us is, less to ask, than to deserve them." This was pretty well for a man who, at the time, was living in the house of Madame de Warens in immoral relations!

It would seem that skepticism cannot abide the atmosphere of real prayer; such as is set forth in the well known definition of the Westminster Assembly of divines: "Prayer is the offering up of our desires unto God, for things agreeable to his will, in the name of Christ, with confession of our sins, and thankful acknowledgment of his mercies." In ascertaining whether the Christian doctrine of prayer rests upon a foundation of reason, it is well to approach the subject gradually, and to gather up the related facts one by one. It may be noticed, then:

1. That prayer appears to be a universal instinct, wherever men have the least conception of a God. Guizot, in his treatise entitled "L'Eglise et la Société Chrétiénne," has a true and eloquent passage on this point, which may be rendered in English thus: "Alone of all beings here below, man prays! Among his moral instincts none is more natural, more universal, more indestructible than prayer. The child inclines to it with eager docility. The old man betakes himself thither, as to a refuge against decay and solitude. Prayer comes spontaneously to young lips, which with difficulty stammer out the name of God; and to dying lips, which no longer have strength to pronounce it. Among all nations, celebrated or obscure, civilized or barbarous, one meets at every step acts and forms of invocation. Wherever men live, in certain circumstances, at certain times, under the control of certain impressions of the soul, the eyes are raised, the hands clasp, the knees bend, to implore aid or to render thanks, to adore or to appease. With transport or with fear, publicly or in the secrecy of his heart, it is to prayer that man betakes himself, in the last resort, to fill up the void of his soul, or to bear the burdens of his destiny: it is in prayer that he seeks, when all else fails, strength for his weakness, consolation in his grief, hope for his virtue."

The case is this: the idea of God seems naturally and instinctively to carry with it the duty and privilege of prayer; the one — except by a few would-be philosophers — is universally associated with and thought to imply the other. This is seen by such a skeptic as Mr. Wm. C. Greg, who, in his "Enigmas of Life" (p. 249) thus writes: "The instinct of prayer, of appeal for help in difficulty and rescue in peril, is an inevitable consequence and corelative of belief in God; in a Being who can hear and answer, who has made us, and who cares for the creatures he has made. It flows from the consciousness of our inferiority and his superiority, of our helplessness and his power. It is an original and nearly irresistible instinct, precisely similar to that which makes the child run to the mother, and the feeble cling to and entreat the strong. We can scarcely imagine its extinction." Professor J. Tyndall himself allows the naturalness and almost inevitableness of prayer, *as a theory*, to every one who has faith in God; even while denying that it has proof as a fact. In the *Contemporary Review* of 1872, in an article on "Science and Religion," he says: "It is matter of experience, that an earthly father, who is at the same time wise and tender, listens to the requests of his children, and, if they do not ask amiss, takes pleasure in granting their requests. We know, also, that this compliance extends to the alteration, within certain limits, of the current events of earth! With this suggestion offered by our experience, it is no departure from scientific method, to place behind natural phenomena a universal Father, who, in answer to the prayers of his children, alters the currents of these phenomena." Now this is to say, that as a child instinctively calls to the parent for help, so a human soul instinctively prays to God the heavenly parent. The act is an outbirth of creaturely and filial dependence, and is a spontaneous utterance.

But nature teaches that every instinct points to a corresponding reality; that it springs from a want, and leads to a supply. Is there in all nature an aimless, or an unrewarded instinct? The new-born child instinctively desires and seeks for milk; and the fountain is at hand, in the mother's breast. The instinct of the bird impels it to build a nest, and the nest is no sooner finished, than nature produces the eggs, and leads to incubation, rewarding the whole seemingly blind process, by a brood of young birds. Instincts, needs and supplies are indissolubly bound together. If this be so, then the instinct of prayer in the human soul indicates a divine plan of procedure. It implies other coincident facts; it tells us that in some way divine power and love are pledged to honor the appeal. The reason for such an instinct, also, is everywhere obvious; for human life is full of events which throw the soul back on a higher power. Individual knowledge and ability are limited, and men continually fall into difficulties, related often to life's highest interests, from which they cannot extricate themselves; when but for prayer the soul would sink into utter despair. And the broader and deeper our experience, the more complete our dependence is found to be; so that eventually, with souls of the noblest and purest type, to breathe is to pray.

2. In noticeable accord with this primary instinct

is the fact that, in all ages, men have insisted that their prayers were answered. It is of little use in philosophy, to argue against an ascertained fact; to show that an event could not have occurred, after it has occurred. Some will remember that the learned scientist, Dr. Dionysius Lardner, of England, published an elaborate paper to prove that the Atlantic could not be crossed by steam vessels, just as the feat was accomplished; and that in a few weeks he made a sudden and a not very honorable flight in a steamer to these shores! It is only a joke, when men tell of the Frenchman who was so wedded to his theory that, when told that certain facts contradicted it, he said, "so much the worse for the facts!" In the case before us the facts can be ascertained. Prayer is as old as the human race, and by this time its effects ought to have been thoroughly tested. If it be a delusion, void of real power, it should long since have gone into disuse. But so far is this from being true, that it was never more widely or more earnestly practised. And men insist—a strange hallucination, surely, the skeptic must think—that they receive that for which they pray, in instances so many and so marked, as to leave no doubt of the agency involved. Here and there a case might be explained as a mere coincidence; but no such disposal can be made of the mass of the facts, in which special characteristics in the petitions have found correspondence in the events. And it is noticeable, that those most accustomed to rely on this source of aid are those who have the strongest faith in it, and who put it to widest use in meeting the requirements of life.

Of course the test of reality must accord with the nature of the case. As prayer is a moral and not a mechanical power, it is not to be tested as if it were a physical force depending only upon physical antecedents, few in number and within the knowledge of the spectators. We judge of water-power or steam-power by the laws of matter; by the number of pounds which can be moved in resistance to gravity through a given space. There is nothing to be done, but to apply the force, and watch for that single result. But mind has other laws than matter; and moral power, unlike physical, cannot be tested by the production of a single outward result on fixed visible conditions. Prayer, as we have seen, has numerous relationships and many conditions, and only God can know, at the time when the petition is outwardly offered, whether the necessary conditions have been met. Hence it may seem to be impotent, when its force has not really been invoked, or when the effect has been produced in an unanticipated form. For prayer does not imply that God will do everything which everybody shall ask. That would involve him in unutterable follies and contradictions, to his own dishonor and to our ruin. But it implies that he who offers it does so with a submissive, conditional faith; trusting God to do the specified thing, if it be specifically promised, and be for the best interests of all concerned: otherwise desiring him not to do it, but to substitute such gift as may be more wisely granted. The prayer being thus conditional in spirit, even when not so in form, may be accepted and answered, when the specific object is not given. And so a form of prayer may be accompanied by a state of heart so selfish, unsubmissive, or unbelieving, as to meet no moral condition, and to fail of influence with God.

Here was the mental confusion of Sir William Thompson and of Professor Tyndall, in the famous communication to the *Contemporary Review*, in July, 1872, which proposed a hospital test of the power of prayer. There can be no objection to the idea that prayer, if a real power, may be tested. Does not the Bible appeal to men, to "prove" God with respect to his promises? Mr. Tyndall had a right to demand that the *theory* of prayer, which he admitted to be natural, should present evidence of being a *fact*. His words were: "But without *verification*, a theoretic conception is a mere figment of the intellect, and I am sorry to find us parting company at this point. The region of theory, both in science and theology, lies behind the world of the senses; but the verification of theory occurs in the sensible world. To check the theory, we have simply to compare the deductions from it with the facts of observation." To this the Christian fully assents, and will allow prayer to stand or fall by such a test.

But Professor Tyndall unfortunately sees fit to add these taunting words: "While science cheerfully submits to this ordeal, it seems impossible to devise a mode of verification of their theory, which does not arouse resentment in theological minds." Not so; theologians only object to proposed tests which *violate the very conditions of the theory*, and which are therefore wholly inappropriate. Professor Tyndall should not have fallen into such an error; for, as an accomplished lecturer on physical science, and a brilliant experimentalist, he understands the necessity of securing with exactness the necessary conditions of the pre-announced phenomena. To his care, in this respect, and the skill of his able assistant, is his success due. What would he say, if theologians should require him to succeed without regard to these conditions? If they should expect him to produce combustion without oxygen; or to explode wet gunpowder; or to confine electricity without insulation? But the moral universe has its laws and conditions, as well as the physical, and these must be as rigidly observed, in order to the success of moral experiments. Let us see whether Sir William Thompson's proposed test, which Professor Tyndall endorsed, conformed to them.

Here is the now celebrated proposal: "I ask that one single ward or hospital, under the care of first rate physicians and surgeons, containing certain numbers of patients afflicted with those diseases which have been best studied, and of which the mortality rates are best known, whether the diseases are treated by medical or by surgical remedies, should be, during a period of not less than three or five years, made the object of special prayer by the whole body of the faithful; and that, at the end of that time, the mortality rates should be compared with the past rates, and also with that of other leading hospitals similarly well managed, during the same period. Granting that time is given and numbers are sufficiently large, so as to insure a minimum of error from accidental disturbing causes, the experiment will be exhaustive and complete."

Probably it so appeared to the two distinguished gentlemen who fathered the scheme; for they were thinking of scientific tests of physical forces, and they reasoned about prayer, as if it operated mechanically; as if it were a head of water, or a pressure of steam, to be turned upon wheel or piston—so many petitions, for such a length of time, for such a number of patients! In other words, they quietly ignored the spiritual laws and conditions which the Scriptural theory of prayer implies. For prayer pre-supposes a moral kingdom, of which it is a leading instrumentality, and in which outward results are wholly subordinated to those of a spiritual character. Prayer must therefore spring from a spirit of faith, love, humility, submission, obedience and perseverance, and must desire that which shall be for the good of the petitioner and for the general welfare. The proposal in question violated the legitimate principles of verification, by paying no attention to what God declares to be essential.

(1.) It gravely asked, what could not be secured—

a ward or hospital, whose patients should be specially prayed for "by the whole body of the faithful" for three or five years! But there is no possible way of thus uniting the prayers of Christendom upon a single institution exclusively, that its results may be compared with those of other institutions. The idea itself is abhorrent to the nature of prayer, which is a spirit of universal sympathy and love, even when it has a specific object. How could Christians, while praying for the unfortunate in one hospital, withhold prayer from the more numerous unfortunates in other institutions; and that for a period of three or five years, and in the face of the Scriptural injunction that "supplications, prayers, intercessions and giving of thanks be made for all men"? The suggestion is preposterous; while there could be no means of ascertaining whether the experiment, if nominally undertaken, was actually carried out. For surely it may be supposed, that the patients in the other institutions would have anxious friends who would pray for them; and that many of the patients would pray for themselves, and all the more earnestly, should they learn that two men of science had arranged with the Christian world that no outside petitions should ascend!

(2.) The proposal encounters this moral difficulty: that God has not been wont to put forth his power to gratify curiosity; and that, in his Word, he has put himself under limitations of human faith. Prayer has its long established place in the ordinary economy of life, in connection with which every sincere and reverential inquirer may test its power for himself. To drag it forth for a public spectacle, at the dictation of skeptics, to be applied to what they shall consider to be proper objects, is not a proceeding warranted by the nature of the case, or by the precepts of the Bible. It will be remembered, that, even in the days when miracles were specially appropriate, Jesus, though working them daily, with great variety and publicity, in all parts of the land, yet refused on a certain occasion, to meet the demand of the unbelieving and scoffing Pharisees for a "sign from heaven." (Matt. xvi: 1–4.) He also declined to perform one for the gratification of King Herod (Luke xxii: 8, 9); and of his visit to Nazareth it is said, that "he did not many mighty works there because of their unbelief."

(3.) The proposal ignores the condition in prayer, of submission as to the answer to be returned. It falsely assumes that when a specific request is made, it must always be granted, or prayer is a failure. But God has never promised in connection with prayer to make our ignorance the law of procedure, instead of his wisdom. Hence he has not promised to heal all the sick for whom his people may pray; or any definite proportion of them. It is not the province of prayer, to countervail death, or to usurp the place of medical skill; but only to secure such aid, spiritual and physical, in the case of illness, as the particular relations of each case may make best. Hence, at such times, God allows us to pray conditionally, with mingled faith and submission; and the prayer often meets with signal answers, in the way of recovery, when such answer can be made to fit into the moral discipline of life with happy effect. It would be presumptuous, therefore, to select a given ward or hospital, which must include cases of the most varied moral conditions and relationships, and to insist that these shall be subjected to the one use of proving the value of prayer in securing recovery from disease. This would be to assume God's place, and to substitute dictation for prayer. Who is authorized to say that the highest interests require that those patients should certainly or in large proportion recover, while the patients in other institutions should be left without divine aid?

(4.) It may be added, that Messrs. Thompson and Tyndall could give no assurance, that a favorable result of the experiment would be accepted by skeptics as a demonstration of the real power of prayer. Experience shows, that these are not much influenced by outward events which seem to others to indicate divine power. The marvels of creation fail to convince some of them that God even exists. The miracles of Jesus wrought no conviction in the minds of his determined opponents. When they could not deny the facts, they referred them to diabolic agency. It was a deep insight into the human heart that led him to the representation of Abraham, replying thus to the prayer of the rich man, to send Lazarus to warn his living brothers: "They have Moses and the prophets; let them hear them. And he said, Nay, father Abraham, but if one went unto them from the dead, they will repent. And he said unto him, If they hear not Moses and the prophets, neither will they be persuaded though one rose from the dead." Modern skeptics, as did the ancient ones, deceive themselves, when they stand in front of the Crucified, and say: "If he be the King of Israel, let him now come down from the cross, and we will believe on him." In the case of marked success, in the particular hospital prayed for, the unbelievers would claim that this was accidental, and due to unknown natural causes; or that it arose from a more salubrious situation; or from better ventilation; or from the excited imagination and hope of the patients, who knew that they were being prayed for by the Christian world, and the proportionate depression of other patients, for whom no prayer was offered; or from some unfairness of physicians favorable to the triumph of Christianity. To suppose that men, who are unmoved by the evidence of the power of prayer from the whole history of the human race, would be convinced by any result of the experiment proposed, is a large draft upon one's credulity.

5. The moral phenomena of the case, as we have seen in a previous chapter, equally sustain the reasonableness of prayer; prayer is an indispensable means of moral training, and is such an arrangement as God would necessarily enjoin for the closest union of his rational creatures with himself. There is no other such powerful means of giving impressiveness to the being and agency of God. The habitual act affects the imagination and the heart, and leads to the asso-

ciation of the divine love, wisdom and will with the events of life. At the same time, it brings out our noblest aspirations, subdues our baser tendencies, and preserves us from discouragement and despair amid the attacks upon our virtue, and amid the trials of our lot.

Here is the reason that the church resists the infidel assault on prayer. It is not that ecclesiastical or priestly power may be made secure; for of all religious rites none is so individual as prayer, carrying the soul, as it does, past the priest, and past the church, directly to God himself. But it is felt that he who would destroy the faith of men in prayer, little as he may suspect it, is the enemy of mankind. He would rob them of their greatest help in weakness, their greatest comfort in sorrow, their greatest hope in danger. This fact comes out strikingly, when those who, in prosperous days, have undervalued and neglected prayer, in time of calamity fall upon their knees, and realize that God might as well not be, as not to hear the prayers of his distressed children. Thus we can understand that God should institute prayer, not for his own information, or as a stimulus to his benevolent feeling, but for our spiritual education. We could better do without the gifts, than fail of the moral training which is secured by their reception through prayer. Therefore Jesus said: "Men ought always to pray, and not to faint"; and Paul wrote to the churches, to "pray without ceasing."

We come then to an important inquiry: if prayer

be a universal instinct, if in all ages men have claimed that they had experience of its power with God, and if it is an indispensable means of moral training, on what grounds do the skeptics object to it? Why, especially, do certain scientific writers make opposition to it? It is because they totally misconceive its office and methods. They strangely imagine that Christian people hold its object to be, to inform an omniscient Being; or to persuade a God of love; or to induce an infinitely wise Ruler to change the plan of his universe! Pope, in his Essay on Man, introduces this objection in the lines:

> "Think we, like some weak prince, th' Eternal Cause
> Prone for his fav'rites to reverse his laws?
> * * * * * * * * *
> When the loose mountain trembles from on high,
> Shall gravitation cease, if you go by?"

But we hold no such theory. God knows our need, he is already compassionate, and he will not swerve from plans which are necessarily perfect. It is because he is wise and good, that he has made prayer a condition of our prosperity, and has provided a place for it in his plans, as truly as he has for the law of gravitation. The scientists must broaden their outlook, and learn that above the physical universe is the moral; the former being quite subordinate to the latter, and in fact, but the platform on which it operates; and that each is true to its own laws. God, who is at the head of each, has ordained their respective arrangements to work in harmony, and he can use prayer, as a means of training his rational creatures, without disturbance in either realm. For when we pass from the office of prayer to the method of its answer, there is no insuperable difficulty. The fact should be credited, on sufficient evidence, even if the method should be wrapped in inscrutable mystery. Science is constantly accepting facts which it cannot as yet explain; and certainly ignorance is not to be made a substitute for knowledge, as is done, when men think that not to know how God can do a certain thing, is the same as to know that he cannot do it!

A very curious distinction Professor Tyndall tries to make, at this point, between physical and spiritual phenomena. He will not admit that, in answer to prayer, God intervenes to produce physical effects; but he thinks that prayer may avail for spiritual aid. He says that, "in its purer forms, prayer hints at disciplines which few of us can neglect without moral loss;" and that "it may strengthen the heart to meet life's losses." But then he asserts that "no good can come of giving it a delusive value, by claiming for it a power in physical nature." Now one cannot well understand the philosophic ground for this distinction. A metaphysical philosopher might indeed exactly reverse the statement, with much greater plausibility. He might affirm that, knowing from constant experience the power of free will over the laws of matter, and the ease with which it can overrule, or combine, or counterbalance them, to work out its own results, he was ready to concede that prayer might lead God to produce physical effects; but that the real difficulty lay in understanding how God could answer prayer by producing mental and moral changes, where he would have to deal not with dead matter, but with living spirits; not with necessitated forces, but with freedom itself. What could Mr. Tyndall reply, except to withdraw also the spiritual realm from the province of prayer? And all because he will not leave the ruts of physical science, and pass to a higher class of phenomena with their superior laws.

An illustration of the principle involved, Professor Tyndall himself indicates, as he notices in a passage already quoted, that a father's will controls physical phenomena. Thus a child asks for an apple; and he steps to the orchard, shakes a tree, picks up the apple which falls, brings it into the house, and gives it to the boy. In moving his own body, in shaking the tree, in picking up the apple, in handing it to the boy, he answers prayer by producing physical phenomena. And it is done in accordance with natural law, which is directed by superior spirit-force, as by turns he opposes and uses the law of gravity. Nor can he explain the phenomenon of this subjection of matter to will. Life is full of these manifestations of the play of spirit-force among material forces; as though to teach us, that much more surely and easily must the Infinite Spirit touch and use the laws of nature, to which he has given efficacy, and thus be able to answer prayer without interruption of natural law. That God does this invisibly, while we act visibly, does not change the principle involved; and then the action of the human will is as invisible as that of God. In both cases we see the effect only.

In the class of answers covered by the proposed hospital test, the cure of disease, the answer to prayer need suspend no natural law. God may operate upon disease through the laws of life, the secret of which he possesses, with or without the instrumentality of medicine; or he may secure the sending for the best physician; or he may bring to notice the most appropriate remedy; or he may lead to the fulfillment of some other natural condition of a restoration to health. The result is brought about in answer to the prayer equally, whatever be the method God shall be pleased to employ. That may be indirect, as well as direct, for the Bible gives us reason to believe that prayers are often answered by angelic agency — which is expressly mentioned in the deliverance of Daniel from the lions, and of Peter from prison. Unseen by us, angels, in the use of natural law, may work effects not more inexplicable to our ignorance, than is our transmission of telegraphic news over the wires, to a savage. If Professor Tyndall, by his superior knowledge of chemical and mechanical laws, can do that which to uneducated men appears miraculous, why should he doubt that Gabriel may possess a knowledge of such forces as far beyond his science, as that is beyond the apprehension of a child; and that God may use angelic agency to work out answers to prayer in connection with physical phenomena? And this idea accords with what the Bible reveals as to the existence and ministry of angels.

It is furthermore to be considered by the modern scientific objectors to prayer, that their favorite theory of evolution or development furnishes a close analogy to one of the theories advanced to explain the harmony of prayer with natural laws. The development-theory teaches, that the unknown, mysterious First Cause, if such there be, formed the universe, not by distinct creations of different objects, but by the production of countless initial atoms, in which inhered certain forces or tendencies, the combined influence of which has developed by necessary law, from stage to stage, the variety of existence which we see in animate and inanimate nature. Now these numberless existences stand related to each other, and are mutually so dependent that the non-production, or different form of almost any one of them, would have prevented, or greatly modified the production of the others; so that it seems incredible that they should all appear in the right time and place to be serviceable to each other, through mere blind forces. But the development theorists assure us, that this only adds to the completeness and wisdom of the original plan; and that their idea is consequently more honorable to God than the ordinary idea of creation by successive fiats; since it represents him as seeing the end from the beginning, and as able to form this marvelous universe, by so pre-arranging the play of independent forces, as they wrought in countless parallel lines, that all the results, at any given date, should have the proper relations of harmony with each other.

We will not pause to dispute this; be it so. Such philosophers ought then to find it easy to believe, that prayers and their answers formed part of this very system of pre-arrangement. For if God could so adjust material forces, as that the combination of results should work advantageously in every direction, of its own nature, surely he could, with similar foresight and skill, arrange that prayers should be occasioned by one set of phenomena, and that answers to them should be provided at the right moment by appropriate forces. This is only the development theory applied to morals and theology; and the scientists should rejoice in the added scope. Neither should they be envious that the theologians, centuries since, anticipated them in this explanation; as was done by those who sought to harmonize the universality of the divine purposes with the duty of prayer. And possibly it may help to reconcile them to it, that the distinguished mathematician Euler, in his "Letters to a German Princess," upon science, clearly sets it forth in these words: "When God established the course of the universe, and arranged all the events that must come to pass in it, he paid attention to all the circumstances which should accompany each event, and particularly to the dispositions, desires and prayers of every intelligent being; and the arrangement of all events was disposed in perfect harmony with all these circumstances. When, therefore, a man addresses to God a prayer worthy to be heard, that prayer was already heard from all eternity; and the Father of mercies arranged the world expressly in favor of that prayer, so that the accomplishment should be a consequence of the natural course of events. It is thus that God answers the prayers of men without working a miracle."

Thus, view the skeptical objections to prayer on whatever side we may, they prove to be as unworthy of a philosophic as they do of a religious mind. The Bible doctrine vindicates itself to reason as well as to faith, and the Psalmist is justified in his declaration: "The eyes of the Lord are upon the righteous, and his ears are open unto their cry."

"Oh, this is blessing, this is rest!
Into thine arms, O Lord, I flee;
I hide me in thy faithful breast,
And pour out all my soul to thee.
There is a host dissuading me;
But all their voices far above,
I hear thy words: 'Oh, taste and see
The comfort of a Savior's love.'
And, hushing every adverse sound,
Songs of defense my soul surround,
As if all saints encamped about
One trusting heart pursued by doubt.
* * * * * * *
O, tenderness! O, truth divine!
Lord, I am altogether thine,
I have bowed down; I need not flee;
Peace, peace is mine in trusting thee."

—*A. L. Waring.*

CHAPTER VIII.

BIBLE-ANSWERS TO PRAYER—OLD TESTAMENT.

THE Bible wisely teaches by example as well as by precept, and on its pages we find the biography illustrating the promises, and history showing the fulfillment of prophecy. We might then expect that it would give us facts as well as theory on the subject of prayer. It does so, and the difficulty is, to make a selection such as the author's limited space and definite purpose require.

Before calling the reader's attention to specific cases, it is well to notice general declarations put upon record by one who had great experience in this respect. David, because of his devotional nature, and of his many and severe trials, was much addicted to prayer, and the book of Psalms contains not a few of his supplications made in seasons of distress. What is now to be observed is, that he distinctly affirms that his prayers had been answered in a signal manner. These are some of his grateful words to that effect: "I cried unto the Lord with my voice, and he heard me out of his holy hill." Ps. iii:4. "In my distress I called upon the Lord, and cried unto my God: he heard my voice out of his temple, and my cry came before him, even into his ear. * * * He

6*

sent from above, he took me, he drew me out of many waters." xviii: 6–17. "O Lord, my God, I cried unto thee, and thou hast healed me." xxx: 2. "I sought the Lord, and he heard me, and delivered me from all my fears." xxxiv: 4. "I waited patiently for the Lord, and he inclined unto me, and heard my cry." xl: 1. "If I regard iniquity in my heart, the Lord will not hear me: but verily God hath heard me; he hath attended to the voice of my prayer. Blessed be God, who hath not turned away my prayer, nor his mercy from me." lxvi: 18–20. "I love the Lord, because he hath heard my voice and my supplications. Because he hath inclined his ear unto me, therefore will I call upon him as long as I live." cvi: 1, 2. It would appear from such expressions, that the large experience of David in the matter of prayer had been eminently satisfactory. And if that be so, how is the skeptic to allege anything to the contrary? For David was not reciting a theory, but thankfully recording facts. He had put prayer to a thorough test, for many years, and the experiment was a complete success.

The answers mentioned by the inspired writers are numerous. There is space only for a few of the more marked, which illustrate classes of cases. We will attend first to the Old Testament.

1. Let us begin with a prayer for personal deliverance from imminent danger. Jacob had deceived his aged and blind father, Isaac, and obtained the blessing which was intended for his elder brother, Esau; hav-

ing also, on a previous occasion, taken advantage of the reckless Esau's hunger, to sell him some pottage at the price of his birthright. He fled from the country, for his life, hearing of Esau's deadly threats. After an absence of many years, during which he had grown rich in flocks and herds, he ventured to return, and, on coming to the confines of the land, heard that Esau was advancing to meet him, at the head of four hundred warriors. Consciousness of guilt, and a remembrance of his injured brother's wrath filled him with fear, lest this should be the hour of bloody revenge. Resistance would be unavailing, and his imagination pictured a scene of plunder and slaughter, in which he, his two wives, his children, and his servants would be the victims. In this terrible emergency the night fell about him. Esau would be there in the morning; his only hope was in God; his only salvation must be prayer! And upon the true principle, that prayer is not a substitute for appropriate human effort, but a means of rendering it successful, he took measures to propitiate Esau, and then, sending his family over the river Jabbock, remained alone in the darkness, to plead with God.

We can understand the earnestness, and even agony, of the prayer, when everything was at stake; as also the arguments he would use. Indeed a prayer of the previous day furnishes an outline of the petition. See Gen. xxxii: 9–12. We thus learn that he fell back upon two arguments—that God was pledged to him by the general covenant made with Abraham and Isaac; and by the special promises given to himself, in the famous vision at Bethel, at the time of his flight to Mesopotamia, and on the occasion of his setting out to return. This was firm ground, upon which a rational faith could plant itself. He also confessed his own unworthiness, and with gratitude acknowledged what had already been done for him. As he was thus praying and humbling himself, in the midnight darkness, he was conscious of a presence with him, as of a human form, which he recognized as a divine manifestation; and he laid hold of the person, to insist upon a blessing. The seeming man struggled to depart, and wrestled with Jacob, to break away. But the patriarch clung to him desperately, even till the day began to dawn, and after his thigh had been dislocated, saying: "I will not let thee go except thou bless me!"

He was rewarded with victory! God graciously allowed himself to be overcome by the importunate petitioner; while, as an encouragement to others to imitate his example, he changed the patriarch's name from one which commemorated his sin, to one which immortalized his victory. "And he said unto him, What is thy name? And he said, Supplanter (Jacob.) And he said, Thy name shall be called no more Supplanter (Jacob,) but Prince of God (Israel;) for as a prince hast thou power with God and with men, and hast prevailed." And so the name Israel, which passed first to the chosen nation, and then to the whole Christian church, is a perpetual reminder of the power of importunate prayer. Scarcely had the assurance of safety been given, than Esau was seen in the distance, at the head of his armed men, mounted on camels, probably, and sweeping down like a modern band of the Bedouin. But lo! when they reached the helpless group of Jacob, instead of drawing their swords and beginning the slaughter, they quietly stopped, while Esau ran to meet his brother, "and embraced him, and fell on his neck, and kissed him, and they wept!" And so, in answer to prayer, fratricidal hatred was turned into fraternal love! It is not surprising that, in every succeeding age of the church, this scene at Peniel (or God's-face,) has given tone to the prayers of believers, and has introduced into religious phraseology the words "wrestling in prayer." From this narrative it was that Charles Wesley drew his inspiration for that marvelous, spiritual poem, the first and third stanzas of which are these:

"Come, O thou traveler, unknown,
Whom still I hold, but cannot see;
My company before has gone,
And I am left alone with thee:
With thee all night I mean to stay,
And wrestle till the break of day.

"In vain thou strugglest to get free;
I never will unloose my hold:
Art thou the Man that died for me?
The secret of thy love unfold;
Wrestling, I will not let thee go,
'Till I thy name, thy nature know."

2. Jacob prayed in his own great peril: let us take

an instance of success in prayer for others. Moses was eminent as an intercessor. Seldom is there a record of his praying for himself. Perhaps it was because he was a distinguished type of Christ, the great mediator and intercessor, that we find him so often supplicating in behalf of those in distress or danger. The point to be noticed is, that he had special power in this respect. For whomsoever he prayed, an answer of mercy came. Thus when Pharoah was suffering under the successive judgments of God, and, at each step of the discipline, agonizingly besought Moses to pray for his relief, Moses did so, and secured the withdrawal of the plague. When the Israelites went forth from Egypt, his imploring cry for deliverance from the pursuing monarch, divided the Red Sea for their safe passage. And so, on each fresh emergency of their life in the desert, his constant petition brought the needed relief.

The culmination came, however, on those two solemn occasions, when the life of the whole nation was at stake, because of their rebellion and ingratitude toward God, and sentence had apparently gone forth against them for their destruction, together with almost a prohibition to Moses to intercede for them. Thus when they worshiped the golden calf at the very foot of Sinai, where the second commandment had been thundered in their ears, God said to Moses (Deut. ix: 14): "Let me alone, that I may destroy them, and blot out their name from under heaven; and I will make of thee a nation mightier and greater than they." Here was everything to discourage petition in their behalf. The people deserved destruction; God seemed to have decreed their doom; Moses was apparently bidden not to pray against it; and provision was made to fulfill the pledges to Abraham and the other patriarchs, by raising up out of the posterity of Moses himself the promised nation. Thus reverence, fear, faith and personal ambition might all be said to withhold Moses from intercession. But love for those threatened with death triumphed over every other consideration, and he had such confidence that God would not be displeased with prayer which came from a self-sacrificing and compassionate spirit, that even when three thousand had already fallen (Ex. xxxii: 25–32), he went up to the mount, and said: "Oh, this people have sinned a great sin, and have made them gods of gold. Yet now if thou wilt forgive their sin—(do so); and if not, blot me, I pray thee out of thy book which thou hast written." And he fell down before the Lord, fasting and interceding for forty days (Deut. ix: 18) till, as he writes it, "the Lord hearkened unto me at that time also."

The other occasion, equally note-worthy, was that of their refusal to enter Canaan, on the report of the spies, when, as Moses records the occurrence (Deut. ix: 23–29): "I fell down before the Lord, forty days and forty nights, as I fell down at the first; because the Lord had said that he would destroy you." At this time his three arguments were; that God after having done so much for his people, and borne so long with them, should not now destroy them; that he should show mercy for the sake of his pious servants, Abraham, Isaac and Jacob, their fathers, and not regard simply the sin of the present generation; and that he must not furnish occasion for the Egyptians to think that he was unable to carry his people into the promised land. And again he succeeded. The case stands as a monument of the value of intercessory prayer, and should encourage Christian patriots to pray for their country, and pious souls to pray for the reviving of religion in a time of declension, and every saint to pray for sinners in danger of perdition.

In all this, Moses is a character of special interest, because he was a type of Christ, the Great Intercessor, who "is able to save them to the uttermost, that come to God by him, seeing he ever liveth to make intercession for them." We read in the epistle to the Hebrews, that "Moses verily was faithful in all his house, as a servant, for a testimony of those things which were to be spoken after." It is not surprising, then, that the same poetic pen, which was moved to apply so happily the scene at Peniel, has brought out, in words which have thrilled with hope thousands of sorrowing souls, the grand fact of the intercession of our High Priest.

"Arise, my soul, arise;
Shake off thy guilty fears;
The bleeding sacrifice
In thy behalf appears:
Before the throne my surety stands;
My name is written on his hands.

"He ever lives above,
For me to intercede;
His all-redeeming love,
His precious blood to plead;
His blood atoned for all our race,
And sprinkles now the throne of grace.

"Five bleeding wounds he bears,
Received on Calvary;
They pour effectual prayers;
They strongly speak for me:
Forgive him, O forgive, they cry,
Nor let that ransomed sinner die.

"The Father hears him pray—
His dear Anointed One:
He cannot turn away
The presence of his Son;
His Spirit answers to the blood,
And tells me I am born of God.

"My God is reconciled,
His pardoning voice I hear;
He owns me for his child,
I can no longer fear:
With confidence I now draw nigh,
And Father, Abba Father, cry."

3. Let the next case be one of parental petition and prevalence. Hannah was the devout wife of Elkanah, who loved her devotedly. But the years of their married life passed, and she bore him no child. This was a natural grief, and to an Oriental wife was a sore reproach. Hannah felt it the more, because Elkanah had another wife, by whom he had numerous sons and daughters, and who taunted her with barren-

ness. On one occasion of the yearly visit to the tabernacle, Hannah's long accumulating desire and grief inspired an agonized prayer to God for help, accompanied by a solemn vow, that the child that should be given her, should be dedicated to divine use, as a token of her gratitude. She would not retain him at home as a gratification to maternal pride and fondness, but she would bring him to the tabernacle, and leave him there with the high priest, Eli, to be trained for religious work. Her agitation was such, as she whispered her prayers, so that others might not hear, that Eli mistook her condition for that of intoxication; but on hearing her statement—"No, my lord, I am a woman of a sorrowful spirit; I have drunk neither wine nor strong drink, but have poured out my soul before the Lord," he prophetically said: "Go in peace, and the God of Israel grant thee thy petition that thou hast asked of him." "So the woman went her way, and did eat, and her countenance was no more sad." The prayer thus born of sorrow, importunity and faith was signally answered. A son was given unto her, and she performed her vow by taking him to Shiloh, and leaving him with Eli, as soon as he was old enough to do without her daily care. Then she broke forth into a sublime prophetic song of triumph, which formed the model of Mary's similar song at the conception of the Messiah. The child became the distinguished Samuel, the last of the Judges, and the founder of the school of the prophets, whose name was venerated by the Israelites, next to that of Moses, for his services to the nation and for the power of his intercessory prayers. See Ps. xcix: 6, Jer. xv: 1.

Here is the encouragement to parental piety and faith. Prayer should begin even before the birth of a child, and the child, when received, should be held for the Lord's service, in such way as he may appoint, in the spirit of genuine consecration. The prayer thus offered will be heard. Many a son has in a similar way been furnished to the Christian ministry, or directed to other means of extensive usefulness.

4. Let us now pass to a prayer for the vindication and revival of true religion. After the secession of the ten tribes, and the setting up of the separate Kingdom of Israel, idolatry, in the form of the worship of the golden calves, was introduced as a matter of state-policy. When Ahab took as his queen, the handsome and haughty Jezebel, the daughter of the Phenician monarch, she introduced Baal-worship as the court-religion. Under such influences the worship of Jehovah declined almost to extinction. Then appeared Elijah, in all the zeal and courage of an inspired reformer, bent upon securing a revival of the true religion and a recovery of the people from their apostacy. Prayer occupied a large place in his plans; for the case was desperate. He had to contend with depraved popular taste and passion, and with a determined opposition from the weak Ahab under the control of the relentless and capable Jezebel.

His first endeavor was to convince the king and the people that Jehovah alone was the true God, by a judgment which should come at his prayer, and should be removed only at his intercession. And so he asked that rain should be withheld; which was done, season after season, for three years and a half, till the drought brought the land to the verge of destruction. The king, in his despair of other relief, sent in every direction, even to neighboring countries, to find Elijah, who had withdrawn from view. (1 Kings, xviii: 10.) The time had now come for the prayer-test between Jehovah and Baal, on his success in which the prophet relied to secure the reviving of the true religion; and so he induced the king to gather to Mount Carmel, nine hundred prophets of Baal and of "the groves" (or rather of Asherah, a female deity associated with Baal), whom he alone confronted, in the name of Jehovah. The test was to be, to see which deity, in answer to prayer, would send down fire, to consume a sacrifice.

A scene worthy of being depicted by the highest order of art was then witnessed. For many successive hours, in the presence of the king and of thousands of spectators, the idolatrous prophets wildly called on Baal, and "cut themselves with knives and lancets till the blood gushed out upon them," while Elijah taunted them with their vain appeals, and bade them cry more loudly. When finally no response came, he repaired the broken-down altar of Jehovah with twelve stones, emblematic of the tribes of the chosen people, laid on it the sacrifice, saturated the wood with barrel upon barrel of water, and then prayed for the descending fire; saying, "Hear me, O Jehovah, hear me; that this people may know that thou art Jehovah God, and that thou hast turned their heart back again." The fire fell, and the people shouted; "Jehovah, he is the God! Jehovah, he is the God!" And in a few hours after, the long-withheld rain descended in torrents. In this case, the interests to be promoted were public religious interests, and the prayer was as when, in a time of declension at the present day, God's people plead for a revival. And lest we should reason that Elijah was so peculiar a man, and was called to so peculiar a work, that he could be no example to us, James wrote in his epistle: "The effectual, fervent prayer of a righteous man availeth much. Elias was a man subject to like passions as we are, and he prayed earnestly that it might not rain," etc. Hence when we find the cause of God languishing, we are authorized to ask and to expect such form of interposition as will most effectually vindicate religion. As fire is a symbol of the Holy Spirit, the descending fire of Elijah's day, may well become the descending power of the Spirit in our day.

5. Let us take as the next instance from the Old Testament, a case in which prayer was put to the test by its enemies. It shall be from the experience of that representative man of prayer, Daniel, the statesman and the saint. In power he was next to the king of Persia, and malignant rivals could find no fault with his official administration; so they assaulted him on the side of his religion, and at the particular point

of prayer. He was known to be a praying man, and a trap was laid for him which hinged on that fact. They applied to the king, without making any reference to Daniel, with a proposition most flattering to the royal pride, to-wit: that no petition should be made to God or man, for thirty days, except to the king himself, under penalty of being thrown into the den of lions. The king, taken with the idea of playing God, for a month, and not once thinking of its bearing upon his loved and trusted prime-minister, rashly consented, and issued the irreversible edict.

Daniel knew what it meant, and what fate it portended, beyond any escape that his conscience would allow. But he made no change in his devotional habits. "When Daniel knew that the writing was signed, he went into his house, and his windows being open in his chamber toward Jerusalem, he kneeled upon his knees, three times a day, and prayed, and gave thanks before his God, as he did aforetime." He was willing to be a sacrifice, if need were, while yet he had hope that God in some way would disappoint his enemies, and manifest the power of prayer. And when he was arrested under the edict, as a criminal, and sentenced to the den of lions, he submitted with such composure, that even the king, struck by his faith, exclaimed: "Daniel, thy God, whom thou servest continually, he will deliver thee." And when the king, after a sleepless night of anxiety and distress, came early in the morning to the den, and called piteously at its mouth, "O Daniel, servant of the living

God, is thy God, whom thou servest continually, able to deliver thee from the lions?" to his joy, the well-known voice of his prime-minister replied: "My God hath sent his angel, and hath shut the lions' mouths, that they have not hurt me!"

This is, in one respect, the culmination of the history of prayer in the Old Testament; in that prayer itself was on trial, and a representative man of prayer was selected to be the victim of a powerful conspiracy which seemed to be irresistible. Need we be astonished, that the result not only made the deepest impression at the time, but that it has strengthened the faith of believers in all the ages since? A touching fact it was, that the slave-songs at the South, in broken utterance, appealed to this ancient fact:

> "My Lord delibered Daniel,
> Why can't he deliber me?"

6. It would be unwise to close the examples from the Old Testament, without noticing a case of patriotic prayer. Many such might be cited from the sacred history; but it will suffice to recall the experience of Hezekiah. The two rival empires for many centuries, in the olden time, were those of Egypt and Assyria. Between them lay the Holy Land — a prize which both coveted, and which each had at times possessed — and it became the pathway of their hosts, as they carried on their conflicts. In the days of Hezekiah, Sennacherib invaded the land, at the head of an immense Assyrian army, and captured the principal walled cities, except Jerusalem. While besieging

Lachish, he sent his general Rabshakeh to Jerusalem, with a large force, to reduce it; who called upon Hezekiah, in an insulting way, to surrender. The king of Judah refused, and besought the prophet Isaiah to intercede with God to save the city, saying: "Lift up thy prayer for the remnant that is left." Isaiah assured the king that God would cause the Assyrian monarch to hear a rumor that would intimidate him, and cause his return to his own land, where he should be slain. When Rabshakeh bore back to Sennacherib the refusal of Hezekiah, and an account of his faith in Jehovah, that haughty monarch dispatched to him a blasphemous letter, in which he ridiculed the idea that Jehovah could deliver Jerusalem, any more than the gods of other lands had saved them from his conquering power. The inspired narrative says: "And Hezekiah received the letter from the hands of the messengers, and read it; and Hezekiah went up unto the house of the Lord, and spread it before the Lord. And Hezekiah prayed unto the Lord." (Isaiah, chapters xxxvi and xxxvii.) His prayer was an appeal to God to defend his people, and vindicate his own claim to be the one living and true God. "Now therefore, O Lord, our God, save us from his hand, that all the kingdoms of the earth may know, that thou art the Lord, even thou only."

Then came a messenger from Isaiah, to assure the faith of Hezekiah, couched in the boldest figures of Oriental style, and telling Sennacherib: "The virgin, the daughter of Zion, hath despised thee, and laughed thee to scorn — the daughter of Jerusalem hath shaken her head at thee." It also assured him that all his past victories were because Jehovah had used him, as an instrument of his wrath, to punish the heathen nations, but represented the God of the Jews as now saying: "Because thy rage against me, and thy tumult, is come up unto mine ears, therefore will I put my hook into thy nose, and my bridle in thy lips, and I will turn thee back by the way which thou camest." And that very night, the angel of the Lord smote one hundred and eighty-five thousand men in the Assyrian camp, who, the next morning were found dead. Sennacherib, hearing a report, also, that the king of Ethiopia was advancing with an army against him, hurried back to Nineveh, and there was slain by his own sons. So signally did prayer bring an answer, when religious patriotism was its inspiration. And this event the world has never forgotten. Even within our own century it so impressed the genius of Lord Byron, with its tragic sublimity, that in his Hebrew Melodies, he paid it the tribute of these well-known lines:

"The Assyrian came down like the wolf on the fold,
And his cohorts were gleaming in purple and gold;
And the sheen of his spears was like stars on the sea,
When the blue wave rolls nightly on deep Galilee.

"Like the leaves of the forest when summer is green,
That host with their banners at sunset were seen;
Like the leaves of the forest when autumn hath blown,
That host on the morrow lay withered and strewn.

"For the Angel of Death spread his wings on the blast,
And breathed in the face of the foe, as he passed;
And the eyes of the sleepers waxed deadly and chill,
And their hearts but once heaved, and forever grew still.

"And there lay the steed with his nostril all wide,
But through it there rolled not the breath of his pride;
And the foam of his gasping lay white on the turf,
And cold as the spray of the rock-beating surf.

"And there lay the rider distorted and pale,
With the dew on his brow and the rust on his mail;
And the tents were all silent, the banners alone,
The lances unlifted, the trumpet unblown.

"And the widows of Assur are loud in their wail,
And the idols are broke, in the temple of Baal;
And the might of the Gentile, unsmote of the sword,
Hath melted like snow in the glance of the Lord."

CHAPTER IX.

BIBLE-ANSWERS TO PRAYER—NEW TESTAMENT.

WHEN we come to the New Testament, the advent of the promised Savior brought heaven and earth together, more surely than the dream-land-ladder of Jacob; as Jesus implied, when he said to Nathaniel, "Verily, verily, I say unto you, hereafter ye shall see heaven open, and the angels of God ascending and descending upon the Son of Man." John, i:51. When men came to know the true High Priest, the finished sacrifice, the one mediator, the divinely appointed advocate, they had a ground of confidence in prayer far beyond anything before known. Hence the commands and the invitations to pray, multiply from the lips of Christ, and, in his human limitations, he adds the power of his own example. Such was the constancy of the application to him for supernatural aid, and so uniformly did he grant it, that his three years ministry might be called one steady experience of answers to prayer. After his ascension, and the descent of the Spirit, the apostles and early Christians felt that they had a new hold on heaven, a more perfect access to the mercy seat, and a surer guide to acceptable petitions; and so prayer became a mighty instrumentality in securing the progress of the church. "Pray without ceasing," might be said to be the motto, as it was the injunction of its chief apostle. The space at command will allow the citation of but four instances; which shall be chosen to illustrate, in connection with prayer, the value of faith, of earnestness, of union, and of spiritual desire; each standing, as in the cases cited from the Old Testament, as the representative of a class.

1. Early in our Savior's ministry occurred a marked instance, in several respects. It was just after the delivery of the Sermon on the Mount, and as he reached Capernaum. There was residing in that city a centurion — a Roman army officer, answering nearly to a captain in a modern army. He, like Cornelius, of whom we read in the book of Acts, had been deeply impressed by the superiority of the Jewish religion, as consisting of the worship of one God without the use of images. He seems to have become a believer in Judaism, and an admirer of the moral superiority of the nation which the Roman army had conquered. Being a man of wealth, he built their synagogue at his own expense—possibly the very one whose ornate remains have lately been discovered at Tell Hum, which many suppose to be the site of ancient Capernaum. At this time, he had a servant, to whom he was much attached, lying at the point of death with the palsy. Hearing of the coming of the wonderful teacher and miracle-worker, this Roman, who had been brought up an idolater, sent the Jewish elders of the city to Jesus, to intercede in his behalf, and to pray

that he would exert his power and heal his servant. He had such humility that he felt unworthy to go in person. (Luke vii: 1–10.) As Jesus was approaching the house, the centurion sent other friends, to say that it was not necessary for the Master to come in, nor was he himself worthy of the honor of receiving him under his roof. It would be quite sufficient for Jesus to speak the word of power, where he was, and the servant should be healed; as when he bade one of his own soldiers go or come, and was instantly obeyed. This was a faith quite unparalleled by anything which Jesus had before met. It was faith, moreover, on the part of a Gentile; so that Jesus exclaimed, "I have not found so great faith, no not in Israel." He then announced that this man was but the representative of a great multitude beyond the boundaries of Judaism, who should enter the kingdom; and he said: "Go thy way, and as thou hast believed, so be it done unto thee." And at the same moment the servant was healed.

Such was, (and still is,) the power of combined faith and humility. The instance is specially instructive, as showing the quick response which God makes to the soul's perfect trust in his love; and as proving that true humility, instead of discouraging a believing applicant, leads to a complete reliance on divine grace and the use of appropriate intercession. As the centurion, with a sense of personal unworthiness, used the advocacy of the Jewish elders, so we, with a far greater certainty, may, in our appeals to God, use the advocacy of the Son of God himself.

2. The next instance will also be that of a Gentile, and will illustrate yet another condition of prevailing prayer. There was one occasion, when Jesus passed outside of what are usually considered the limits of Palestine, and went "into the coasts of Tyre and Sidon;" that is into Phenicia, whose population was descended from the old Canaanites. He sought to remain unknown, having gone thither probably for rest; but it was soon reported that he was there, and instantly a woman of the country, whose daughter was a demoniac, called earnestly upon him, as the "Son of David," praying that he would cast out the demon. This was a believing acknowledgment of his Messiahship, on the part of a Gentile, and might well appeal to him on her behalf. Yet he made no reply, seemed indifferent, and acted as if he did not hear her. He wanted to have it appear of what spiritual stuff she was made, and to what kind of a spirit a favorable response would be given. She continued her entreaty so piteously, that the disciples interceded for her, and asked the Master to dismiss her with a blessing. But he, using the figure of a shepherd, replied: "I am not sent but unto the lost sheep of the house of Israel." By this he meant that his public ministry was, for good reasons, limited to the Jews, as a nation, and he had not entered into Phenicia with any purpose to extend it thither. Possibly, also, he hinted at the under-lying fact, which John the Baptist had noticed, that God honored a spiritual connection with Abraham more than a blood connection. Mat.

iii: 9. Then the determined mother came still closer, and threw herself at his feet, (Mark, vii: 25,) crying out in her agony, "Lord, help me." (Mat. xv: 25.) How could his compassionate heart resist this appeal? But he repeated the same idea as before, changing the figure to that of the father of a family: "Let the children first be filled; for it is not meet to take the children's bread, and to cast it unto the dogs." The Greek original has the word for "little dogs," as referring not to the wild dogs of the streets, but to the tame dogs of the household, which were allowed about the table. Intent on her point, and not meaning to relinquish the object dear to her maternal heart, and, with a woman's quickwittedness, she replied: "Yes, Lord: yet the (little) dogs under the table eat of the children's crumbs." (Mark, vii: 28.) The victory was hers. Her true character stood revealed. Canaanite though she was by race, she was a daughter of Abraham in spirit, and must have the reward of faith. Humility, that took no offense at seemingly harsh words, and perseverance that would not yield to repeated repulse, were the very conditions of successful prayer; and the Savior said: "O, woman, great is thy faith; be it unto thee even as thou wilt!" There is such a thing then, as a will, on the part of an importunate petitioner, at which God takes no offense, when it means perishing want and firm trust.

3. Now let us test united petitions as a condition of success. Leaving, for the present, a notable instance which would illustrate this point, because it may be

used for another important purpose, we will take the deliverance of Peter from prison, as recorded in the twelfth chapter of the Acts of the Apostles. It was a time of persecution, which had burst out afresh, coming now from the civil power, in the person of Herod, the king. He first beheaded the apostle James, the brother of John; and when he saw that this act gave special satisfaction to the Jews, he seized Peter, the very leader of the apostolic band, at the time of the passover, and put him in prison, till that sacred festival should be over; when he purposed his public execution. It was a delay of but a few days, and the case seemed desperate. No doubt the apostle himself prayed earnestly that, if God had no further use for him on earth, grace might be given to meet death calmly, and to bear an unwavering testimony for Christ. Quite probably, in view of the fate of James, he had little expectation of deliverance, and thought that, as ten or twelve years had elapsed since the ascension of Jesus, the predicted time had come, of which Jesus spake, when he said to him: "When thou wast young thou girdest thyself and walkest whither thou wouldst, but when thou art old, thou shalt stretch forth thy hands, and another shall gird thee, and carry thee whither thou wouldst not." Nothing is said, however, as to Peter's prayers.

But we do read of the united prayers of others in his behalf. "Peter therefore was kept in prison; but prayer was made without ceasing of the church unto God for him." This was a matter of absorbing interest to the whole flock; for Peter was not only the spiritual leader, but the beloved father of that original church. Many of the members had been converted under his preaching, and all had been guided by his counsels. James had been murdered, and must Peter die also? They could not endure the thought. There was no resource but prayer, as Peter was in the inner prison, and four companies of soldiers took turns in guarding him, by day and night. There was no specific promise to plead; only the general provisions for the wants of the church could be applied. Yet there was the providential indication of a few days delay, during which God might cause the king's heart to relent; for was it not written in Scripture: "The king's heart is in the hand of the Lord as the rivers of water; he turneth it whithersoever he will"? Importunate supplication was therefore made; for the word in the original means not "without ceasing," but "earnest," "intent," or literally, "on the stretch." This was the subject weighing upon every mind, and no one could rest till the momentous matter was decided. A column of prayer rose up before God, from the church meetings and from the closets of the saints. And such united and fervent pleading had its reward; for God sent his angel, the very night before the day fixed for the execution, and brought him out of the prison; and while one of the companies of Christians were at prayer at the house of Mark's mother (probably intending to spend the whole of that last night in petition), they were astonished to learn that Peter himself was at the door. Their surprise should not be construed as a weakness of faith; for as they had no specific promise to urge, so they had no right to feel assured of the particular kind of answer which would be given. It might not have been best, that Peter should be spared, any more than James; and if best, no one could foresee the time and manner in which the deliverance would come.

4. We come, now, to one of the most interesting cases of answer to prayer in the whole record of the church of God; one in which we have an illustration of the value of combined union, earnestness, perseverance, and faith in a specific promise, to secure a wide spread spiritual blessing — that connected with the day of Pentecost. We can look back, and see that the occasion was, in an important sense, the birth of the Christian church, and that it was appropriately preceded by spiritual travail. Jesus had ascended to the Father, to act as the Intercessor for his people. Before his crucifixion and also after his resurrection, he had instructed them as to the advent of the Comforter, the Holy Spirit, who was to be his substitute, as their everpresent companion and friend. See John xiv: 16–26, xv: 26, xvi: 7–14. In addition to this specific promise, he gave a command, which partook also largely of the nature of a promise: for we read (Acts i: 4–8), "He commanded them that they should not depart from Jerusalem, but wait for the promise of the Father, which, saith he, ye have heard of me. For John truly baptized with water; but ye shall be bap-

tized with the Holy Ghost not many days hence. * * * Ye shall receive power after that the Holy Ghost is come upon you." In these circumstances, they were prepared for a clear exercise of faith. They had been taught also their pressing need, by the declarations of Jesus, by their sad and mortifying weakness at the time of his apprehension and condemnation, by their sense of loneliness since his ascension, and by their felt inadequacy to the work of going forth to preach his gospel to an unbelieving world. If ever men needed a special divine qualification for a momentous mission, they were the little band of disciples, one hundred and twenty in number, who waited at Jerusalem for this heavenly baptism.

But how did they wait? Not idly and impassibly. They waited *on* the Lord, and not simply *for* him. They knew the divine law of procedure, in cases of spiritual blessing. A promise was meant to encourage prayer. And so the apostles "all continued with one accord in prayer and supplication, with the women and Mary, the mother of Jesus, and with his brethren." It was after ten consecutive days had been thus spent, that "suddenly there came a sound from heaven, as of a rushing mighty wind, and it filled all the house where they were sitting; and there appeared unto them cloven tongues, like as of fire; and it sat upon each of them; and they were all filled with the Holy Ghost." In this occurrence there is to be noted, the essential and the incidental, the permanent and the temporary. That which was incidental, though important for the immediate occasion, was the tongue of fire and the gift of speech in foreign languages. For even miracles are only "signs" of something higher. The flame did not abide, and there is no evidence that the gift of tongues was permanent with all who then exercised the power. Paul even speaks slightingly of the latter, in a long passage, (1 Cor. xiv,) in the course of which he says: "I thank God, I speak with tongues more than ye all; yet in the church, I had rather speak five words with my understanding, that by my voice I might teach others also, than ten thousand words in an unknown tongue." The really essential and permanent thing on the day of Pentecost was, the spiritual influence or baptism. The outward miracle was only a wonder, to attract attention, to gather the crowd, to impress with a conception of supernatural power, and to prepare for the spiritual effect.

What was actually accomplished, for the advancement of the kingdom and the establishment of the church, was the revolution in the mind and heart of the disciples, and the conversion, in one day, of three thousand opposers. The disciples were evidently lifted into a new and higher religious life. They received both light and love. Their minds were enlightened to understand the Scriptures, and especially to interpret the prophecies and explain the mission of Jesus as the Messiah. At the same time, they were "strengthened with might by the spirit in the inner man," so as to lose their former timidity, and to be filled with zeal and courage. From that moment, the change was such, that their enemies took note of it, and marveled that obscure, uneducated men should speak with boldness and freedom. Acts iv : 13. They braved the lion in his den. They, who had all fled, when the Master was arrested in the garden, not only preached courageously in the temple, but faced the Sanhedrim in full session, and refused to forbear their testimony even under threats of death, and the actual infliction of stripes and imprisonment. Acts iv : 18–21, v : 17–42. Yea, these experiences only led them to assemble and pray more earnestly still, and the record is: "And when they had prayed, the place was shaken, where they were assembled together; and they were all filled with the Holy Ghost, and they spake the word of God with boldness." iv : 31. It is no matter of astonishment, then, that this inward renewing should be accompanied by corresponding outward success in preaching the gospel; that the converts numbered three thousand, the very first day, and five thousand, a few days after, counting the men alone; and that the historian inserts such significant words as these: "And the Lord added to the church daily such as should be saved," or literally rendered, "added saved ones." "And believers were the more added to the Lord, multitudes both of men and women." "And the word of God increased; and the number of the disciples multiplied in Jerusalem greatly; and a great company of the priests were obedient unto the faith." Acts ii : 47, v : 14, vi : 7.

We have thus reviewed ten cases of answers to

prayer; six being taken from the Old Testament and four from the New. These have illustrated earnest wrestling for personal deliverance from outward peril, individual intercession for others, parental yearning and petition, prayer for reviving amid widespread declension and apostacy, the testing of prayer itself as a means of rescue from death, patriotic appeal for the nation, the exercise of faith in connection with requests, the value of importunity in one's appeals, the effect of union in soliciting a needed boon, and the result of waiting upon God for spiritual blessings. Many others equally striking might have been cited, but these have a variety of object and of characteristic spirit sufficient to instruct and encourage all saints. Studied carefully, as one would other historic facts, they give us the law of prayer, precisely as physical phenomena give us physical laws. And the law thus ascertained proves to be identical with that which was deduced from Scriptural principles and promises, and from the affirmations of reason, and which was stated in the preceding chapters. A certain right state of mind prompts to prayer, and is found to be linked to the purposes and providence of God.

> Of what an easy, quick access
> My blessed Lord, art thou! how suddenly
> May our requests thine ears invade!
> To show that state dislikes not easiness,
> If I but lift mine eyes, my suit is made;
> Thou canst no more not hear than thou canst die.
>
> Of what supreme, almighty power
> Is thy great arm, which spans the east and west,

And tacks the centre to the sphere!
By it do all things live their measured hour:
We cannot ask the thing which is not there,
Blaming the shallowness of our request.

Of what unmeasurable love
Art thou possest, who, when thou couldst not die,
Wert fain to take our flesh and curse,
And for our sakes, in person sin reprove;
That by destroying that which tied thy purse,
Thou mightest make way for liberality.

Since then these three wait on thy throne,
Ease, Power and Love; I value prayer so,
That were I to leave all but one,
Wealth, fame, endowments, virtues, all should go,
I and dear prayer could together dwell,
And quickly gain, for each inch lost, an ell.

— *George Herbert.*

CHAPTER X.

PRAYER FOR SUPPLY OF TEMPORAL WANTS.

For many centuries, God's people have been accustomed to refer to the daily fall of manna for the Israelites, in the desert, and to the similar supplies brought by the ravens to Elijah, as encouragements to faith. It is not that they expect the same method to be used now as then, or other than ordinary means to be employed; but they believe that God, through human and other natural agencies, will, in answer to prayer, supply the temporal need of his people. Do the facts bear them out in this faith? Let us see.

A German Mother. — There has been circulated in Germany a tract called "*Eine Mutter*," or "A Mother." It was written by Dorothea Trudel, of whom we shall hear in the next chapter, and is a brief account of her own mother. She was a woman of great faith in prayer, and though her husband was a drinking man, who made little or no provision for the family, and the children numbered eleven, and their straits were sometimes great, they always were saved from suffering. The tract says: "There were times when we had not a farthing left in the house. None but God knew of our condition, and he who feedeth the young ravens when they cry, was not unmindful of the petitions of his faithful child. He ever helped us in our time of need. It is on this account that our mother's favorite motto, 'Pray, but do not beg,' has been so impressed upon our minds. In the course of this discipline, many striking deliverances were afforded us, and every one around could bear witness that we were not allowed to suffer want." When one of the children was asked on what her mother relied, in her poverty, the child said: "On God alone; she never tells us how God is going to help, but she is always certain his aid will come at the right time." "But," answered the man, "we must be governed by reason." "Nothing is said in the Bible about reason," replied the child; "but it is written, 'He that believeth shall not be confounded.'" When the mother learned of this conversation, she said: "You will experience that they who always get help just at the right time, are those who look in steadfast faith to God, expecting him to act for and aid them."

The Case of Stilling. — Henry Young Stilling was a physician at the court of the Grand Duke of Baden, and was noted for his skill as an oculist. He was an intimate friend of Goethe, who urged him to write an account of his life, because of his remarkable experience of providential responses to prayer and faith. He was desirous to study at a university, so as to be a physician, and he prayed to be directed as to the particular institution, and was led by a singular occurrence to Strasburg. His plans would require a thousand dollars, while he knew not how to raise a hundred. But he only remarked to his poor relatives, "I wonder from what quarter my Heavenly Father will provide me with money." He started with forty-six dollars, but found himself at Frankfort, three days' distance from Strasburg, with but a dollar left. He said nothing, but to God, to whom he made his case known. While walking and praying, he met Mr. L——, a merchant from his town, who, learning his purpose, asked where the money was to come from, and was told, from his rich Father in Heaven. Finding that Stilling had but a single dollar, he said: "Well, I am one of your Father's stewards," and handed him thirty-three dollars. But when this became reduced at Strasburg to one, again, he prayed earnestly, and one morning his room-mate unexpectedly presented him with thirty dollars. His fee to the lecturer came due, and must be paid by Thursday evening, or his name be stricken from the rolls; and he had no money. He spent Thursday in prayer, and at five o'clock P. M., nothing had yet come, and he broke out in perspiration, while the tears rolled down his cheek. There was a knock at the door. It was his landlord, Mr. R——, who inquired how he liked his room, and then asked whether he had brought any money with him. "No, I have no money." Mr. R. was surprised, and then said: "I see how it is; God has sent me to help you." He left, but soon came back with forty dollars. Stilling threw himself on the floor, and thanked God with tears. His whole university experience was of the same character. He was often in want, and God always relieved him in answer to prayer. And although he was surrounded by skeptics, whom he could not always answer, his faith in the power of prayer kept him from wavering in his loyalty to Jesus Christ.

A California Experience. Rev. Horace Bushnell, D.D., in his "Nature and The Supernatural," refers to an interesting character with whom he met in his visit to California. He says of him:

"He had hired his little house of one room, in a new trading town, that was planted last year, agreeing to give a rent for it of ten dollars per month. At length, on the day preceding the rent day, he found that he had nothing in hand to meet the payment, and could not see at all whence the money was to come. Consulting with his wife, they agreed that prayer, so often tried, was their only hope. They went accordingly to prayer, and found assurance that their want should be supplied. That was the end of their trouble, and there they rested, dismissing farther concern. But the morning came, and the money did not. The rent-owner made his appearance earlier than usual. As he entered the door, their hearts began to sink, whispering that now, for once, they must give it up, and allow that prayer had failed. But, before the demand was made, a neighbor coming in called out the untimely visitor, engaging him in conversation, a few minutes, at the door. Meantime, a stranger came in, saying, 'Dr. I owe you ten dollars, for attending me in a fever, at such a time, and here is the money.' He could muster no recollection, either of the man or of the service, but was willing to be convinced, and so had the money in hand, after all, when the demand was made. When Stilling and Francke recite their multitudes of specific answers to prayer, their reports are very hastily discredited by many, because of their strangeness. But I have heard so many examples, personally, of the kind just cited, that I begin to think they are even common."

DELIVERANCE FROM DANGER AT SEA. The Rev. Dr. Wilson of Philadelphia, had the following fact from the pastor of the lady mentioned. The packet ship Albion, full of passengers from America, was wrecked about fifty years ago, on the coast of Ireland, and the news was, that all on board had perished. A minister near Philadelphia on reading a list of the lost, found among them the name of one of the members of his congregation, and went immediately to inform the wife of the sad fact. She had been earnestly praying, during the voyage of her husband, and had received assurance of his safety amid great danger. Hence, to the astonishment of her pastor, after he had informed her of the shipwreck, and showed her the list of names of those who were lost, she told him that it was a mistake; that her husband had been in extreme peril, but was not dead. When the next tidings were received, it proved that her husband was among the passengers, and had been in great peril; but that he had escaped, and was the only one saved!

Direction Singularly Given. The famous Samuel Rutherford, whose piety is fragrant to this day in Scotland, had a friend, a Mr. Blair, who was on his way from London to Port Patrick, and who greatly desired to make two visits, on his road, but had only time for one; as the persons whom he wished to see lived on different routes. One of these was Mr. Rutherford, who resided at Anworth, and the other was a lady of special piety, Marion Macknaught, who lived at Kirkcudbright. Coming to the parting of the road, where he must decide to which of the two places to go he dropped the bridle on the neck of his horse, and prayed earnestly to be divinely directed. He allowed the horse, then, to take his own way, which proved to be the road to Kirkcudbright. When he reached that place, behold there were both of the friends whom he desired to see; for Mr. Rutherford was on a visit to Marion Macknaught! Here is a case to which applies the statement of the wise man (Prov. xvi: 33): "The lot is cast into the lap; but the whole disposing thereof is of the Lord." Even the apparent accidents of life, and the movements amid the lower orders of creation enter into the divine plans, and are subordinated to prayer; even as Jesus assured his disciples that God's purpose was concerned with the falling of a sparrow.

Prayer for a Result in Parliament. — In the memoirs of Sir Fowell Buxton, who was one of the champions of freedom, in the long conflict in the British Parliament over West India emancipation —

occurs a letter to his daughter, in reference to a recent "division," or vote in the House of Commons, in which he says: "What led to that division? If ever there was a subject which occupied our prayers, it was this. Do you remember how we desired that God would give me the Spirit in that emergency? How we quoted the promise, 'He that lacketh wisdom, let him ask it of the Lord, and it *shall* be given him?' And how I kept open that passage in the Old Testament, in which it is said, 'We have no might against this great company that cometh against us, neither know we what to do, but our eyes are upon thee'— the Spirit of the Lord replying, 'Be not afraid nor dismayed by reason of this great multitude, for the battle is not yours but God's!' If you want to see the passage, open my Bible; it will turn of itself to the place. I sincerely believe that *prayer* was the cause of *that division;* and I am confirmed in this by knowing that we by no means calculated on the effect. The course we took appeared to be right, and we *followed it blindly.*" What a pity it is, that men do not resort more continually to God for needed wisdom, and for important success. Especially how desirable it is, that philanthropic reforms should be conducted in a spirit of prayer and faith, and not from mere natural impulse.

PRAYER DECIDES THE DESTINY OF A COLLEGE. — One of the most flourishing and influential literary institutions in the land is that at Oberlin, Ohio. More than a thousand students gather there, every year, in the different departments, and the ministers and teachers who have thence gone forth into every part of our land, and of the world, have been an incalculable power for good. Oberlin has been a center of piety and of reform. A continuous revival has marked its history for forty years, and it has stood in the forefront of the witnesses against sin. Its part in the anti-slavery conflict is well known, and especially because it dared from the beginning to open its doors to the proscribed colored race, giving them equal literary advantages and kind personal treatment with others. This stamped upon the institution what, at the time, was a most unpopular characteristic, yet one which, in the end, made it strong in influence for good, and rallied around it a host of devoted Christian friends, who have grown in numbers with each successive year.

But this step, we may be sure, was not taken without a conflict of opinion among the good men who were founding the institution. When the proposition came up, in the board of trustees, it gave rise to an earnest and protracted debate; for many of them thought that thus to defy public sentiment would be the ruin of the college. Funds would not be contributed, parents would not send their children, odium would be excited, and quite likely mob violence would be aroused. It was replied, that Christian men should stand by truth and right, and should live out, and not live down, their principles. God could be trusted to take care of the consequences. Finally, amid great excitement and agitation, the vote was taken, and stood a tie! The president of the board cast the deciding vote in favor of the proposition, and the glorious future of Oberlin was decided! But that it may be known that prayer directed the momentous decision, let this extract be read from a letter written to the author by Mrs. E. R. Shipherd, widow of the founder of Oberlin; who still lives, to rejoice over the events of that fateful day, and at whose house the trustees held their meeting. Little did those brethren, in their warm discussion, think that God was giving, in answer to the prayers of a circle of sisters then in supplication over that very matter, one of the most signal proofs on record of his readiness to fulfill the promise: "If any of you lack wisdom, let him ask of God, that giveth to all men liberally, and upbraideth not, and it shall be given him." James i: 5.

CLEVELAND, O., Sept. 1, 1875.

Dear Sir: Your communication is before me, and I cheerfully give you the particulars of the scene which transpired during the discussions as to receiving the colored people into the institution. The trustees met at our house, and my room was adjoining, and all their deliberations were easily heard. As there was a difference of opinion expressed with some warmth, a couple of our sisters retired for prayer, while I remained to give the progress of the discussion. They would call occasionally to inquire, and I kept them posted, until at length, Father Keep, who had just been elected president of the board, threw in the casting vote, and came to my room, to relieve our minds; as we felt that nothing could decide that question but the Spirit of God, which we felt had commenced the work, and would direct it aright. As to facts respecting answers to prayer, I have no more doubt than I have of my own existence. In the early history of the Oberlin work, the closet was their only bank, and that never failed. Time and again Mr. Shipherd would come from his study and remark that they were in need of a certain amount of money, and he knew not where it was to come from. But, he would add, "*it will come!*" and he would call a few of the brethren together to pray; and I never knew it to fail, that, within twenty-four hours the money would come, in a perfectly unexpected way.

Truly yours, in Christian sympathy,

MRS. E. R. SHIPHERD.

HOW WASHINGTON ALLSTON WAS RELIEVED. This celebrated artist had to struggle, at first, with great difficulties, and to endure the pinchings of poverty. At one time, he was reduced to such straits, that he locked himself in his studio, and gave himself to prayer for a loaf of bread, for himself and wife. While thus engaged, there was a knock at the door; and when it was opened, a stranger appeared, who inquired whether the beautiful painting, "The Angel Uriel" was still in the artist's possession. Mr. Allston produced it from a corner, and wiped off the dust. The stranger said that he had greatly admired it at the Royal Exhibition, and inquired the price. The artist replied that as nobody had appreciated it, or been willing to give anything near its price, he had ceased to offer it. "Would four hundred pounds purchase it?" said the stranger. "I never dared to ask half of that." "Then it is mine," exclaimed the visitor, who explained that he was the Marquis of Stafford, and took possession of the treasure, leaving the artist overwhelmed with grateful astonishment at the sudden answer of his prayer.

Prayer for Rain. Nothing has excited more ridicule, on the part of the skeptical physical philosophers than the practice of Christian communities to pray for rain, in a time of drought. They admit that men may have such knowledge of nature's laws as to put them to use, for the production of desired effects; but they have no faith that God may do this on a larger scale, in answer to the supplications of his people. They even concede that men have produced rain at times, in limited localities, by conflagrations and cannonades; yet they do not see how God could possibly do the same thing, by a control of natural laws infinitely easy, without overturning the physical universe! But, for aught they know, any angel may understand and control the conditions of rain-making, as readily as a philosophic skeptic on earth can produce and condense steam. Let us examine facts.

Statement of Rev. Enoch Pond, D.D. This venerable father in the ministry in a letter to the author, dated Bangor, Me., August 24, 1875, says: "I had this account from the late Dr. Snell, of North Brookfield, Mass. It was a time of severe drought in all the northern part of Worcester County, and the Rev. Mr. Tomlinson, of Oakham — a man eminent for the fervor of his piety and the efficacy of his prayers — appointed a day of fasting and prayer on account of it; and Dr. Snell, who was settled in a neighboring town, concluded to ride over on horseback, and attend the meeting with his Brother Tomlinson. The day was fair, and the sun hot, and everything seemed parched and ready to die with thirst. The meeting was well attended, and Mr. Tomlinson was specially earnest and importunate in his prayer for rain. He could not give the matter up. God only could grant the help that was needed, and he must grant it. After meeting, Dr. Snell mounted his horse, to ride home, some six or eight miles. He saw a little strip of cloud in the western sky, but thought nothing of it, at first. Soon, however, it began to enlarge, and gather blackness, and 'before I got out of Oakham,' said Dr. Snell, 'I was drenched with rain.' Oakham was thoroughly wetted, and (which was very remarkable) but little rain fell on any of the neighboring towns."

Statement of Professor Henry Cowles. In the *Oberlin Evangelical* of August 31, 1853, edited by Professor Cowles, is this editorial statement of recent facts in that place:

"The scenes in our church, on Sabbath, August 14th, demand a suitable notice, in honor of divine mercy. A heavy drought lay on us, coupled with intense heat. It affected our mind the more, perhaps, for our having noticed, the day previous, that the autumn grains were wilting under the scorching sun, and that the potatoes, yet small, had apparently ceased to grow. There had been rain in the counties west of us, from fifty to a hundred miles distant; but we could see only the dim form of spent showers: no rain reached our village. Under these circumstances, we met for Sabbath morning worship. Our pastor prayed for rain. His prayer expressed our entire confidence that God always did things well; that he knew, infinitely better than we, the reasons for giving or withholding rain; but that he would not be offended with us, if we should express before him our views of the case, as far as we could see, and our feeling of intense desire, that he would grant us what seemed to us so great a blessing. * * * The prayer closed, we sang a hymn, and the pastor gave out his text and entered upon his discourse, when the rain broke upon us in torrents. It is rare that we have felt God's presence more deeply than in that solemn moment. Our first thought was, let us suspend this sermon, and give public thanks to Almighty God. Soon the pastor did pause, the storm roaring so loud he could scarcely be heard over the house, and said: 'Perhaps I ought to stop preaching, and lead out in thanksgiving.' After a short sermon, we had a thanksgiving hymn, in which all the people seemed to praise God with one consent. The rain continued with little cessation for four hours, and then onward for four days, before the weather became again settled; so that the earth is supplied with water as we rarely see it in the middle of August. It was noticed by those without the house, on that Sabbath morning, that it began to rain almost without clouds; that they swept up from every quarter of the heavens, showing that our village was the center of the storm."

Statement of Rev. Charles G. Finney. About three months before his lamented death, Mr. Finney gave a reminiscence, which Professor Cowles has kindly furnished for use in this volume. Better to understand it, one must remember that Oberlin lies about ten miles south of Lake Erie, which is the lake referred to below. Professor Cowles writes:

"Somewhat more than twenty years ago, the village of Oberlin and its adjacent country along the lake shore, suffered severely through the hot season from a total failure of rain, for nearly three months. Clouds, that seemed to promise rain, were repelled from the heated dry atmosphere over the land, and attracted by the more moist atmosphere over the lake, to pour out their waters there. On one such occasion, the clouds had gathered dark, low, and heavy over the lake, and lay there with no particular indication of rising. President Finney walked out with his eye on these clouds. I give the sequel in his own words, as they fell from his lips, less than three months since. 'In this walk, I met Ralph, who turned sharply upon me. 'Mr. Finney, I should like to know what you mean, in preaching that God is always wise and always good; when you see him pouring out that great rain upon the lake, where it can do no good, and leaving us to suffer so terribly for the want of that wasted water?' His words cut me to the heart; I turned, and ran home to my closet, fell on my knees, and told the Lord what Ralph had been saying about him; and besought him, for the honor of his great name, to confound this caviler, and show forth the glory of his power and the greatness of his love. I pleaded with him, that he had encouraged his people to pray for rain, and that now the time seemed to have come for him to show his power in this thing, and his faithfulness as a hearer of prayer. Before I rose from my knees, there was a sound of a rushing mighty wind. I looked out, and lo! the heavens were black; that cloud was rolling up, and soon the rain fell in torrents, two full hours.' The writer himself remembers how that cloud lay over the lake; how it drove him, also, to his closet; and that soon and signally the prayers of that hour came back to us in mighty rain."

THE BANK OF FAITH. This is the title of a little book, quaint and curious, by a very eccentric Congregational minister in England, who died in 1813. He was noted for his faith in divine providence, even to the minutest events of daily life, and used to write his name thus: William Huntington, S. S. The S. S. meant Sinner Saved! The book is an autobiography from this one point of view, and every page discloses events in answer to prayer for temporal relief. There is space here for but a brief extract, which may be taken as a specimen of the entire volume. Of a time when he was in great need, he says: "However, I found that God now began much to try my patience, and that I ought to importune and watch, and wait upon the Lord, and to keep my eye fixed on him, as a servant's eye is on the hand of his master, until I obtained an answer. And I never waited on his Blessed Majesty in vain; for it was sure to come at length. After putting up many petitions, and having been kept long in suspense, I one night called on Mr. and Mrs. Smith, in Chandler Street, Oxford Road, who were great friends to me. Before I departed, they generously made me a present of three guineas. I humbly beg their pardon for mentioning their names, and exposing their secret alms; but as I prayed to my Father, which seeth in secret, and he in mercy rewarded me openly, I therefore must proclaim it upon the housetop, to encourage the weak faith of others, that they may make God their Guardian and their Bank."

Again: "The next morning a person knocked at my door, desiring to see me. When he came into my study, I looked at him, and perceived him to be a gentleman that I had never seen before. He told me that he had once heard me preach at Dr. Gifford's meeting-house, and once or twice in Margaret Street Chapel, and that he had heard me greatly to his satisfaction; and the reason of his coming to see me now was, that he had been exercised, the last night with a dream; that he dreamed the word of God came to him, saying, 'if thy brother be waxen poor, thou shalt open thy hand to thy poor brother,' etc. He asked me if there was such a portion of Scripture. I answered, the words were these: [the whole connected passage being given.] He told me many of these words came to him in his sleep; and in the morning, when he awoke, he felt the power of them. In wondering who this poor brother could be, he informed me, it was impressed on his mind that I was the poor brother about whom he had dreamed, and asked me concerning my circumstances. I then told him of the trial I was in, and as he was fully satisfied it was of God, he wondered much at it. At his departure he gave me a new pair of doeskin gloves, two new white handkerchiefs, and a guinea. He then blessed me, and left me; and I do not remember ever seeing him before that time, nor but once since. Thus God, who had commanded a widow to sustain Elijah, commanded this man to relieve me. The next day, a friend told me that a person had left a guinea with him for me; and while at Mr. Byrchmore's, in Margaret Street, a lady came to his door in a coach, inquiring for me. When I went to the door, she put her hand out, and gave me a guinea, and then ordered the coachman to drive away, having done all the business God sent her to do.

Thus our Most Bountiful Benefactor answered these, my poor petitions, also, after he had been pleased, for a time, to exercise my faith and patience, in order to encourage me to a stronger confidence in his grace and providence. * * * At another time, when Providence had been exercising my faith and patience, till the cupboard was quite empty, in answer to simple prayer, he sent me one of the largest hams that I ever saw. Indeed I saw clearly, that I had nothing to do but to pray, to study and to preach, for God took care of me and of my family also, agreeably to his own promise: 'Seek ye first the kingdom of God and his righteousness, and all these things shall be added unto you.'"

A College Student Supported.—The case of Stilling at the German university can be paralleled by many cases in our own land. Rev. Wm. L. Bray, of Kalamazoo, Mich., writes thus: "My college chum, Andrew J. Clapp, now in heaven, went through college *on prayer*. He had no means of his own. He would not beg, and was not able to teach; so he laid himself on God's promises, and *never* was disappointed. Many times, just when he must have money or leave, the money came, and very often from unknown sources. Often it was enclosed in an envelope, with not a word to tell where it came from. He believed God sent it. We were in Amherst College; entered in 1854, and graduated in 1858."

Experience of Mrs. Jane Conry Pithey.—Mrs. Pithey is a member of the Centenary Methodist Episcopal Church, in Chicago. She has become known to a wide circle of Christian friends, as one who lives wholly by faith. For several years she has been disabled by the shaking palsy, and has received all her supplies in answer to prayers. She lives in a small frame house, on a narrow and unpleasant street; but, though suffering much from disease, being quite helpless in her chair, is uniformly patient and cheerful. She told the author of this book, that her first experience of the readiness of her Heavenly Father to hear prayer, was when she was living in Dublin, Ireland, and was but sixteen years of age. Having learned to play on the piano, at school, she was very anxious to possess one; but the ordinary price was far above the family means. One day it occurred to her that God heard prayer, and that it might be he would give her a piano. So she expressed to him her desires with childlike simplicity and faith. A day or two later, she was walking along the street, and saw a music store, which she entered, and then inquired the price of a piano which stood before her. To her amazement, the man replied, "five pounds." Seeing her surprise at the low price, he added, "I know nothing of this piano, except that it was brought here to be sold for five pounds. She hastened home, told her mother, obtained the money, and secured her heart's desire. This fact taught her a life-long lesson — to carry all her wants, small or great, to her Heavenly Father.

When her husband died, he left in his pocket book only two silver quarter-dollars. Besides the little cottage, this was all with which to support herself and a bed-ridden mother of nearly ninety years.

But she went to God in prayer, and day by day, ever since, each want has been met. Each needed article was asked for by name, until her hired girl, a Roman Catholic, was astounded at the constant answers given. One morning, as Mrs. Pithey was rising from her knees, at family worship, the girl burst out: "You have forgotten to pray for coal, and we are entirely out." So, as she stood, she added a petition for the coal. About an hour after, the bell rang, she went to the door, and there was a load of coal! She opened the kitchen door and quietly said, "the coal has come;" when the girl clapped her hands together, and, with an exclamation of astonishment, leaped from the floor. The coal was sent by a Mr. Schufeldt, who knew nothing of her want, and who had never sent anything before, nor ever has since. She felt the want of a carpet, and thought that her Father in Heaven would be pleased to give her one. She asked him for it, and in a few days came a present of a sum more than sufficient to buy one. And her sympathy with others equals her freedom from anxiety in her own behalf. When the Foundlings' Home was started, she gave the first dollar toward a permanent building, long before any one else had thought of such an idea; and Dr. Shipman, her physician, and also the superintendent of the Home just referred to, says that he never knew her to worry but once, and that was when she had unexpectedly two barrels of flour in her house, instead of one, and had not been able to get one of them carried to the Foundlings' Home. Wishing, lately, to give a marriage present to a girl who had lived with her, she fixed upon a certain sum, in her mind, as appropriate, and then asked the Lord for the money. In a short time, Miss D——, a city missionary, handed her that exact sum, which had been sent to her from Massachusetts.

Welsh Caleb.—Rev. Dr. Joseph Stennet was a Welsh minister, settled in Abergavenny. One of his parishioners was named Caleb, and lived eight miles away, in a solitary place, among the hills. There came severe winter-storms, which blocked the roads for weeks, and Dr. S. feared his poor parishioner would suffer, and perhaps starve. But it turned out that, all the time, he fared uncommonly well. When, after a few days, the last morsel of food was gone, he went to prayer over the matter with his family, and then retired to bed with a peaceful faith. He slept soundly till day broke, when there was a knock at the door, and a horse stood there, loaded with provisions. The man who rode the horse refused to tell whence they came, except that God sent them. The load contained bread, flour, oat-meal, butter, cheese, salt and fresh meat, etc., enough to last beyond the weeks of imprisonment. It was two years before Dr. Stennet was able to ascertain who the benefactor was. He was calling in the neighboring city of Hereford, on a Dr. Talbot, who had a pious wife, though himself an infidel. In the course of conversation, he alluded to the case of Caleb. At that Dr. Talbot said he knew the man, and related how he once conversed with Caleb as he was coming from a meeting held in a barn; but thought no more of him till that severe winter. Then he was in bed, one night, and, either asleep or awake, thought he heard a voice say, "Send provisions to Caleb." Thinking it a dream, he tried to go to sleep, but heard the same words again, more loudly. He awoke his wife, who also thought it a dream; but, on a third call, he got up, called his man, loaded his horse, and sent him off among the hills to find Caleb. It is no wonder that the man's only story on delivering the load was, "God sent it, I believe."

O God of Bethel! by whose hand
  Thy people still are fed;
Who, through this weary pilgrimage
  Hast all our fathers led—
Our vows, our prayers we now present
  Before thy throne of grace:
God of our fathers! be the God
  Of their succeeding race.

Through each perplexing path of life,
  Our wandering footsteps guide;
Give us each day our daily bread,
  And raiment fit provide.
Oh spread thy covering wings around,
  Till all our wand'rings cease,
And at our Father's loved abode,
  Our souls arrive in peace.

Such blessings from thy gracious hand,
  Our humble prayers implore;
And thou shalt be our chosen God
  And portion evermore.

—*John Logan.*

CHAPTER IX.

PRAYER FOR SUPPLY OF TEMPORAL WANTS.

(Concluded.)

This subject is of such importance that another chapter must be devoted to it, and the more so, that even the church has so little faith in the promise: "Trust in the Lord, and do good: so shalt thou dwell in the land, and verily thou shalt be fed." Ps. xxxvii: 3.

THE EXPERIENCE OF MISS LUCY R. DRAKE. When this page meets the eye of the reader, Miss Drake will probably be on her way to India, whither she goes as a faith-missionary, relying on God for support. The author's acquaintance with her is limited, though he has long and intimately known some of her relatives. Her experience of the healing power of the Lord will be found in a succeeding chapter. In connection with the present topic, she has kindly written out a narrative, which is now presented with slight abridgement. It is dated, Grove Hall, Boston Highlands, Mass., Sept. 10, 1875.

"Many years ago, I wished to go as a missionary to India, but I knew that I could not obtain a certificate from any physician that I was in health, and therefore it would be useless to offer myself to any Board of Missions. It had never entered my mind, that I might go as an independent missionary, and trust God to support me, instead of leaning upon a pledged salary; or, in other words, I never had seen the great practical power in the words: 'Seek first the kingdom of God and his righteousness, and *all these things shall be added unto you.*'

"Upon entering a work where the manager and laborers were having faith in God to care for their temporal wants, while they obeyed his call, [the Consumptive's Home, Boston,] I began to have some of the same faith in God, and relinquished my salary, which in this way would go into the Lord's treasury. But still I clung to the annual interest of a few hundred dollars I had saved, thinking that if I should come into great straits, I should have something to which I could turn. This implied a fear, a lack of trust, and I had according to my faith; for while this fear continued, I was obliged to live almost wholly upon this interest. I had held the three hundred dollars for some time as the Lord's, and finally he called for it to be put into the same treasury where my salary went. I simply asked that I might know his will, and be *convinced* that he did call upon me to give up all my dependence. I did so; without any eye but his beholding it, and he richly poured his blessings into my soul. I never have regretted it.

"Full trust in him for temporal wants and money began now to work. The first launch of faith was in reference to giving. One evening, my heart had been wrung in deep anguish for my heathen sisters, and I wished I had money to give toward their enlightenment. The thought came, why not ask God for it; and I believed I might. In two hours — no person knowing of my prayer — a stranger came to me, at the close of a meeting, and said: 'I know nothing of your circumstances, but I cannot help giving you five dollars.' At once I knew that my father had fulfilled the 'desire of them that fear him,' and I told the stranger where and how the money was designated. Similar instances have frequently occurred since.

"As to temporal wants for myself, I soon came where I must ask, or go without positive necessaries. As a husband would not wish to have a wife going about and telling others her wants, but would wish to have the honor of supporting her, so I believed that my Savior wished me to whisper my needs in his ear alone. While seriously thinking what I was to do, in my then present need, the following passed in my mind: 'What do you want?' I want money. 'Then ask for it.' And I did, and I went home, that night, with the firm assurance that I should find much money; which I did in a letter sent by a friend, who knew nothing of what I was passing through. In less than six months, the Lord gave me more than half of the three hundred dollars. I look to the indwelling Spirit to teach me how to pray for temporal things as well as spiritual, and I must say to his praise, that I never prayed for one, two, ten, twenty, thirty, or fifty dollars, without obtaining *exactly the sum* I asked. Again, when it has appeared to me, that I needed certain articles of clothing, but still I did not *know*, I have asked him to send the money for them, or the clothes, if he saw it to be a need. Sometimes they have come, but not always: still it was blessed to know that if they did not come, it was not a need; for he hath promised to 'supply our need.'

"I have been engaged in evangelistic work, in different parts of our country, for years, and never once have I been permitted to know a real necessity unmet, though sometimes placed in a strange city, not knowing how I was to have the means to return home. Yet it always came, though sometimes by the hand of a stranger. I might be left, also, without a cent, but money came, ere I needed it. Trust for books and opportunities for mental improvement, to assist me in my work for souls, has also been rewarded most wonderfully.

"Having been thus educated by the Lord, it need be no matter of surprise, that, when the Lord Jesus commissioned me, last February, to go to India, to point those who 'sit in darkness' to the blessed Lamb of God, while no support was pledged by man, yet I could have no fear that he who cares for the sparrows, would for me. I have only looked to the Lord, and after I was willing to go out as the disciples did, (Mat. x: 9, 10,) he most abundantly supplied; so that even every thought and wish has been met by a tender Father, into whose ear alone my wants have been breathed. If my eyes had been opened, years ago, to see my privilege as a 'child,' or 'heir,' eight years more might have been given to work in India. Every soul that shall find Christ through my instrumentality there, will praise God that he gave me faith to trust him for care of the body while engaged in his work. If a human parent only desired to have his child spiritually enlightened, but cared not whether he was fed or clothed, and did not provide for both, all would exclaim against him; yet our unbelief in our divine parent for these things robs him of much glory, and our souls of much comfort and freedom from anxious care about those things 'after which the Gentiles seek.' This life of trust in my Father for all my need, as the little child trusts its earthly parent, has become so delightful, that I rejoice in the prospect of going to India without any pledged support from man, to teach them there what a Father they have in heaven, who will 'freely give them all things,' with his dear Son." Rom. viii:32.

This is a narrative of extraordinary interest, and modestly points out the way in which one soul thinks it has been divinely led, in answer to prayer. Miss Drake does not assert that all souls are to be led in precisely the same way, or are to imitate the specific acts which she has performed. It does not follow that missionary societies are unwise, or that ladies who seek a missionary work are to refuse to go to the heathen under their auspices, merely because Miss Drake, with her peculiar training, finds the independent method best suited to her aims and habits. Faith need put us in bondage to no one method. The important thing is to follow the movings of God's Spirit, the indications of his providence, and the directions of his word. Many have had the same spirit of consecration and of faith, who have found their work in other ways, and have been prospered in it marvelously. Each may be permitted to testify what God has done for and through him or her; but no one may make personal experience an iron rule for others. God led John the Baptist to a different work, and a different method, from that which he assigned to his Son Jesus. Yet each was accepted—John in his strict, ascetic life and legal preaching, and Jesus in his free social converse and doctrine of loving liberty.

Billy Bray's Pulpit. Billy Bray was a Cornish miner, very poor, but very zealous and prayerful, and full of faith. He built several chapels, where he ministered, as opportunity offered. One of these was at Kerley Downs, and it lacked a pulpit. Billy saw, at an auction of old furniture, a three-cornered cupboard, which he thought he could alter into a pulpit. He asked a man near him what it would go for, as he wanted it for a pulpit; and the man recognizing him, said it would bring about six shillings, and handed him the money as a gift for the object. When it was put up, Billy immediately bid six shillings; but, to his surprise and chagrin, a man behind him bid seven, and took it, as Billy had not a penny to add. "Well, Father do know best," said he, falling back on his faith; and down he went to his chapel to pray about it. Gaining fresh assurance there that all was right, he came out and saw the cupboard going along on a cart. He followed it, and it was carried to a house, where they tried in vain to get it through the door; it was just too large! "Here's a mess," said the purchaser; I've given seven shillings for it, and now shall have to chop it up for firewood." Now was Billy's opportunity, and with twinkling eyes he stepped up, and said, "I'll give you six shillings for it, if you will carry it down to my little chapel." "That I will," cried the man, glad of the chance. "Bless the Lord!" ejaculated Billy; "'tis just like him. He knew I couldn't carry it myself, so he got this man to carry it for me." And was it not so?

HOW A SLAVE OBTAINED FREEDOM. In Prof. Park's memoir of Rev. Dr. Samuel Hopkins, he gives an account of a remarkable African, who was a slave in Newport, R. I., and who made great progress in self-education. The following account of the manner in which he gained his freedom rests on the authority of several eminent men, who knew the facts. The slave's name was Newport Gardner. "He was allowed to labor for his own profit during whatever time he might gain by extra diligence. The slave devoted all this *gained* time to procuring the means of liberating himself and family. He was finally advised by a deacon of Mr. Hopkins' church, to spend this time in *fasting and prayer* for his liberation; and he was assured of more rapid success in this course than in that of manual labor. Accordingly, having gained a day, this pious negro, without communicating his plan to any but Mr. Hopkins and two or three Christian friends, spent that day in secret fasting and prayer, that he might obtain his freedom. His master, totally ignorant of his slave's occupation, sent for him about four o'clock in the afternoon, but was told that Newport was engaged for himself, this being his *gained* day. 'No matter; call him,' says Captain Gardner. After some hesitation the slave was called, and his owner gave him a paper, on which was written: 'I, Caleb Gardner, of Newport, Rhode Island, do this day manumit and release forever, Newport Gardner, his wife and children,' etc., etc., adding some conditions which could easily be complied with. The slave received his manumission with gratitude to his owner, but with still deeper gratitude to his all-wise Disposer above, who had signally answered his request for freedom, *even before he had finished his supplication.*"

Escape From a Bear. Rev. James French, a Baptist Home Missionary, in Colorado, writes to the author, that in 1874, Mr. I. H. Wilt, a devotedly pious brother, clerk of the Baptist church in Bear Cañon, Douglas Co., Colorado, was hunting for cows, in the Foot Hills of the Rocky Mountains, not far from his home; when he was attacked by an enraged cinnamon bear, which had probably been wounded by some one shortly before. Having no means of defense, he sought to escape by climbing a tree, but was overtaken by the bear, who seized him from below by the feet, and tore his boots with his teeth, and mangled his flesh to the bones. In his extremity he remembered that God of whom David said: "The Lord that delivered me out of the paw of the lion, and out of the paw of the bear, he will deliver me out of the hand of this Philistine." 1 Sam. xvii: 7. To use his own words, "I cried unto the Lord." The prayer was instantly heard; for the bear at once released his hold, and ran away. Mr. French says: "I saw him, when he was a cripple from his wounds, and heard him relate how the Lord heard his prayer, when hope from all earthly sources had gone." Of course, in this, as in a multitude of other cases, one may say, that there was a mere natural coincidence; that just at the time the man called on God for help, the bear had exhausted his rage, and was ready to leave. But even a determined unbeliever must think the coincidence not only marvelously happy, but very singular, seeing that the bear not only ceased inflicting wounds, but, instead of sitting down to watch, as if seized with a sudden panic, incontinently ran away! Certainly one cannot censure the saved man, if in his gratitude, he thinks that God heard his prayer, and as surely delivered him from death, as he did Daniel in the den of lions.

Repeated Instances of Help. A lady-missionary writing, Sept. 17, 1875, from a New England city, bears this testimony to the author, of God's faithfulness in sending needed aid: "In my own case, it has occurred several times. Once, being out of money and provisions, I asked my dear Heavenly Father to give me my daily bread. In less than an hour, one nearly a stranger handed me three dollars. Several times, when away from home, and nearly out of money, my wants have been met, in answer to prayer; and in every instance, the persons giving me the money knew nothing of my special needs. Once, when house-rent became due, and I had no money, I asked the Lord for it, and a person called and paid a debt amounting to more than was needed. One morning, two years ago, the promise in my Text-book was, 'He shall give thee the desire of thy heart;' and feeling the special need of counsel and advice, I asked the Lord to send to me Rev. Henry Belden, of Brooklyn, N. Y., from whom we had not heard for many months. He came that day, on the noon train. One bitter cold night, two years ago, last winter, a widow lady living in Connecticut, being very destitute, arose at the midnight hour, and asked God to send help. That same night, a cousin of hers, living in Louisiana, from whom she had not heard for years, was so exercised in mind that he could not sleep, and he arose and asked God to bless the suffering poor. While praying, he thought of this cousin, though not supposing her to be needy. Yet his impressions became such that, at day-break, he rode several miles on horseback to a bank, and sent her a check of fifty dollars."

ANTICIPATIVE ANSWER TO PRAYER. One of the peculiarly interesting facts brought out in the experience of God's people is, that he often anticipates their wants and provides a supply; but does not reveal what he has done, till the exigency arrives, and earnest prayer is offered for divine aid. Then it appears that God had planned that the help should come just at the time when the soul, through a sense of want, prayer and faith, was prepared to appreciate the gift, and to receive with it a spiritual blessing. The following incident occurred among the family connections of the author.

A lady in a New England city, who was possessed of some property, made her will two or three years before her death. In planning for the wisest disposal of her estate, she determined to remember quite a circle of relatives and connections whose means were limited. Among others to whom a bequest of five hundred dollars was made, was one from whom she had not heard for years, and who had removed to some unknown part of the great West. After the lady's death, her brother, the executor, proceeded to carry out her bequests. In a letter to the author he says:

"Five hundred dollars were left to a lady whose residence I did not know. Upon inquiry, I heard she was in California or Oregon. I sent a notification to her, by letter, of the bequest, wishing to know how I should forward it to her. After awaiting reply for several months, and hearing nothing, I made further inquiries, and learned that she was in Ohio; and, the same day, I received my original letter from the dead letter office, Washington, with an inscription on it, that it had been advertised and not called for. I immediately wrote to Ohio, saying I had this $500 for her, and was desirous of paying it, to close the estate. The within extract from her reply will give you the result:

"I cannot express the pleasure with which I have received your letter. The gift itself came so opportunely, and so much as if sent from God, that I could but say, *Praise the Lord!* As you, I believe, are a Christian, I will, for your own encouragement in the Christian life, tell you my experience of an answer to prayer. Last Friday night was almost a sleepless one to me, on account of a pecuniary pressure, just at that time, for five hundred dollars. I will not detail all the circumstances: sufficient to say, that after a sleepless night, and seeing no way out of the darkness, I was led to throw my burden on the Lord, and ask him if he would not please to send help *that day*. This I did sincerely, and left it all there, feeling easy then, in my mind. I did not worry at all through the day, Saturday, and at the close of the day, your letter was brought to me. Can I ever do anything else but trust my Heavenly Father? While my angel-mother is walking those golden streets, will it not please her, if her children live by faith, here below, and trust him who has said, 'Leave thy fatherless children with me.'? 'When my father and mother forsake me, then the Lord will take me up.'"

Here was a case in which the words of Scripture were fulfilled: "And it shall come to pass, that before they call I will answer; and while they are yet speaking I will hear." Is. lxv: 24. This language implies, that God foresees both the wants and the prayers of his people, and provides the needed answer by way of anticipation. He kindly led to the remembrance of this needy lady in the will of her relative; for wise reasons he allowed her place of residence to remain unknown to the executor, till the exact time when it was necessary that he should learn it, so that the requisite aid should be sent to his praying child; he inspired his child to come filially to her Heavenly Father; and then he rewarded her faith. This is an illustration of the fact that God makes prayer an element of his plan of the world; that he so orders his providences, that they leave a place for prayer in the midst of second causes, and thus secure temporal and spiritual good at the same time.

Another Similar Case. As it is instructive to notice how God plans, on the one side, to allow trials to lead his people to prayer, and on the other, to provide the answer for that prayer when it shall have been offered, the author would add another case, both of the parties to which are personally known to him, and from one of whom he obtained the facts. Mr. T—— was a gentleman, doing business at the time in the city of Philadelphia. He had set apart twenty-five dollars for Home Missions, and was about to enclose that sum in a letter to the Society at New York. Suddenly the thought occurred to him that Rev. Mr. L—— was doing home-missionary work in Illinois, and that it might be well to send the money to him. He did so. And what was happening in Illinois, in the home of

Mr. L——? His good wife was in great distress over an empty family-treasury. Bills were coming in, and there was no money with which to meet them. Having no human resource, she went to her closet, and prayed earnestly that God would send help. Receiving comfort from this appeal, she went about her domestic duties, and a little after, a letter was brought from the post-office, which proved to be the one from Philadelphia with the twenty-five dollars.

PRAYER DELIVERS FROM UNJUST WRATH. All the parties to the following narrative were well known to the author, who received the account from the person principally interested:

A pastor at the east, Rev. Dr. P——, visiting Mr. E——, a sick parishoner, found him so evidently marked for death, that he advised him to attend, without delay, to any worldly arrangements he might wish to make. Mr. E—— desired the pastor to call upon his lawyer, and send him to the house, that he might draw up a will; which he did. The pastor had been intimate with the family for many years. The father-in-law, Mr. A——, on coming home, and learning that the pastor had been there, and afterwards the lawyer, became very angry, and sent a most insulting letter to the pastor, forbidding him ever again to call at his house. The pastor wrote back a kind note of explanation, which was returned unopened, with another angry and insulting letter, refusing to receive any explanations. The pastor then requested a common friend of both parties, Mr. S——, to call upon

Mr. A——, and read to him a full statement of the facts. He called, but was not allowed to read the communication, or to make any verbal statement. The pastor then laid the whole matter before God in prayer, for several days. One morning, when in his study, and on his knees, pleading with God to take away the unjust wrath of Mr. A——, and to restore the warm friendship which had long existed between the two families, there was a ring at the door. A servant knocked at the study, announcing a gentleman. The pastor opened the door, when in rushed Mr. A——, the tears running down his cheeks, and crying out: "O, my dear pastor, can you forgive me the deep wrong I have done you?" He fell upon his knees, in his earnestness, and begged for forgiveness. Thus the answer came, even while the prayer was on the lips.

Reconciliation Effected. A letter from a lady to the author gives this further illustration of the value of prayer in reconciling those alienated: "The writer knows a Christian woman, who, on account of business matters, had brought on herself, without just cause, the dire displeasure of another woman, nearly allied to her; and for a long time all intercourse was denied her by the latter. Having occasion to go to the same place, the first mentioned, on the journey, laid the case before the Father, who hears when his children cry to him. She begged him, if he so pleased, to heal this breach in his own way, though to her it seemed almost an impossibility. Some hours after her arrival, a note from the offended one was brought to the house where she was, inviting her to dine; as though nothing unpleasant had existed. The first expression of her heart was, 'What hath God wrought!' With thankfulness she accepted the invitation, and so those two near and dear ones, alienated for so long a time, were joined in loving intercourse."

ANOTHER PRAYER FOR RAIN. This same lady writes also, that during the ministry of Rev. Mr. R., in the village of C., there was a season of drouth, so severe and long-continued, that the church felt that they must meet and call on God to grant them the blessing without which both man and beast must suffer. They met, and earnest, believing prayer was made. On their way from the meeting, they saw, like Elijah, signs of rain, and ere long copious showers testified to the goodness and faithfulness of a prayer-hearing God.

MISS ANNIE SHIPTON AND THE BLIND BOY. Miss Shipton is the author of several spiritual books, which have been widely circulated, on both sides of the Atlantic. One of these is called, "The Secret of the Lord," in which she gives this bit of experience. She read in a religious paper an account of a blind boy, who was learning to read by means of raised letters; and was deeply impressed with the conviction that she should send him something, and the amount also seemed to be fixed at eighteen pence. She believed it was of the Spirit of God, and although she did not know the boy's exact direction, she wrote a letter, enclosed in it the money and a text of Scripture, which occurred to her, placed it in a large black-bordered envelope, and sent it to a friend, who lived in the same village with the boy. Two months after, during a season of deep depression, a christian friend called on her, and in conversation said: "So you have a correspondent at K——?" "No," she replied; "I have none there." "That is strange," he answered; "I thought I knew your handwriting. I was in a cottage there, one day, and among the papers and letters in the casement I saw a black-bordered envelope. This attracted my attention, and I said to the woman, 'Who is your correspondent?' 'Ah, sir,' she replied, 'that is a wonderful answer to prayer. Poor Leonard has his blind-books, you know. He has almost all the Testament now, and he wanted a box for them. The carpenter said he would make him one for fifteen pence. So Leonard prayed to the Lord to send him the money. There came this letter, as you see, with eighteen pence, in stamps, and this text, which was indeed for him. We don't know the name, but Leonard always prays for his 'friend in London.'" Miss Shipton naturally adds: "Precious, precious return! A flood of thanksgiving rushed through my clouded heart, and carried doubt and distrust away."

Prayer in Sundry Exigencies. It is often a question, how far we may refer the smallest matters of life to God; and no other reply would seem to be appropriate except this: that God is interested in everything which affects the happiness of his children. A letter, now before the writer, from Rev. S. A. Dwinnell, of Reedsburg, Wis., communicates a series of facts as follows: A Mr. H——, a man mighty in the Scriptures and in prayer, said to Mr. D.: "At one time, while in Baraboo, we were reduced to great straits for food. I said to my wife, we are shut up to God, and must carry our wants to him in special prayer. We did so. About two hours afterwards, I sent my son to the post office, and he returned with a letter from England. I opened it, and found a five pound note ($25) enclosed. It was from an old friend, who said, 'I have a strong impression that you are in want, and hasten to send you the enclosed bank-note, without waiting to get a draft.' The impression was evidently from God directly, as he had no earthly reason for supposing that I and my family were at that time in want."

Mr. D. continues: "In the summer of 1870, I was teaching a Bible-class, on Sabbath mornings. One day, two ministers were present, and the subject for examination was prayer in secular matters. One of the ministers, Rev. Mr. Snell, related the following: Some years ago, one of my neighbors, a wicked man, had legal possession of a land-title, which morally belonged to me. He had for a long time refused to give it up to me. There seemed to be no hope of obtaining it, unless God should directly influence him. The document was of great value to me. Having made the case a matter of special prayer, I went to see him. I found him with several companions in a bar-room, somewhat under the influence of liquor. Unfavorable as were the circumstances in which I found him, I took him to a retired part of the room, and made an earnest effort to obtain the paper. He refused to give it up. I started for home, and got as far as the door, when he called me to come back. I again used every argument in my power to move him; but he was inexorable. I was about to leave, when he again recalled me. This was three times repeated, when he finally yielded, and gave up the document. It seemed to me that God directly moved him to do it."

The other minister, Rev. H. H. Hinman, said: A few years ago, when I was a missionary at Meudi, on the western coast of Africa, I was sent, one time, with my family, into the interior, one hundred miles from our base of supplies, and entirely among the heathen. After a time, from some failure in forwarding provisions, we were left in utter destitution, and could only appeal to God for help. Soon after, a native, whom we had never seen before, and never saw afterwards, came and left us a supply of food, which lasted us until more was forwarded us from the mission. It seemed that God directly moved upon the mind of that native to help us in our extremity. We could see no other reason.

Mr. D. continues, with reference to answers received when he was superintending the repairs on his church: "One day I sent an order to the furnace at Ironton, for weights to hang the window-sash. I learned, when too late to change the order, that they each should have been a pound heavier than I had ordered. I could only carry the case to God, and ask him to rectify the mistake. After a few days, I received a letter from the proprietor of the foundry, saying: 'I have filled your order, but by some unaccountable mistake on the part of my pattern-maker, they are each a pound too heavy. If you can use them you can have them at a discount; otherwise I will keep them.'"

THE SMALLER EVENTS OF LIFE. A letter from Mr. F., a Massachusetts pastor, relates his unsuccessful search for a valuable knife, prized as a present from a friend, on a laurel-covered hill-side; a pause for prayer, and immediate success thereafter. It also mentions the case of a friend in a responsible position under the government, whose accounts failed to balance by reason of an error, which, after long search, he could not detect. In great distress, he betook himself to prayer, and then opening his books, on the very first page which he happened to glance at, and at the top of the colnmn, he saw instantly the looked-for error standing out so plainly, that he wondered he had not seen it before. A lost rubber shoe promptly recovered after prayer, is also mentioned, and the writer of the letter suggests that such cases are "quite as convincing as some of more dignity and importance."

Another correspondent, Mr. T. S. Goodwin, M. D., of Staten Island, is of the same mind, and writes of his boyish experience, when thirteen years old. He lost a choice penknife, while collecting and driving several cows, from a pasture covered with grass two inches high. Having read Huntington's Book of Faith, he bethought him of prayer, and, in child-like trust, he knelt under a tree, outside the bars, and prayed for his lost treasure; for he was a farmer's boy, and his spending money amounted to only about fifty cents a year. His words are: "I rose up, cast my eyes down on the ground, and without planning my course, or making any estimate of probabilities, walked across the meadow centrally to near its farther edge, saw the penknife down in the grass directly before me, and picked it up — all as readily as I could have done had any one stood there pointing to the exact place. Had I gone two feet to the right or left, I could not have seen the knife, for the grass." This fact is inserted the more readily because it may encourage children to go to their Heavenly Father with their troubles, believing that he is not above listening to their prayers. It is a blessed thing to learn early to make God our confidant.

Still another writes of his experience as a teacher. He lost a silver-mounted penholder, which had been presented to him, and feared that some scholar had stolen it. Unwilling to charge or suspect the school, he knelt in prayer, during recess, when all the pupils were out, and asked God to help in the emergency. He called the scholars in, and then went out himself, to bring in wood for the fire; and as he stooped down, at the wood-pile, there lay the lost penholder on the ground, where it had dropped the previous day, from behind his ear. He was thus saved from even mentioning the matter to the school.

God's people should consult him frankly in whatever concerns their welfare. Parents should pray about the little matters which pertain to their children; ladies should talk over their domestic affairs with the Lord; business men should spread out their plans and wants before the mercy-seat; and the poor, who need employment, or a specific supply, as of a hat, a coat, or a pair of shoes, should tell the fact to their Heavenly Father. They would receive many gifts by so doing.

"Thy thoughts are good, and thou art kind,
  E'en when we think it not;
How many an anxious, faithless mind
  Sits grieving o'er its lot,
And frets and pines by day and night,
As God had lost it out of sight,
  And all its wants forgot.

"Ah, no! God ne'er forgets his own,
  His heart is far too true;
He ever seeks their good alone,
  His love is daily new,
And though thou deem that things go ill,
Yet he is just and holy still,
  In all things he can do.

"The Lord is ever close and near
  To those who keep his word;
Whene'er they cry to him in fear,
  Their prayer is surely heard;
He knoweth well who love him well;
His love shall yet their clouds dispel,
  And grant the hope deferred."

—*Paul Gerhardt.*

CHAPTER XII.

PRAYER FOR PHYSICAL HEALING.

(Commenced.)

There is a great truth, with much adjacent error, connected with the subject of physical healing in answer to prayer. The famous words of James are frequently misunderstood: "Is any sick among you? Let them call for the elders of the church, and let them pray over him, anointing him with oil in the name of the Lord; and the prayer of faith shall save the sick, and the Lord shall raise him up, and if he have committed sins they shall be forgiven him. Confess your faults one to another, and pray one for another, that ye may be healed." James v: 14, 15. It will be seen that sickness and sin are here connected, as are also healing and forgiveness. This naturally points to the fact that God had sent upon some of the churches physical judgments for their sins; as Paul informs us, in the words: "For this cause many are weak and sickly among you, and many sleep (die)." 1 Cor. x: 30. John also is supposed by some, to refer to the same fact (but this is more doubtful) when he says: "If any man see his brother sin a sin which is not unto death, he shall ask, and he shall give him life for them that sin not unto death. There is a sin unto death: I do not say that he shall pray for it." 1 John v: 16. If James had in view only this class of cases, then he simply authorizes a specific faith for such persons; that on confession of their sin, and the offering of prayer by the officers of the church, they should be forgiven and healed.

Or James may be speaking in a general way of the value of faith, not pausing to name other qualifications, which were to be taken for granted. Mere emphasis of faith must not be mistaken for the assertion of a narrow rule, to cover all cases of illness. That would be to abolish death in the Christian church. It would also seem probable, that the apostles and others in the primitive churches who had the miraculous "gift of healing" (1 Cor. xii: 9–28), received an inward intimation from the Holy Spirit, when they were to exercise the gift, and feel assured of a specific answer to prayer. Otherwise Paul, instead of having occasion to write to Timothy, "Trophimus have I left at Miletum, sick," would have healed his friend, and taken him with him. The gift was only for use on fit occasion suggested by the Holy Spirit.

We come, then, to the conclusion that, in all cases of illness, it is our privilege to offer prayer for recovery, with a submission of the case to the divine will, and an assured faith that God will actually secure the healing, if such a result is best; that fact being sometimes preintimated. A multitude of instances will be found in which the answer comes in a way so striking — it may be, in the assurance gained, the means used, the person called in, the peculiar effect produced, or the time when it took place — that one cannot fail to recognize the divine intervention. The prayers being conditional, however, those are not to be considered unanswered, which are not followed by healing; since other needed blessings may be attached to the sickness, or to its results. What we really ask is, that our Heavenly Father will do the best thing possible, in each case; adding his blessing to the means which we appropriately use; whether it be anointing with oil, as in James's day, or resorting to other remedial agencies, now deemed beneficial. There is no reason why prayer should not be accompanied by appropriate effort, in this class of cases, as it is in other cases. We will attend to the testimony of facts as to its success in healing in our own days.

Dorothea Trudell's Prayer-Cure. If the reader has never met with a little volume, entitled "Dorothea Trudell, or The Prayer of Faith," he will do well to obtain and read it, It is but a brief sketch that can here be given of its contents. Dorothea Trudell, who lived in Switzerland, inherited her faith in prayer; for she said: "Our mother was permitted in a wonderful manner to meet with events which passed all general experience. We were taught to acknowledge that the Lord alone is the true Physician, by the fact that no other were summoned, when we or she herself were ill; and when I was attacked by small-pox, at four years old, and almost blinded by it, while my brother, who was fourteen, was seized with epilepsy, our mother believed and trusted; that the Lord would help; and in a short time we both recovered." Dorothea's own experience in that line began when, among a number of workmen employed by her nephew and herself, four fell seriously ill, and steadily grew worse under the care of the physician, until their case became quite alarming. Then she bethought her of the promise in James, and laid the matter earnestly and believingly before the Lord, and all four recovered. Her prayers in other cases were so signally answered, that the wife of a nobleman urged her to open her house to receive patients; and, notwithstanding her refusal to do so, sent patients to her. One, a Madame M——, the mother of twelve children, had been sent away from a a lunatic asylum uncured; but after being with Dorothea a few weeks, she went away permanently cured. The patients so increased, that a second little house had to be purchased. After a time, a storm of persecution burst upon her head. She was prosecuted for practicing as a physician, and the two lower courts fined her, and ordered her houses to be closed to patients. She says: "Though it was the most grievous day in my life, I obeyed the command; but houses so hastily emptied filled as fast as ever with the blind, the lame and the deaf, for whom the Lord did great things." An appeal was taken to a higher court of law, where hundreds of testimonials were presented in her favor, and Bishop von Kapff and Professor A. Tholuck bore witness to her self-denying zeal and earnest prayers. Her counsellor, Mr. Spöndlin, of

Zurich, made a powerful speech in her behalf, in which he urged that Miss Trudell's whole influence was brought to bear on the soul; that she promised no one a cure, nor yet pronounced any sickness incurable, but said to each patient: "If you only believe, you *may* be healed by prayer; let God decide;" that most of her patients were such as had already exhausted medical assistance without avail; and that the doctors had brought the charge against her, without once examining her establishment, nor could they show a case in which a single person had experienced any evil effect. The prosecution admitted it all, and only argued that so many sick people must not be allowed to crowd to one place. But the Court decided in favor of Miss Trudell, and threw the costs on her prosecutors. The trial lasted from March to November, 1861, and drew such attention to the house that only a small proportion of the applicants could be received. On carefully reviewing the facts detailed in the volume, they may be thus classified:

1. Miss Trudell felt that a thorough self-abnegation and consecration on her own part was essential to success. She declared that she had now learned what it was to "be nothing." When a rationalistic clergyman asked her how these wonders were performed, she replied: "Nothing is done by us; all these marvels in bodies and souls are wrought by the strength of Christ's blood!" When he answered that he did not believe in the blood of Jesus, she said: "It would be a poor thing for me to say only that I *believe* in the

blood; no, it is my element, and it is only because Christ has become an offering for my sins, by the sacrifice of his body and blood, that I can stand here and perform all these wonders."

2. She aimed primarily at spiritual results in her patients. This she did, because she deemed them the more important, and because they had a bearing on the cure of disease. She believed disease to be aggravated, if not caused by sin; and she wished the prayers of the patient to be added to her own, for the desired blessing. Hence she sought the conversion of the unconverted, and the elevation of the piety of others. For this purpose, she held every afternoon, from three to four o'clock, a Bible-lesson with them collectively, and during the rest of the day she talked with them singly. The physical improvement often kept exact pace with their spiritual healing.

3. While she prescribed no medicine, but only anointed with oil, laid on her hands, and offered prayer, she yet did not neglect all natural auxilaries. Her patients were most carefully and wisely nursed, and their minds were brought out from under the depressing influences. No doubt good nursing and a cheerful, patient and hopeful mind are better than medicine alone, in an average of cases. Yet it would hardly be advisable for physicians to attribute Miss Trudell's success to those agencies alone, lest they discredit the value of their own professional services. As some insisted that her influence was simply mesmeric, it may be well to state, that her slight touch,

as she prayed, would hardly supply the necessary mesmeric conditions, especially as her own health was very feeble; and that a French gentleman, who came as a patient with that idea, carefully investigated the proceedings in the institution, and left thoroughly satisfied that that theory would not answer. Once, Dorothea made this point a subject of special prayer, at a time when she was asked to visit an out-patient. She refused to go to the lady's house, but made her the subject of special prayer, and she was speedily cured, without any contact.

4. She promised no cures whatever, nor looked for instantaneous relief. She did not claim to be clothed with any miraculous power. She asserted that, in answer to believing prayer, by truly consecrated souls, God often healed the sick; but that no one could tell in advance what God would see to be for his glory in a particular case. Usually, the recovery, though prompt in commencing, was gradual in accomplishment. Yet many very striking cases occurred. We are told that on one occasion a young artisan arrived, in whom cancer had made such progress as to render any approach to him almost unbearable. At the Bible-lessons this once frivolous man became an earnest inquirer, and learned that he must seek first a spiritual improvement; and from the day he confessed his sins, the disease abated. Some time later, he acknowledged a sin previously concealed, and then speedily recovered his bodily health, and returned home cured in body and soul. A lady in S——, fell and

injured her knee, so that for weeks she lay in the greatest agony, and the physician declared that dropsy would supervene. But when Dorothea, in her usual way, prayed, and laid on her hands, the knee was cured in twenty-four hours.

5. Her assistants were her sister, four nurses, and Mr. Samuel Zeller, brother-in-law of Bishop Gobat, of Jerusalem — all like-minded with herself, and serving night and day without remuneration. No fee was taken from the patients, but a small sum was accepted from the rich for their board, while the poor were fed gratuitously.

The institution, which was at Männedorf, a little village on Lake Zurich, is still carried on since the death of Miss Trudell, by Mr. Zeller, who reports that while cures are by no means invariable, a multitude of favorable results are obtained, even in apparently desperate cases, such as epilepsy, which is a peculiarly obstinate disease, and in lunacy, and maladies occasioned by Spiritualism. The prayers seem also to be as prevalent when offered for patients who cannot come to the institution, and who are aided in soul as well as in body. One such case has, incidentally, a peculiar interest. A gentleman wrote to have prayer offered for his niece, who was threatened with blindness. Soon after, he wrote again as follows: "In answer to your prayers for our niece, I must thankfully tell you, her eyes are so much better, that the doctor this morning told her to thank God for having saved her from the most dangerous kind of a cataract.

While examining her eyes, the doctor, who is a Jew, took up a book lying near, and opening it, told her to try and read, which she was able to do with ease. It was a hymn-book, and the words on which her eyes fell were these:

> "Christ Jesus, glorious King of Light,
> Great Conqueror, David's heir,
> Come, now, and give my blind eyes sight;
> O Savior, hear my prayer!"

"'That will do,' said the doctor; 'you are much better.' I, for my part, hastened to my chamber, and, shutting the door, fell on my knees with a cry of joyful praise." Patients continue to arrive in such numbers that larger accommodations are pressingly needed.

CASE OF MRS. JANE C. MILLER. The author of this book has the pleasure of a slight acquaintance with Mrs. Miller, and her husband, Rev. Daniel R. Miller, and has heard the facts stated below from their own lips. Rev. Charles G. Finney, ex-President of Oberlin College, furnished to *The Advance*, then under the writer's charge, her statement, with these remarks: "Mrs. Miller is the wife of a Congregational minister, and a lady of unquestionable veracity. However the fact of her healing is to be accounted for, her story is no doubt worthy of entire confidence, as we have known her for years, as a lame, suffering invalid, and now see her in our midst, in sound health. This instantaneous restoration will be accounted for by different persons in different ways. Mrs. Miller, and those who were present, regard the healing as supernatural, and a direct answer to prayer. The facts must speak for themselves. Why should not the sick be healed in answer to the prayer of faith? Unbelief can discredit them, but faith sees nothing incredible in such facts as stated by Mrs. Miller."

Mrs. Miller's own statement was published in *The Advance* of Dec. 26, 1872, and is as follows:

"From my parents I inherited a constitution subject to a chronic form of rheumatism, which affected my whole system. For nearly forty years I was subject to more or less suffering from this cause. For seven years, until the last three months, I have been unable to get about without the aid of crutch or staff; generally both. I have used many liniments and remedies, but with no permanently good result. Last summer (1872), several of us, Christian sisters, were in the habit of spending short seasons of prayer together. Some of our number had read the narrative of Dorothea Trudell, and had spoken to me on the subject of healing in answer to prayer. My faith had not then risen to this elevation. I had, in fact, accepted what I supposed to be the will of God, and made up my mind to be a lame and suffering invalid, the rest of my life. I had long since ceased to use remedies for the restoration of my health, and had not even thought of praying in regard to it. Notwithstanding what had been said to me, I remained in this opinion and attitude until the 26th of September last, when several ladies met at our house, by appointment, for a prayer meeting. I had grown worse for some time, and was then unable to get out to attend a meeting. I was suffering much pain, that afternoon; indeed, I was hardly able to be out of my bed. One lady was present, who could speak to me, from her own experience, of being healed in answer to the prayer of faith. She related several striking instances in which her prayers had been answered, in removal of divers forms of disease to which she was subject. She also repeated a number of passages of Scripture, which clearly justified the expectation of being healed, in answer to the prayer of faith. She also said, that Jesus had shown her that he was just as ready to heal diseases now, as he was when on earth; that such healing was expressly promised in Scripture, in answer to the prayer of faith, and that it was no where taken back. These facts, reasonings, and passages of Scripture made a deep impression on my mind, and for the first time I found myself able to believe that Jesus would heal me in answer to prayer. She asked me if I could join my faith with hers, and ask for present healing. I told her, I felt that I could. We then knelt, and called upon the Lord. She offered a mighty prayer to God, and I followed. While she was leading in prayer, I felt a quickening in my whole being; whereupon my pain subsided, and when we rose from prayer, I felt that a great change had come over me — that I was cured! I found that I could walk without my staff or crutch, or any assistance from any one. Since then my pains have never returned. I have more than my youthful vigor. I walk with more ease and rapidity than I ever did in my life; and I never felt so fresh and young, as I now do, at the age of fifty-two. Now the ciii Psalm is my Psalm, and my youth is more than renewed like the eagle's. I cannot express the constant joy of my heart, for the wonderful healing of my soul and body. I feel as if I was made every whit whole.

JANE C. MILLER."

A year later, Mrs. Miller wrote to a friend, under date of Dec., 1873, a letter in which she says: "I know not of any one who is able to perform the amount of labor I am; was out all day, yesterday, canvassing for the *Advocate and Guardian*, and soliciting funds to fill our box, and have done this, day after day, besides doing most of my housework and out-chores, as my husband is always absent in winter, laboring as an evangelist. It has rained most of the week, yet I have not felt it, and am not only healed, but all *tendency* to the old difficulty seems removed. 'Bless the Lord, O my soul!'"

Rev. Daniel R. Miller, her husband, confirms the statement of his wife, in these words, under date of Oberlin, O., August 6, 1873: "She had been unable to walk without crutches, for a series of years. A long time ago, we tried many remedies and physicians, with no lasting good results, and were expecting she would remain an invalid. Of late she had applied no remedy, nor taken any medicine. At the time of her cure, she was much worse than for a long while before, being in great pain continually, until the moment she fully believed, and *in an instant* she was restored to perfect soundness."

Another confirmatory statement is signed by seven of her nearest relations and connections, and by four neighbors, including a deacon of the church and two ministers of the gospel.

THE HEALING OF A CHILD. The case just stated led to another, an account of which was forwarded by a friend to *The Advance*, and it was published in that paper. A more careful account was afterwards prepared by the mother, and also by the father, with whom the author has conversed personally, in respect to his daughter. The parents are Rev. Albert Connett and Mrs. Anna E. W. Connett. At the time referred to, he was settled at Carbondale, Kansas, but has since removed to Solsberry, Ind. The mother's account is as follows: "About the middle of September, 1871, our eldest girl, Nettie, then nearly eight years old, began complaining of her left leg. The physicians pronounced it sciatic rheumatism. At times her sufferings were very great. Frequently she would not walk for a week. She was lame all the time, and never free from pain. In the fall of 1872, she seemed worse; one limb seemed higher than the other, and that limb shrinking away. It was not nearly so large as the other. We called in the physicians again. They said the indications were, that it was hip-disease. We wrote to the Surgical Institute, at Indianapolis, in regard to her. They thought she could be cured there; but that if she did not have treatment soon, she would be a suffering cripple for life. We wanted to send her there, for treatment, but found it impossible to raise the means. The child grew worse, and on the 29th of December, 1872, she had not left her bed for several days, and her sufferings were intense. That Sabbath morning we read an article in *The Advance*, 'Prayer for Healing: A Remarkable Case' [it was the account of the healing of Mrs. Miller]. Then came the thought, Why cannot we have faith to believe that Jesus will cure our child? Myrie and Orthie, of seven and five years, talked together about asking Jesus to cure Nettie. She told one of the children to come to her, and I kept on reading, as though I had read nothing remarkable; though I am sure that I knew not what I was reading about. I dreaded any conversation with the children. At length I could stand it no longer, but left the room, and prayed for faith to believe that my child could be cured. I then went to Nettie. She asked me if I would pray, and ask Jesus to cure her? She thought he would, and the little ones expressed the same opinion. My faith was growing stronger. I told them that we would read about Jesus curing sick folks. I then read aloud all the instances of healing recorded in Matthew. We all felt, then, that all we had to do was, to ask Jesus to cure her. I prayed, and was followed in prayer by Nettie. We asked for her cure that day. After prayer, I discovered that a change had come over the child. She looked worse than ever before. The thought occurred to me, that God was going to answer the prayer by taking her to himself. At her request, I read to her awhile. She then wanted to be helped into the rocking chair, though she could sit only on one side. I helped her up, and, while doing so, such a sense of weakness came over me, as I never felt before. I lay down on her bed, and immediately fell into a deep sleep. How long I slept, I know not; perhaps half an hour; or may be an hour. I was then awakened by Nettie telling me she was cured. She would say: 'O mamma, I am a new girl: Jesus has cured me. How I do love Jesus!' She was the happiest person I ever saw. For the first time in fifteen months she was entirely well, and free from pain. She could run, jump, stand on one foot; in short, do any of the many things a well child could. I then took off the plaster which the doctor put on her hip, a few days before, to make a sore, and we quit giving the medicines. That night we were a happy family, and it was late before the child could compose herself to sleep. On Wednesday following, the doctor came to see her. He could find nothing ailing the child. He seemed to think Mesmerism, or something of the kind, had been used; but after we gave him a plain statement of the case, he said he wished his daughter, who is an invalid, could be cured by prayer, or any other way. When he was ready to go, I brought him the medicines, which he took, but said I had better keep the plaster, as I might need it. He has been here two or three times since. He always questions her closely. The last time he was here, a few days ago, he found her with a big apron on, doing work in the kitchen. He said: 'Nettie, does your limb pain you much?' She said: 'No, sir; it doesn't pain me any at all.' Mr. Connett was away, at his appointments, when the child was restored. She continues well of the disease up to the present time."

About eight months after the cure, the physician M. T. Perrine, M. D., gave the following statement in writing:

CARBONDALE, Sept. 22, 1873.

The Rev. Mr. Connett's daughter was lame from sciatica, fifteen months before I was called to treat her. I used the common homœopathic remedies. They heard of the prayer-cure, and resorted to it. She seemed to become better, at once. She has continued better since—with the exception of a few days, caused by slipping down. They now consider her well."

The author of this book has heard quite recently of the continued health of this little girl, from a friend who has visited the family at their present home in Indiana, and also from the father, who writes, Oct. 11, 1875: "Our girl, whose case you published in *The Advance*, still continues well. She is now twelve years old, large of her age, and doing most of the work for our family of six persons."

THE HEALING OF A MINISTER'S WIFE. A few months subsequent to the case last named, occurred the one now to be described. The parties are not personally known to the author, who first learned of the facts from the statements made in the secular and religious papers of the region, but has since met with a carefully prepared account, written after a visit to the place and a diligent investigation of the facts, and printed in a little pamphlet entitled, "*Were they Miracles?*" which can be found at the Willard Tract Depository, Boston, and to which reference can be had for more extended details. A condensed account is as follows:

Mrs. Ellen Clark Sherman is the wife of Rev. Moses Sherman, who, in August 1873, was in the third year of his pastorate of the Methodist Episcopal Church of Piermont, N. H. Mrs. S., when a girl, twice fell and badly injured her left knee, so that it became partially stiff, and was pronounced incurable by the physicians. Subsequently she strained herself, so as to bring on serious female-diseases. Twice she fell down steps or staircase, striking her backbone, nearly paralyzing the spinal cord and causing serious and permanent spinal disease. In September, 1872, she took to her bed, where she lay helpless, except when lifted from it, till August 27, 1873. She could not walk a step or stand; nor could she even sit up a short time, without great distress. Medical skill proved unavailing. During the last two or three weeks, it required two persons to move her. She had come to think that her lot was to be a bed-ridden, suffering invalid. At the date just named, she was left alone in her room for the night, and lay awake revolving various sore trials, and was led to commit them by faith to Jesus, and to feel perfect rest of soul. She made a renewed consecration of her all to God, surrendering herself completely to do and suffer all God's will, when a delightful consciousness of acceptance came over her. She then felt a special presence of Jesus, and what some would call a dream, and others a vision came to her. What followed is given in her own words abridged; which certainly record a strange experience:

"Then I became conscious of a movement of the Presence, and it seemed to be filling the room more and more. From the foot of the bed the Presence whispered, 'Believest thou that I am able to do this?' This was repeated many times, while I lay there, and reasoned the matter all over. The power to yield and believe was given, and I said: 'Lord, I believe; help thou my unbelief?' At once the Presence seemed to press up to me over the foot of the bed, and whispered to me the words, 'And he breathed on them, and said, Receive ye the Holy Ghost;' and they were accompanied by a warm breathing upon my face. This was repeated many times. Each new pulsation of the Holy Breath flowed deeper through my body; and as it went, all pain ceased. After a little time, I was told by a whisper from the Presence, to raise my left arm, the worse one, to my head. Before, I was not able to raise either without the aid of the other; but now I raised this easily and without pain. Then I was told to raise the other; which I did with equal ease. Then, to turn over. At once I came over, like a cork in water. Then to ring the bell. I did so, and my husband came in, but half-awake, and lighted the candle. I said, 'There is a strange influence in the room: the Savior is here, at work upon me;' when the words were inwardly spoken, with great emphasis, 'That the people may know that the Son of man hath power on earth *still* to forgive sin, *Rise up and walk!*' At once I, who had been bed-ridden, and incapable of stepping a step for months, threw off the clothes with my left arm, sprang out of bed upon my feet, and started to walk across the room."

Her husband's first thought was that she was crazed, and he sprang to help her. But she refused his aid, walked back and forth across the room, and insisted that Jesus had healed her. He called up his son of twelve years, and a woman in the house, and they rejoiced together from one to three o'clock, when all retired. In the morning, her son came in to find out whether it was real, or a dream; when she sat up, on the side of the bed, picked up and drew on her stockings, which she had not been able to do for more than a year, and lifted the left foot upon the other knee, and found it wholly restored. From that time all her troubles — neuralgic sick-headaches, lack of appetite, dyspepsia, costiveness, feminine difficulties, kidney disease, etc. — entirely left her, and she has gained steadily in strength to this time.

A HOME MISSIONARY SAVED TO LABOR. A missionary in Kansas writes of his personal experience, to this effect. He had just begun to preach somewhat, as a young Christian, under the direction of his pastor, and in a fit of deep depression was returning from what he meant should be his last appointment, when he took a severe cold in a storm. In a few days he was so low, that the physician pronounced his case hopeless, and he put his affairs in order, arranged for his funeral, and calmly awaited his end. The pastor was away, at the first, but coming home, called and found him speechless, and received answers about his spiritual condition only by signs. He then called on two church members present to pray, and when they had finished, began himself. With the greatest simplicity he spoke of the Lord's goodness, and of the chastening which he had sent, and then turned to the world's need of laborers, and quoted Mat. ix: 37, 38, from which two years before he had preached a powerful sermon, which had led several young men to devote themselves to the gospel ministry. "And now," said he, "Lord, wilt thou take them away again?" And he pleaded as did Jacob, when wrestling with the angel. Then he quoted the text in James, v: 14, 15, as to the prayer of faith healing the sick, and cried out, "Lord, I do believe." At that moment the young man seemed to hear a voice saying, "You must preach the gospel," and at once began to amend. For nearly forty years he has now been obeying that command, and receiving souls for his hire.

TESTIMONY OF CHARLES CULLIS, M. D. Dr. Cullis is widely known among Christians, as the superintendent of the "Consumptives' Home," in Boston; which is wholly supported by voluntary contributions received in answer to prayer. His success in this respect led him to consider whether healing, as well as money, might not be received from the Lord, and a perusal of the memoir of Dorothea Trudell convinced him, that we ought to expect God to do in America what he was doing in Europe. The results of his experience were clearly and frankly given in the "Ninth Annual Report of the Consumptives' Home." From the many cases described are taken the following, in the words of Dr. Cullis:

"At this time I had under my professional care a Christian lady, with a tumor which confined her almost continuously to her bed in severe suffering. All remedies were unavailing, and the only human hope was the knife; but feeling in my own heart the power of the promise, I one morning sat down by her bedside, and taking up the Bible, I read aloud God's promise to his believing children: '*And the prayer of faith shall save the sick, and the Lord shall raise him up; and if he have committed sins, they shall be forgiven him.*'

"I then asked her if she would trust the Lord to remove this tumor and restore her to health, and to her missionary work, She replied, 'I have no particular faith about it, but am willing to trust the Lord for it.'

"I then knelt and anointed her with oil in the name of the Lord, asking him to fulfill his own word. Soon after I left, she got up and walked three miles. From that time the tumor rapidly lessened, until all trace of it at length disappeared.

"Some time afterward, this lady gave testimony in a public meeting to the cure wrought in her by the prayer of faith, and a sorrowing wife present, whose husband was sick with consumption, went home and repeated to him the story. At my request he has written out the case as follows:

"'W——, NEAR BOSTON, March, 1872.

"'I was first confined to my house in November, 1870, with a violent cold. I lost my voice completely, suffered with pain in my lungs, and expectorated almost constantly. I grew worse every day, and in a week called in a physician. On examination he found my lungs diseased. I also had fever. With all his care my cough grew worse, and night-sweats set in. A few weeks later, my wife was told by the doctor that my lungs were badly ulcerated, and that, my case being hopeless, it was not worth while for him to attend longer; also that she must not be surprised if I should pass away suddenly. I then tried some highly recommended patent medicine, which seemed only to increase my disease.

"'When I became so weak as to be nearly helpless, Dr. Cullis was called in. He sounded my lungs and gave the same verdict, saying that my only hope for recovery was in the Lord. My wife pleaded in the name of Jesus for my restoration; but diarrhœa set

10*

in and my feet began to swell. She, however, continued to pray earnestly, urging me to pray for myself. I could not do it, as I had no desire in the matter apart from the will of God, who had dealt with me so graciously in all my sickness, that I delighted in his will. If it was alone of his goodness to me that you desired me to write, I would not know where to end. During the next summer I seemed to gain, but was so dependent on my medicine, that a single day's omission would aggravate my distress. As autumn advanced, I felt that my disease was gaining ground.

"'At length my wife heard, at a meeting for Christian holiness at the house of Mr. Cullis, Miss D. narrate her recovery from a tumor by the power of faith. Returning home, she repeated it to me. I knew that our Father in heaven was no respecter of persons, and the more I thought upon it and read the precious promises of God, the more I was convinced that '*the prayer of faith shall save the sick, and the Lord shall raise him up.*' Believing that he *is* faithful that promised, I now sent for Dr. Cullis to come and pray with me. Dr. and Mrs. Cullis, with my wife, went with me into an upper room, where we knelt before God. Dr. C. prayed, anointed me with oil, and in the name of the Lord Jesus commanded me to be healed. Instantly my whole being was thrilled with an unknown power, from the top of my head to the soles of my feet. From the moment I believed, the work *was done!* My lungs, so long diseased, breathed with new vigor, and I returned thanks to God for the results of faith. Since that memorable night I have taken no medicine, and my health has been constantly improving, so that I am feeling better now than I did before my sickness. To God be all the glory!'

"It is now more than two years since the above incident took place. The writer continues perfectly well, and is engaged in active business, walking before the Lord in humble, fervent spirit.

"A lady came to me with a cancer in the cheek, which had attained the size of a filbert. It had a very red and angry appearance. After prayer for her healing, she went into the country, when some one remarked: 'E. thinks that faith will cure her; but that is something that will have to be burned or cut out.' Her friends tried to induce the use of various applications, all of which she firmly refused. She returned home in eight weeks, entirely cured. The friends acknowledge that 'faith did do good, once.'

"A lady of East Cambridge writes: 'For nineteen years I have been afflicted with neuralgia; added to this, of late years a combination of diseases has rendered life an intolerable burden, and baffled the skill of every physician to whom I have applied. By the prayer of faith I have been healed, both body and soul, and made to rejoice continually. For the first few months, Satan was busy with me; and when I gave way to doubt, pain again racked my body God has strengthened my faith continually. I can now say I am entirely well, and engaged in arduous work, often among the sick, losing whole nights of rest.'

"It is right to add, that a few instances have occurred in which I seemed in my own consciousness to have the same faith, and yet the healing did not follow. I offer no theory upon this subject. I simply state facts, and leave the rest with God. And yet I can conceive wherefore he who alone knows the end from the beginning, decides why some should be saved, and others left to suffer and to die. It is not always that even those who are Christians have used a restoration to health or to life, to their own blessing and the glory of God."

The closing paragraph of Dr. Cullis, deserves attention, as showing the limitations of faith in this prayer for healing. There are two theories which seem dangerous, to which allusion was made in the chapter on the prayer of faith. One of these teaches, that we can have anything through prayer, by simply believing that we shall have it; which would imply that we could obtain on that condition the healing of any case of disease. This is attended, as was shown, by too many absurd implications to be admitted. Prayer certainly was never intended to be a universal panacea, and to do away with the skill of physicians, any more than with nurses, or than with any class of appropriate agencies for securing desired results. More plausible is the theory that only now and then is it the divine purpose to grant healing in answer to prayer, and that in such case the Holy Spirit not only awakens the desire, and inspires the petition, but also creates in the soul the positive assurance, or faith, that the blessing will be granted. Some of the facts seem to favor this idea; but others do not. Thus, confident expectation and assertion are often not followed by the result desired. This makes a stumbling-block for the theory; which also acts discouragingly upon cases where prayer is offered, and no such specific assurance is obtained. And yet these latter prayers are often followed by favorable results. It is better, then, to say that the requisite faith is simply that God will secure the healing, if it shall be best for all interests, and suddenly or gradually, with or without medicines and physicians, as he may choose, in each instance. Iron rules are of human rather than of divine ordering in these matters.

DR. CULLIS' VISIT TO MANNEDORF. In his tenth annual report, Dr. Cullis gives an interesting account of his visit to the institution which Dorothea Trudell founded at Männedorf, which is now under the charge of Mr Zeller, who originally came as a patient. He says: "Mr. Zeller had not only been restored, but was praying with the sick, God honoring his faith. Dorothea in looking to the Lord for a successor, felt it to be his will that Mr. Zeller should be the one, and accordingly, after much prayer, made over the entire property to him, so that when in the autumn of 1862, she fell sick and died, there was no change of hands — no trouble or expense — the work going on as heretofore. Mr. Zeller is thirty-seven years of age.

"Service is held in the chapel every morning, attended by the household, and any persons in the village who so desire; also a prayer-meeting every other evening. Every day at five o'clock, Mr. Zeller meets such as are able, for praying, and anointing for healing. Preaching every Sabbath morning. All these services are conducted by Mr. Zeller, who is not an ordained clergyman, but called of the Lord for this his own work; and his power rests upon him. Persons are often cured while listening to his preaching, though he may not at the time say anything about the healing of the body — only of the healing of the soul by the blood of Jesus. There is one marked feature of the work — that not unfrequently the soul is saved and then the body cured. * * * Nettie Weber was a faithful worker with Dorothea, and now spends her whole time ministering to the sick. Many are healed in answer to her prayers, especially among the insane, of whom there were thirty at the time of our visit. There were about fifty patients in the house, subject to various diseases; among them several paralytics and epileptics. Many others, who avail themselves of the privileges of the house, and take meals there, lodge in the village. Anna Barbara Meili was another healed in Dorothea's time, when far gone in consumption, who remains to devote the life that God has given, to his service.

"We next visited the churchyard, to look upon the spot where Dorothea was buried. A small iron cross, overgrown with ivy, bearing name and dates of birth and death, alone distinguished her lowly resting place. Accepting an invitation to dine, we sat down with about one hundred and fifty persons of different nationalities; these all waiting upon the Lord for healing. We enjoyed the simple meal, and would fain have lingered in the home, so hallowed by the Holy Spirit's presence. * * * On asking the question, whether *all* were healed, the reply was: 'No; but none die until the soul is healed.'"

A Further Report of Cases. This tenth report of Dr. Cullis also gives a number of new instances of healing during the year. As many suppose these cases to be limited to nervous disorders, rheumatism, paralysis, etc., it may be well to mention, that one of them was a person long afflicted with a painful heart-disease, and others were cases of consumption. One of these latter is thus described by the patient himself, who signs his initials as S. B. P.:

"Boston Highlands, July, 1874.

"During the winter of 1869, which I spent in England, from the effects of a severe cough lasting several months, the lower part of my right lung became hepatized. About the middle of last March, I was taken with congestion of the lungs. Our family physician was called; he visited me for nearly three weeks, and I have no doubt did all that medical skill could do. He succeeded in checking my fever, but I grew weaker day by day; a subtle disease was evidently preying upon my nervous system; I lost my appetite, coughed and expectorated a great deal, and had night-sweats. My wife became alarmed, and after consulting our physician, (who is also my dear friend and shared all her anxiety,) called as counsel Dr. Charles Cullis. The doctors examined my case very carefully, and found I had no use of my right lung; they gave very little if any encouragement. From that time I grew rapidly worse; my disease, as the doctors feared, was evidently tending to the brain. The second night after the consultation I was sleepless and quite delirious; in the morning I was so wild that my family could not control me. Both doctors were called, and as they came into my room I cried out in my delirium, 'I want none of your medicine, only your prayers.' I felt a consciousness that deliverance had come; I threw my arms around Dr. Cullis and wept like a child. The doctor knelt with me by my bed, offered a short prayer for my recovery, anointing me with oil in the name of the Lord. My nerves immediately became quiet; I lay down and remained in a semi-conscious state for about two hours. From my appearance my wife feared that I was dying, but the doctor assured her that that was not the case; that he felt confident the Lord would raise me up. Soon after the doctors left, in spite of the remonstrance of my wife, I got up, dressed, and went below, and for some ten hours I was in an almost constant struggle, trying, as I told my friends, to get myself into the hands of the Lord. At last I said to those around me: 'In a few minutes I shall go to sleep; as soon as I am asleep you can put me where you please, I shall sleep two or three hours.' In a few minutes I fell asleep; they lifted me from the floor, where I had persisted in lying for several hours, and laid me on a sofa. I slept quietly for about two hours; when I awoke, I felt a wonderful sense of relief. I had during my illness felt sick from the crown of my head to the soles of my feet; that feeling was all gone. I went to bed, and for the first time since I was taken ill, I slept quietly nearly all night; I slept a good part of the next day, like a weary man. *I took no more medicine*, but from the hour I went to sleep I commenced improving, which has continued until I feel as well as ever, except that I have not the full use of my hepatized lung, but I breathe the whole length of it, including that part which I had not used since 1869. My breathing is improving constantly, and I have no doubt it will recover entirely.

"For all this I give God the glory. It is said to me by those to whom I relate this experience, 'It is wonderful.' I say to them, 'Yes, it is wonderful; but not that God fulfills his promises; it is wonderful that his children should doubt his word.' It is certainly wonderful that Christians should read the fourteenth and fifteenth verses of the fifth of James, and think it means nothing now—it is not for them. I have a friend who has a daughter who came home from the West last May, apparently in consumption; she had a bad cough, expectorated a great deal, and had profuse night-sweats. She arrived in Boston on Thursday of the week; on the following Monday she had a stroke of paralysis, completely paralyzing her left side. The doctor gave no hope, said she could not live; I advised them to call Dr. Cullis and have him pray for her. He consented to do so, if they would abandon the use of medicine and simply trust her case in the hands of the Lord; to this they assented, and Dr. Cullis prayed for her. To-day she is free from cough, night-sweats, and all other signs or symptoms of consumption, and has been for nearly two months. Her paralysis is so far removed that she walks about the house."

We may not climb the heavenly steeps,
  To bring the Lord Christ down;
In vain we search the lowest deeps,
  For him no depths can drown.

But warm, sweet, tender, even yet
  A present help is he;
And faith has still its Christ,
  And love its Galilee.

The healing of the seamless dress
  Is by our beds of pain;
We touch him in life's throng and press,
  And we are whole again.

—*John G. Whittier.*

CHAPTER XIII.

PRAYER FOR PHYSICAL HEALING.

(Concluded.)

LUTHER AND MELANCHTHON. The prayer of Luther for the recovery of Melanchthon, who lay apparently at the point of death, is well known to every student of the history of the Reformation. Melanchthon's learning and facile pen were invaluable to the cause, while his milder manner avoided the offense often given by Luther's impetuosity and occasional coarseness. Hence, when Luther was summoned to the death-bed of his dearly loved friend, he burst into tears and an exclamation of agony. This roused Melanchthon, who said: "O Luther, is this you? Why don't you let me depart in peace?" "We can't spare you yet, Philip," was the Reformer's answer; and then he spent more than an hour on his knees, pleading for his recovery, until he felt that the prayer was heard. Then he turned to Melanchthon, again, whom he took by the hand, and who said: "Dear Luther, why don't you let me depart in peace?" and received as an answer: "No, no, Philip, we cannot spare you yet from the field of labor." Luther had some soup brought, and when his friend declined it, saying, "Dear Luther, why will you not let me go home?" again replied: "We cannot spare you yet, Philip," and added, in his droll way: "Philip, take this soup, or I will excommunicate you." The soup was taken, Melanchthon began to revive, and he lived to labor for many years. When Luther went home, he told his wife with triumphant joy: "God gave me my brother Melanchthon back, in direct answer to prayer." And can anyone doubt this, who considers the promises of God, and the peculiar circumstances of the case?

THE HEALING OF REV. S. H. PLATT. Rev. S. H. Platt is at present stationed in the De Kalb Avenue Methodist Episcopal Church, Brooklyn, N. Y. He has been lame, and a great sufferer in one knee, for twenty-five years, and in both for three years, and has never been able to preach standing until since his recent cure. For many years he has been a believer in the gift of healing in special cases, but could not see any reason to think that it was God's will to heal him; especially as in 1872, he visited Dr. Cullis, at Boston, without gaining permanent relief.

In the summer of 1875, he went to Ocean Grove, for a vacation, and took with him a collection of narratives of faith-cures, which he carefully read, and by which he was much impressed. Sunday, July 25th, two ladies called at his cottage, one of whom was a Miss Mossman, who claimed that the Lord had sent her to tell him that he might be cured of his lameness, if he would only believe. He mentioned his experience with Dr. Cullis; and she said his faith had subsequently failed, and she related to him a marvelous cure of a broken ankle at Syracuse, N. Y., by the simple prayer, repeated several times, "Please, Lord, heal my foot." She stated that hearing of his case, she felt divinely impressed to go to him with the message mentioned, as she had successfully gone to several others. Says Mr. Platt: "Kneeling, she rested one hand upon each knee, just as she would upon a chair, with no pressure and no motion of any kind, and in a short prayer, of not even two minutes, she asked for 'the healing of these knees.' * * * I was conscious of no change whatever, either mental, spiritual or physical, until about a minute after she had resumed her seat; when a sensation, unlike anything ever before or since experienced by me, began about four inches below each knee, and slowly swept upward with a sort of enveloping, condensing and toning up feeling, seeming to permeate every fibre of tissue about the joints, and then faded out at about the same distance above the knees. I mentioned this sensation; 'oh yes, you are cured' was her confident reply; 'only hold on and don't lose it. * * * When pain comes, trust in Jesus. Ask God to put power into your knees whenever you want to go anywhere, but don't go anywhere, unless he wants you to; and if he wants you to, you can walk any distance.'"

Since that time, Mr. Platt has walked without his canes, has preached standing, and has gradually been delivered from pain. Miss Mary H. Mossman is the daughter of a Congregational Deacon in Massachusetts, who for sixteen years has been leading a life of faith in Christ and the leadings of the Holy Spirit, and is of slight build and feeble health. Her prayers avail only in cases in which she is specially impressed by the Spirit to pray for the recovery of the person. Mr. Platt had previously tried medical and surgical remedies in vain; as also electricity and magnetism, without any permanent benefit. He has published the full particulars of his case in a pamphlet.

STATEMENT BY REV. HORACE BUSHNELL, D. D. In his valuable book, entitled "Nature and The Supernatural," Dr. Bushnell makes known some very interesting facts as follows:

"I became acquainted, about two years ago, in a distant part of the world, with an English gentleman, whose faith in the gift of healing had been established by his own personal exercise of it. He gave me a full account in manuscript of some of the cases. * * * It became a question with him, soon after his conversion, whether, as he had been healed spiritually, he ought not also to expect and receive the healing of his body by the same faith; for he had then been an invalid for a long time, with only a slender hope of recovery. After a hard struggle of mind, he was able, dismissing all his prescribed remedies, to throw himself on God, and was immediately and permanently made whole. At length, one of his children, whom he had with him away from home, was taken ill with scarlet fever, and 'now the question was'—I give his own words—'what was to be done? The Lord had indeed healed my own sickness, but would he heal my son? I conferred with a brother in the Lord, who, having no faith in Christ's healing power, urged me to send instantly for the doctor, and dispatched his groom on horseback to fetch him. Before the doctor arrived, my mind was filled with revelation on the subject. I saw that I had fallen into a snare, by turning away from the Lord's healing hand, to lean on medical skill. I felt grievously condemned in my conscience. A fear also fell on me, that if I persevered in this unbelieving course, my son would die, as his eldest brother had. The symptoms in both were precisely similar. The doctor arrived. My son, he said, was suffering from a scarlet fever, and medicine should be sent immediately. While he stood prescribing, I resolved to withdraw the child, and cast him on the Lord. And when he was gone, I called the nurse, and told her to take the child, and lay him on the bed. I then fell on my knees, confessing the sin I had committed against the Lord's healing power. I also prayed most fervently that it would please my Heavenly Father to forgive my sin, and to show that he forgave it, by causing the fever to be rebuked. I received a mighty conviction that my prayer was heard, and I arose, and went to the nursery, at the end of a long passage, to see what the Lord had done; and on opening the door, to my astonishment, the boy was sitting up in his bed; and on seeing me, cried out, 'I am quite well, and want to have my dinner.' In an hour he was dressed, and well, and eating his dinner, and when the physic arrived, it was cast out of the window. Next morning, the doctor returned; and, on meeting me at the garden gate, he said, 'I hope your son is no worse.' 'He is very well, I thank you,' said I in reply. 'What can you mean?' rejoined the doctor. 'I will tell you; come in and sit down.' I then told him all that had occurred, at which he fairly gasped with surprise. 'May I see your son?' he asked. 'Certainly, doctor, but I see that you do not believe.' We proceeded up stairs, and my son was playing with his brother on the floor. The doctor felt his pulse and said, 'Yes, the fever is gone.' Finding also a fine healthy surface on his tongue, he added, 'Yes, he is quite well; I suppose it was the crisis of his disease.'"

"Another of the cases which he reports shows more fully the working of his own mind, on the instant of healing. It was the case of a poor man's child, who had heard him advocate the faith of healing, and now that the physician, after attending him for many months of illness, had given the little patient up, saying that he could do no more, the parents sent for him, in their extremity, to come and heal their son. He replied to the father: 'My dear friend, I cannot heal your son; I can do nothing to help him. All that I can do is, to ask you to kneel down, and pray with me to Christ, that we may know what is his will in this matter.' 'He immediately knelt down with me,' the written account continues, 'and my prayer was a reminding of the Lord Jesus Christ of his mercy to the sick, when he was on the earth, and that he never sent any sick away unhealed. I then presented the petition of the father and mother, that their son might be healed, and besought the Lord to show what his will was in the case. Whilst I was making the supplication, it was revealed to me, through the Holy Spirit, that I was to lay hands on the boy; and receiving at the time great faith to do so, I arose, and not wishing to be observed by the father, I laid my hand on the boy's head, and said in a low tone of voice—'I lay my hand on thee in the name of Jesus Christ.' In an instant, I saw color rush into his pale cheeks, and it seemed as if a glow of health was given, insomuch that I said involuntarily, 'I think your son will recover.' I then hastily left the room. In less than an hour, the mother came to my house, and insisted on seeing me, to tell me the wonderful things that had happened to her son. The result was, that the boy was about, the next day.' "

The other cases narrated by him are scarcely less remarkable. At the same time, he admits, with characteristic ingenuousness, that no such gift has been vouchsafed him now for a number of years, and that most of the expectations he had, in connection with the apostolic wonder thus restored, have been disappointed.

Insanity Cured. A recent event has kindly been communicated by Rev. S. J. Humphrey. A physician of his acquaintance, of devoted piety and great faith in prayer, needed seven thousand dollars, that he might add a new building to his medical establishment. Just then a banker brought his insane wife, whose case was considered incurable, and said to him, "Cure her, and I will loan you the money!" The doctor called in as witnesses some others who believed with him in the power of prayer, and had the proposition repeated in their presence. For some days earnest prayer was offered by them all, while the doctor used such remedial means as seemed to him wise. In less than a week, she returned to her husband in sound mind, and the promise was redeemed.

Another Instance. President Wm. M. Brooks of Tabor College, Iowa, communicates an instance of recovery from insanity, in answer to prayer, which is as follows; the names being suppressed: A young lady of his acquaintance, of a finished education, lost her reason in the winter of 1871–2, and in August, 1872, was placed in the institution for the insane, at Mt. Pleasant, Iowa. No encouragement was given of her recovery, and a year later, when her father visited her, in June, 1873, she appeared so badly, that he said it would be a relief to know that she was dead. Soon after, Mrs. H. the wife of a Baptist minister, who had long known and loved her, being shut up for days in a dark room, because of inflamed eyes, felt drawn out in special prayer in her behalf, and finally sent for the father and told him of her exercises and of the assurance gained that his daughter would be fully restored. In a few days, came news of a sudden change for the better, and in a little over two months she returned home well, and is now teaching, with all her powers in full vigor. The acting Superintendent of the Hospital, who is not a professed Christian, and who knew nothing of the prayers referred to, said that when the change occurred, there was not a case among the five hundred inmates of which he had less hope, and that it was the most remarkable case of recovery which he had known during the eight years of his connection with the Hospital.

A Young Lady Healed in Pennsylvania. The author has received, from the subject of the healing described, the following letter, which will be read with great interest by those who are studying the phenomena of prayer in its relation to physical cure. Its writer so expresses her own view as to give one a clear conception of the psychological conditions of her recovery:

Harrisburg, Pa., Sept. 9, 1875.

Rev. Wm. W. Patton: More than three years since, when fourteen years old, I received an injury, the result of which was miletus, or inflammation of the sheath surrounding the spinal cord; the suffering from which was heightened by a complication of diseases of a chronic nature. Although never well, I had repeated attacks, during which I was obliged to lie in a horizontal position for many months at a time. I had two very kind physicians; but the aid afforded me was only temporary, I never getting free, even for the shortest space of time, from pain in the region of the spine. The pain was severe; yet precious was my Savior's promise: "My grace is sufficient for thee."

Although having the witness of my acceptance with God, in the light of justification, I found there were remains of the carnal mind in the heart. Knowing there is efficacy in the blood of Jesus Christ, to cleanse from every stain, and thus seeing my duty, accordingly on Dec. 15, 1873, I asked the Lord for a pure heart, and was led to see the necessity of entire consecration to God. I found my consecration to God incomplete, in that I was not giving the body so as he would receive it. I found that to consecrate the body, I must give it to be healed in a way the Lord would reveal. * * * * *

After considering and reconsidering the subject for fully thirteen months, knowing that God declares, "With Christ, I freely give you all things;" "He beareth our sickness, and healeth our diseases;" "The prayer of faith shall save the sick;" "All things are possible to him that believeth," I saw it would honor God more, to exercise faith and live; as I had the assurance of an instantaneous healing, as I believed. On Tuesday, January 26, 1875, at 7½ P. M., I realized my Savior's words: "Daughter, thy faith hath made thee whole." Taking *now* as the accepted time, I said: "Lord, I believe; help thou my unbelief;" the utterance of the lips corresponding with the desire of the heart. "Ask what ye will in my name, and I will do it," was suggested. My reply was: "To be wholly the Lord's—in a word, to enjoy a pure heart, and to be well physically." I was enabled to rise, walk, and show the truly great thing, the Lord had done for me. I have not taken medicine since the day previous, or been abed [confined to the bed] since the moment of healing. * * * Wonderful art Thou, in all thy works, and that my soul knoweth right well! Unto him be glory and praise evermore.

Yours, with respect, MINNIE H. WALTERS.

BISHOP SIMPSON'S LIFE SAVED. Bishop Bowman, of the Methodist Episcopal Church, gives this account (which has been published in the papers) of the unexpected recovery of Bishop Simpson at a time when he was supposed to be dying:

"I remember once, when there was a Conference at Mt. Vernon, in this State (Ohio), at which I was present. Bishop Jones was presiding, one afternoon, and, after reading a dispatch stating that Bishop Simpson was dying in Pittsburg, asked that the Conference unite in prayer, that his life might be saved. We knelt down, and Mr. Taylor, the great street-preacher of California, led in one of his beautiful prayers. After the first few sentences, in which I joined with my whole heart, my mind seemed to be at ease, and I did not pay much attention to the rest of the prayer, only to notice its beauty. When we arose from our knees, I turned to a brother and said: 'Bishop Simpson will not die; I feel it.' I then told him how the feeling had come over me, and he assured me that he had experienced the same impressions. The word was passed around, and over thirty ministers, who were present, said they had the same feeling. I took my book, and made a note of the hour and circumstance. Several months afterwards, I met Bishop Simpson, and asked him what he did, to recover his health. He did not know; but the physician had said, it was a miracle. He said that, one afternoon, when at the point of death, the doctor left him, saying he should be left alone [by the doctor] for a half hour. At the end of that time, the doctor returned, and immediately noticed a great change in the patient. He was startled, and asked the family what they had done for the Bishop; and they replied: Nothing at all. That half hour, I found, by making allowance for difference of localities, was just the time when we were praying for him at Mt. Vernon. From that time on, he steadily improved, and has lived to bless the church and humanity. If the Lord could touch vitality in one direction, he could in another. Bishop Simpson's case, and ten thousand others are living examples of that to-day. God does answer prayer for physical good, I know he does. On the God, who has so often answered my prayers, I will still rely, scientific men and philosophers to the contrary notwithstanding."

A Deafness of Twenty Years Cured. Rev. Franklin Fisk, who has been forty years in the Methodist ministry, and now resides in Wilbraham, Mass., says, in a letter to his friend, Mrs. (Rev.) David Sherman, D. D., of Malden, Mass., the original of which lies before the author, bearing date August 30, 1875:

"I find in my diary, under date of April 17, 1837, that I called on 'Father Harding,' in the town of Wellfleet, Mass. He was a venerable octogenarian, had long been a member of the Methodist church, and was highly esteemed by all who knew him, as a man of great purity of character. He told me, that when past forty years of age, he was deaf; so that he could hear no human voice. He had been in this condition twenty years. One morning, while contemplating the miracles of Christ—his restoring sight to the blind, hearing to the deaf, etc.—that he is 'the same yesterday, to-day and forever,' and the promise that he will 'withhold no good thing from them that walk uprightly,' he was impressed with a strong conviction that, if he should ask for it, his hearing would be restored. He said he immediately began to pray, and continued with increasing earnestness and faith all the forenoon. Soon after noon, he began to realize a strange rumbling in his ears, which continued until evening; which so wearied and worried him, that he retired earlier than usual, and immediately went to sleep. In the night time he awoke, hearing the wind blow violently, as he thought. He awoke his wife, and asked her if she ever knew the wind to blow so hard before. She was surprised at his idea, and assured him there was no unusual gale. He again went to sleep, and did not awake till the sun had arisen, and was shining into his room. He said it seemed to have a charm and a glory in it, as did all other objects, such as he had never known before. He arose and dressed himself, and, going out at his front door, ascended a wooded hill directly opposite his house. He heard the birds sing, and leaves rustle as they were moved by the gentle breeze. He said he came down, and, entering the house, told his folks he could hear now as well as any of them. And he added: 'I have continued to hear to the present time, a period of more than forty years.'"

MISS LUCY R. DRAKE'S ACCOUNT. The reader has already learned of Miss Drake's faith and its reward, in reference to the supply of ordinary wants. In the narrative of Dr. Cullis, reference was made to a Miss D., who was healed of a tumor, in answer to prayer. This was Miss Drake, and she has now written out for this volume her experience of cure from consumption, in like manner, as follows:

"In 1866, I was in consumption, and the disease had made such progress, during the years I had been afflicted with it, that in the judgment of a skillful physician, I was not expected to live through the summer. Of a decidedly consumptive family, and having all the symptoms of the disease in an advanced stage, humanly speaking, I could not have a ray of hope. But for several years I had left my body with its disease in the hand of the Lord, and consequently was without any anxiety about it; having asked that, if he saw it would be for his glory to spare me, he would raise me to health; and if not, he would take me to 'behold his glory.' One evening in July, (the 5th,) while reading one of the promises given to an ancient patriarch, my soul was exceedingly stirred with its richness, and, as it met *the* longing desire of my heart—to win souls to Christ—I inquired of the Lord, and studied his revealed will, to know if it was his pleasure to give that promise to me. By faith in the promise to give wisdom (James i:5,) having asked, I was thoroughly persuaded that it was mine. It related to future usefulness, and in a few minutes it occurred to me that if it was fulfilled, I must be cured of my disease. I had been, and was then so weak, I could not sit up fifteen minutes at a time, without keen suffering. I said at once, 'Of course I must; but the Lord knew that when he gave me that promise; and consumption is as easy for him to cure, as to sway yonder branches with his winds.'

"From that moment not a doubt entered my mind about my recovery; for God had promised it, included in that spiritual promise. I do not remember about that evening; for it was quite late, but the next day great strength was given me, and I did work that would have affected me seriously, for months following, if I had performed it at any time within months previous. I gained constantly. My physicians and friends were astonished, and only found refuge in saying, 'She will be sick again soon.' But sickness did not return, and my lungs gradually healed, and, in a short time, I became engaged in preaching to the multitude the glad tidings of the gospel; and I have continued this work since that time. I mention this to show, that the voice required in this public work, could only be forthcoming *when the lungs were in a normal condition.*

"There have been several other times, when, having other diseases, recovery was considered doubtful, that after exercising faith in Christ for healing, I have been cured; several times *immediately*, and at others gradually. I mention this to show that it is our privilege not only to take Christ as our physician, once in a lifetime, but whenever we need him; as we may continually live by faith in him, to be kept from the power of sin."

The last paragraph surely cannot mean that no Christian need die, but may always be healed of every sickness; but only that oftentimes God is pleased to cure more than once.

Testimony of Mrs. C. S. Whitney. This lady, who resides in Hartford, Ct., where she is extensively known by her Christian labors among the poor, kindly furnishes the author the following statement of her personal experience:

"Three years ago, I was healed of a bodily disease. I had been troubled from my birth with canker, and at times suffered greatly. I had consulted some of the best physicians in the land, and had been treated by the most skillful. My case was said to be incurable. When I learned to trust Christ for everything, I applied to him for healing. My husband joined with me, in this prayer, for three weeks; but all the time I was growing worse. I then prayed for entire submission. About the first of October, 1872, my stomach, throat and mouth were so cankered, I could scarcely eat anything. One day, I took up the little book, entitled 'Dorothea Trudell'; and while reading, I seemed to hear a voice saying unto me, 'All things are possible unto him that believeth.' 'According to thy faith be it unto thee.' I claimed the faith, and immediately asked God to heal me, and in his own way. While yet on my knees, it seemed very clear to me, that I should go to Boston, and ask Dr. Cullis to pray with me. I obeyed that leading, and made preparation to go, the day following. Just as I was ready to start for the depot, I realized that I was cured. An entire change was wrought in my system, and my soul was filled with joy and gratitude. Soon I began to wonder why I had been thus strangely led, and the dear Lord made it all plain by directing my attention to the story of Abraham, teaching me the beautiful lesson of obedience, and again assured me by the voice of his Spirit, saying, 'Thy faith hath saved thee.'"

TWO CASES OF CHILDREN. It may be well to cite two cases in which the patients were, by age and physical condition, unable to take any part in the process of recovery, in the way of an exercise of imagination or faith, which often has great nervous influence. Rev. T. W. Greene, a Baptist minister at Denver, Col., furnishes the following from his own experience:

"While I was pastor of the Baptist church at L——, in Central Illinois, in the year 1868, I learned, one day, that a family belonging to my congregation, and living some two miles in the country, was in deep distress, because of the momentarily expected death of their little child. Making no delay, I hastened to the house. It was very hot weather, and the child was suffering from a low fever. The opposite doors of the room were standing open, to furnish a current of air;

but the little patient had sunk to a condition in which he did not seem to breathe at all. The doctor had given the child up to die, and gone away. The father had left the room, being unwilling to witness the death. The mother and nurse were the only attendants at the bedside; though I believe a neighbor was sitting in the opposite corner of the room. The child showed no signs of life, that an ordinary observer could detect. It had no perceptible pulse, and made no cry or movement of any kind. Its eyes were fixed. But I at once felt, that I could pray in faith for its recovery. I knelt down by the bedside, prayed with much composure, and went back, feeling that my prayer would be answered. I was not surprised to hear, in a day or two, that the child was rapidly recovering; and soon after that it was running about the house.

"In the same place and year, I visited another family, under very similar circumstances. The child, in this instance, had been sick for some time with a violent form of dysentery, if I remember correctly. The doctor in attendance was an avowed infidel — a disbeliever in the inspiration of the Scriptures, in the sinlessness of Christ, in the influence of the Holy Spirit on the heart, and, indeed, in his existence altogether. All the while I was in the room, he sat on the side of the bed, holding the child's wrist. In reply to my inquiry, How is the child? he gave me to understand that he had no hope of its recovery. The parents and friends had also evidently given up hope. They were waiting, in tears and silence, to see it die. I asked the

Lord, in my prayer, to spare the child, not forgetting to mention the condition — always to be remembered, in praying for temporal blessings — if it was in accordance with his will. The Holy Spirit, we know, he is always ready to bestow on those that ask him — more willing than earthly parents are to give good gifts unto their children. The prayer was answered by the speedy restoration of the child to comparative health: though it took a relapse after a month or so, and died. The doctor said to a number, though not to me, that he could never again deny the reality of prayer, for that, during my prayer, he felt the pulse quicken and grow stronger, all the time. He mentioned it himself, as a case altogether remarkable in his estimation. A third case, so similar that it would hold no interest, occurred while I was pastor, some time before, at W——, in Illinois."

A Freedman Cured of Consumption. Miss Rachel C. Mather, who has charge of a Colored Orphan Asylum, at Beaufort, S. C., sends to the author, under date of Oct. 20, 1875, an account which, somewhat condensed, is as follows: "I's come, missus, to say good bye, afore you go Norf; 'spec I'll neber see you agin, in dis yere world; de doctor's given me up; he can do no more," said Noble Mitchell, a freedman, to me, on my piazza, one June morning, panting for breath and having every appearance of a man in the last stages of consumption. "I's jes' waiting for de Lord to call me home; I's ready to go; I wants de Lord's will to be done." "So do I," I replied; "but I believe it is his will that you should live and labor. Your wife and six little children need you; all your neighbors need you, to repair their rickety cabins, in cold weather; I need you to build another school house." "It will be a miracle, missus; my cough tears me, day and night; my appetite has lef' me; de night-sweats worry me a heap; when I tries to walk, I staggers." "Faith is a miracle-worker. Did not Jesus say, 'Thy faith hath saved thee'? 'All things are possible to him that believeth.' I then read him the account of Hezekiah's recovery, how Jesus healed the sick, and a few pages from Dorothea Trudell, to which he eagerly listened. After prayer, he left, saying: "I's got new light. I's got new joy in my heart. I's better already. I'll pray de Lord to cure me, an' I hopes he will.'"

One month later, while in Boston, Miss Hildare, who took charge in my absence, wrote: "Noble Mitchell is well, and passes by here every day, to work in Beaufort—it is wonderful." And so it was; for he had not worked at his trade for five months, and his friends had for sometime looked to see him sink into his grave. He has been at work ever since, and the last six months for me, putting up a new school house. He is a faithful man, a useful neighbor, and an exemplary christian.

A Girl Cured. Miss Mather sends an account of a girl, Laura, thirteen years old, who came to her with a hard cough and a pain in her side and steadily grew worse. Her appetite failed, night-sweats came on, and she was confined to the bed most of the day. At last the end seemed near, and Miss M. says: "I lingered by her bed till near midnight, in prayer for her recovery. I could not give her up. Again, in my own room, I poured out my soul in prayer for the child, and then slept. About two o'clock I suddenly awoke, and seemed to hear a voice saying: 'Go to Laura; I can heal her now; the conditions are right; you are both calm and truthful.' 'Well, Laura,' I went and said, 'Jesus has told me to tell you that he will cure you now. Do you believe he will?' 'Yes, missus, me do believe. O, Jesus, do, please make me well; let me live a long time and be a good and useful woman.' The burden rolled off my heart. From that night, Laura rapidly recovered; in less than a month she was strong and well. During four years since, she has been a good, useful girl."

A Case in New York City. Rev. Edwin F. Hatfield, D. D., who is widely known throughout the Presbyterian Church, has kindly obtained and forwarded, at the request of the author, the following letter from Mrs. K., the mother of the young girl referred to below, who resides in Brooklyn, N. Y.:

"*Dear Sir:* I have a daughter who was for fourteen months, afflicted with hip disease. It was brought on by a fall and a consequent dislocation, when she was eight years of age. Her right side was paralyzed, and she had an abscess. I placed her in a hospital, under the care of good nurses and the very best medical advice. Everything possible was done for her, but all to no avail; she grew worse instead of better, and the doctors directed me, as there was no hope for her, to take her home to die.

"But I did not cease to hope. I did as the doctors directed, but continued to pray the prayer of faith for her recovery, for two weeks. One morning, at the end of this period, we were conversing together about the wonderful cures wrought by the Savior, when on earth, and particularly that of the man at the pool of Bethesda. In the midst of our conversation, my daughter rose to obtain a drink of water, when she exclaimed, 'Mother, I can walk!' 'Thanks be to God!' said I; 'come, and let me see you.' Her crutches, the only means by which she could move about, before, were now useless. Upon examination, I found that the abscess had entirely disappeared, and that the paralyzed limb was restored whole, like the other. She was again dangerously ill, five months afterwards. I prayed for her recovery, one night, before retiring, and the next morning she arose, perfectly cured. She is now twenty-one years of age, and during all this intervening time, has been free from any trouble of this kind. To-day she is as well as any one, walking and running about without the slightest trouble."

CURE OF BRIGHT'S DISEASE AND PARALYSIS. The author has received a letter from Mr. James H. Blackman, of Sharon, Mass., (P. O. address at Canton, Mass.,) which is of extraordinary interest. Some of the facts have been given before, but never so fully as now.

Slightly abridged, it is as follows; under date of Oct. 23, 1875:

"In the spring of 1870, my wife was taken sick with the kidney complaint. She continued to grow worse during the summer. I took a bottle of urine to Dr. Erasmus D. Miller, a celebrated physician of Boston, to be tested. He sent me a note saying: 'Her disease is Bright's disease of the kidneys, in a far advanced stage, and incurable.' The water was afterwards tested by several physicians, who coincided with Dr. Miller. An increase of albumen was apparent at every test, and the last, (a 2-oz. bottle,) tested by Dr. A. A. Holmes, of Canton, contained nothing but albumen. The water gradually decreased in quantity, and finally stopped altogether, and for two years nothing passed. It is well known that physicians do not profess to cure this disease. During my wife's illness, her left limb became completely paralyzed, and withered away to the size of a man's wrist, in the largest place, and without any feeling, even to pins and boiling water. She tipped a milk pan of boiling water upon her feet, but did not know that this limb was scalded, till she began to dress the well foot. For three years and two months she did not walk; for two years she crept upon her knees, drawing the lame leg after her; and for the last year she moved herself around in a wheeled invalid chair. During these three years, she was taken out of her bed in the morning, and put into it again at night. For the two years and four months, no physician had been in the house, and she had taken no medicine, and resorted to no bathing or rubbing. She ate but once a day and immediately vomited.

"During her sickness God gave me a new heart, and I prayed for her conversion, which occurred in January, 1874, and then for that of our daughter, which took place in February. Previously I was a Unitarian, unacquainted with evangelical doctrines. Not knowing that the Christian world had decided that the day of miracles was past, in my ignorance and simplicity I went to praying, with faith in Christ's promise, that my wife might be healed; my wife and daughter joining, after their conversion. God gave me the assurance that our prayers were accepted, and I became bold to say to others that she would soon walk. I made this declaration to Rev. James Jennison, Congregational minister at Canton, and he replied, 'Why, you can't expect God to do a miracle!' My assurance grew stronger and stronger, and filled me with joy and gratitude. Just then, the water came back in large quantity, and, on being tested by Dr. Holmes, proved free from albumen. On the morning of February 25th, 1874, I prayed earnestly in secret, and then placed my wife on her knees, at the family altar, and again prayed earnestly that she might walk. At the close of the prayer, she was unconscious and apparently dead. She remained thus about three minutes, when she raised her head and exclaimed: 'I can walk! I know I can walk! Praise God, I can walk!' She got up off her knees, and walked twice around the room, exclaiming, 'Praise God, I can walk! Why don't you praise God that I can walk?' We then commenced shouting, Glory to God! Oh the rapture of that moment! We bowed before God and thanked him for the great miracle he had performed.

"I opened the door, and she walked out upon the piazza, and about an hour afterwards she walked out and shook hands with a neighbor, who was so surprised, that he lost all power of speech. The paralyzed limb became immediately enlarged, and in a few days was plump and round, and stronger than the other. The appetite came back, the vomiting ceased, and Bright's disease, with all its attendant pains, passed away. She is in better health than ever before, and like the impotent man at the Beautiful Gate, goes about leaping and praising God, often walking eight and ten miles in a day, without limping or fatigue. * * * We got our faith by prayer and reading the promises. How could we, after having been born again, refuse to accept those promises as true? Our hearts had been given to him, and we prayed for her recovery, that each might be enabled to go out into the world, and make known the wonderful things God had done for us in giving us clean hearts; and by the grace of God, so will we ever do."

Remarks Upon the Various Cases Cited. The instances which have filled these two chapters will not make the same impression upon every mind; nor are they all of the same convincing power. It may be well to notice several of the characteristics, and to consider their bearing.

1. A large proportion of the cures are gradual. In this they differ from the miraculous healings by the Savior and the apostles; which were instantaneous and complete, and needed to be such, to make the desired impression, and to serve their peculiar purpose at the introduction of the gospel, as indubitable signs of divine power. But it is not at all necessary to consider answer to prayer as miraculous; and the moral end sought in the discipline of prayer is sufficiently gained, if the petition, or its equivalent, is finally granted in any of the various methods; God using natural laws, and therefore working out the results, oftentimes gradually.

2. In some cases medicines were employed, and in others they were not. Why should their use be considered as indicating any lack of faith? Why should God be expected to exempt those who pray, from the necessity of using means, in this relation more than others? We must labor as well as pray, in order to succeed in business, or to be useful spiritually. Why not apply the same rule in reference to the removal of disease? Hezekiah prayed for recovery, and it was granted; but the prophet put a poultice of figs on the boil or carbuncle. It was just as well for God to bless that as a means, as to answer the prayer in any other way. Timothy was troubled with dyspepsia, and Paul directed him to confine himself no longer to water, but to "use a little wine for his stomach's sake and his

often infirmities." Why did not Paul direct him, instead, simply to pray in faith? Because he might as well, in this as in other things, use wise means and then pray with faith for a blessing. It is not even certain, but that James ordered the anointing with oil, for medicinal as well as for symbolical purposes; for olive oil was extensively used at that day in the healing art, both internally and externally. At all events, it is not easy to see on what authority the use of medicine or of other helpful appliances is to be ruled out as inconsistent with faith. It will hardly be doubted, that Mr. Müller, of the Bristol orphan houses, is a man of faith, and is ready to carry out his faith to the farthest Scriptural warrant, fearless of the ridicule or contempt of the unbelieving. Yet, recently, his institution was visited with typhoid fever, and five hundred cases occurred. He prayed earnestly, but he also used all known appropriate means. He had every appliance for ventilation and disinfection recommended by the medical authorities; he isolated the sick; and he had the physician visit them twice every day. And by God's blessing only five or six deaths occurred. There was no weakness of faith in this, but only a fulfilling of the words of James: "Seest thou how faith wrought with his works, and by works was faith made perfect? * * * For as the body without the spirit is dead, so faith without works is dead also."

3. Many of the sudden or instantaneous cures are to a certain extent naturally explicable. They are dis-

orders of the nerves, cases of rheumatism, paralysis, weakness, etc. It often happens, in such disorders, that persons fancy their inability to be greater than it is; that they firmly believe in the impossibility of their doing certain things, when the impotence is largely in their wills. Furthermore, whether the impotence be imaginary or real, it is often true, that anything which sufficiently excites the mind, to induce determined action, restores nervous energy; sometimes temporarily, sometimes permanently. Thus the *Independent* mentions a girl, who supposed herself to be helpless, but was told by a physician, that he would horsewhip her, unless she rose from her bed; which she immediately did! It is said that, at the time of the great Chicago fire, a lady who had been bed-ridden for years, escaped for her life, and was permanently cured. A friend tells the author, of a lady thus bed-ridden, whose friends conspired with a noted tramp, to startle her into action. The tramp came into her room, and took off his coat, announcing his intention of undressing and getting into the bed. In her terror, she arose and rushed out, and was permanently cured! Now it may be argued, that such is the tonic influence, on the nervous system, of any excitement—whether it be that of fear, joy, surprise, expectation or imagination of supernatural power—that nervous maladies may be suddenly relieved, or even entirely removed; and that this is the explanation of the Romish and Protestant faith and prayer-cures. Though some of the instances are of disorders of quite a different nature — such as cancer, tumor, Bright's disease, consumption, canker, deafness, etc.— yet it may be admitted, that even these might be favorably affected, by a powerful determination of will and a settled expectation of cure. But when this is conceded, nothing is subtracted from an intelligent theory of prayer; which includes the divine use of natural causes, physical or mental, that conduce to the desired end. It still remains true, that only prayer has sufficed to bring to bear the favorable influences of mind upon body, and that the physicians having utterly failed, in many cases, after years of effort, a quiet confiding in God has at once developed the power of the human and divine spirit over matter. Who shall say that prayer is then useless, either as an act of submission and consecration, or of faith and petition?

4. It will be observed that a close connection is traceable between the physical and spiritual experiences of those healed. This is marked in the whole course of things under Dorothea Trudell, as also in many of the single cases of which the particulars have just been given. The removal of disease was the culmination of a spiritual process, in which the soul sought forgiveness and purity, and emerged from darkness into light. This suggests the connection of sin with disease and death, to which the Bible often alludes, and also the probable relation of holiness and health. For aught we know, the faith of a saint, by which he opens his soul to an influx of divine grace, may stand related to a quickening of the mysterious

life-principle, which is the gift of God. Whatever act or exercise brings God into the soul, must strengthen life, *in every sense*. Prayer may then be precisely the means which stand related appropriately to the removal of disease, presenting the soul, in all respects, in the position favorable, morally and physically, for securing divine intervention. And yet there may be nothing traceable by the eye, in the mode of the answer, which contravenes natural law.

5. The seeming law of a specific faith, in the matter of healing, is worthy of notice. What is claimed by those who have had most experience in that line is, that, while a conditional prayer of faith is proper and necessary, in all our supplications, the Holy Spirit commonly begets within the soul peculiarly intense longing and assured expectation, when it is the will of God to grant a specific answer to prayer. Thus, Miss Mary H. Mossman, who prayed so efficaciously for the cure of the lameness of Rev. S. H. Platt, when asked by him, "Have you ever been sent in this way before," said "Yes;" and when asked, "Have you ever been mistaken and failed, upon such an occasion?" replied, "No, never, when I have been impelled to go as I have been to come here. I have had people come to me, and urge me to pray for their recovery, and it has done them little or no good." In a subsequent interview, she "utterly repudiated the notion that there is resident in her a gift of healing in any other sense than this; and she believes that it is a privilege which all God's people, who live in close communion with him,

may enjoy. Hence the afflicted, instead of running to this or that one, who is supposed to have peculiar power in this direction, should gather a few praying friends, and lay their case before God in earnest prayer: when, if agreeable to his will, they will be healed by the prayer of faith; or, if more be needed, the Holy Spirit will impel some devout one present to supply the lack, either by anointing with oil, or laying on of hands." This view at least recognizes the common sense truth, that prayer is not intended to cure every case of disease among believers, and to release the church from the sentence of mortality. A special faith is inspired for special cases, in which God sees fit to put marked honor on prayer, for the encouragement of his people, or the confounding of the enemy. On any other supposition, how are we to account for the lingering illness and final death, at the age of only fifty years, of Dorothea Trudell, herself—the eminent exemplifier of faith in the prayer-cure? Had she no faith for herself? Had her co-laborers in the institution no faith in praying for her? Undoubtedly they had faith in the general and warranted degree; but God wrought in them no such specific faith as to her recovery, as served to indicate that to be his will.

Rev. C. B. Boynton, D. D., of Cincinnati, Ohio, in a letter to the author, makes the following thoughtful suggestion:

"There have been instances, in my own church, of persons being raised from sick beds, in answer to prayer, as I and others *believe*. So also in my personal experience, I *believe* that God has answered prayer; but the circumstances, sometimes minute and not to be explained to others, cannot be so set forth as to produce in others the conviction which I feel myself. The New Testament seems to me to teach, that to spiritual humanity, the true church, belongs the exercise of spirit, or *supernatural*, power, through faith in Christ, who is the source of that power. I think he endowed the church with this power, to be conferred on her, on the prescribed conditions. It has been lost, in great measure, by unbelief and 'non-user.' May we not hope for its re-appearance, as the church becomes more spiritual, and understands better her royal prerogatives? Doubtless there are more cases, even now, of answers to prayer, when more than natural power was exerted, than the world or even the church is aware of. May your researches bring them to light!"

MEDICAL EXPLANATIONS BY H. M. LYMAN, M. D. Since the foregoing was written, and just as it was passing to the printer, the author's eye fell upon the lucid and interesting essay of Dr. H. M. Lyman, in *The Advance*, of October 14, 1875, entitled "The Faith-Cure." He comments, from a medical point of view, on four of the cases here given, and attributes them to purely natural causes. It does not furnish occasion, however, for additional remark, as the most of its suggestions and cautions were anticipated and briefly stated in the foregoing pages. It may be well to observe, nevertheless, that the instances referred to in these chapters cover a much larger field of disease than is allowed in the explanation of Dr. Lyman; that many of the cures indicate no excitement whatever, in the person healed; and that, in some cases, the faith and excited imagination were not at all in the patient, but in those who prayed for him. There is plainly a larger range for spirit-influence over a diseased material organization than physicians are wont to recognize; and the fact opens the way for prayer to invoke that divine aid which can touch the secret springs of life.

Lord, a whole long day of pain
  Now at last is o'er!
Ah, how much we can sustain,
  I have felt once more;
Felt how frail are all our powers,
  And how weak our trust;
If thou help not, these dark hours
  Crush us to the dust.

Draw my weary heart away
  From this gloom and strife;
And these fever-pains allay
  With the dew of life:
Thou canst calm the troubled mind,
  Thou its dread canst still;
Teach me to be all-resigned
  To my Father's will.

Then, if I must wake and weep,
  All the long night through,
Thou the watch with me will keep,
  Friend and Guardian true:
In the darkness thou wilt speak
  Lovingly with me,
Though my heart may vainly seek
  Words to breathe to thee.

—*Heinrich Puchta.*

CHAPTER XIV.

PRAYER FOR SANCTIFYING GRACE.

It is noticeable in the narratives of Scripture, especially in connection with the ministry of the Savior and his apostles, that there was usually a marked connection of outward and inward bestowments. If Christ healed the sick, it was to draw attention to the moral diseases of men, and to himself as the Great Physician. If he fed the hungry multitude with miraculously increased loaves and fishes, it was to tell them afterward of their spiritual need, and of himself as the Bread of Life. If he opened the eyes of one born blind, it was that he might also clear the inner vision, and pour light on a dark soul. And the recipients of his benefactions seem to have exercised faith in him for salvation from sin as well as from bodily maladies. Their completed prayers had a double object, and in the end secured a double answer. And so Jesus taught his disciples that the highest exercise of prayer was in obtaining God's divinest bestowment, the gift of the Holy Spirit. It was to this power that he made the parental analogy apply: "If ye, then, being evil, know how to give good gifts unto your children, how much more shall your Heavenly Father give the Holy Spirit to them that ask him." Luke xi:13. Prayer for the in-dwelling of the Spirit, with all the fullness of his sanctifying grace, ought then to be the most natural and continual of the petitions of the Christian.

There is reason to fear that too many of our prayers in this connection are verbal only; that is, we have not faith to expect actual results from them. Yet here the greatest certainty is to be expected; because we can be certain of our real wants and of the divine will. Both are plainly stated in Scripture. One difficulty is, that *ministers so widely preach a philosophy instead of a gospel*—a self-healing, through natural laws, instead of a divine healing by supernatural grace. They do this, in a measure, unconsciously, in harmony with the spirit of the age. As Dr. H. Bushnell remarks, in his "Nature and The Supernatural": "Calling the God we prove, a personal being, and meaning it in good faith, we yet find ourselves living before causes and looking for consequences. We only half-believe in prayer. We expect to be delivered of sin, by a long course of duty and self-reformation, that will finally pacify the offended laws of nature, and bring them on our side again. That God will do anything for us, himself, or hold any terms of real society with us, we but faintly believe."

It is therefore important to revive the faith of the church in the *direct* efficacy of prayer in the matter of spiritual healing. Indirectly it operates, in the ordinary course of mental law, to elevate, awe, refine and purify the soul, by the impression it gives of God and duty; much as reading a good book, or conversing with a good man would do. But, rightly used as a petition to God, it will accomplish vastly more: for it will also bring the power of the Holy Ghost into the soul as a supernatural grace.

This was the testimony of Paul in the matter of the "thorn in the flesh": "For this thing I besought the Lord thrice, that it might depart from me. And he said unto me, My grace is sufficient for thee; for my strength is made perfect in thy weakness. Most gladly, therefore, will I rather glory in my infirmities, *that the power of Christ may rest upon me.*" 2 Cor. xii: 8, 9. The fact seems to have been, that Paul was subject to attacks of a disease, which came upon him suddenly, which subjected him to much mortification, and which seemed to him to interfere greatly with his usefulness. He refers to the same thing, apparently, in Galatians iv: 13, 14: "Ye know how through infirmity of the flesh I preached the gospel unto you at the first. And my temptation (or trial) which was in my flesh, ye despised not, nor rejected, but received me as an angel of God, even as Christ Jesus." Also in 1 Cor. ii: 3: "And I was with you in weakness, and in fear, and in much trembling." The apostle naturally made this a matter of prayer, that the disease might be healed. He did this, at three separate times; probably at three separate places, where he had gone to preach the gospel, and had experienced these mortifying attacks. His prayer was answered; but not in the manner anticipated. God told him that, on the whole, grace to bear the trial would be better than to have the trial removed; and that this would not only benefit him the more, but would be the more helpful to the progress of the gospel. And Paul cheerfully accepted this solution of the difficulty; this response to his prayer for aid. "The power of Christ" thenceforth was made to "rest upon" him, so that he could easily and joyfully endure the trial, and could say, "I take pleasure in infirmities, in reproaches, in necessities, in persecutions, in distresses, for Christ's sake; for when I am weak (naturally), then am I strong (spiritually)." We are then to expect precisely the kind and degree of grace which our peculiar circumstances may require, and special prayer for such grace will be specifically answered.

An English Lady's Experience. An estimable Christian lady, who resides in London, and with whom the author has had a personal acquaintance for more than thirty years, thus writes to him, under date of Sept. 1st, 1875, concerning her combined bodily and spiritual experience. Her account makes an instructive transition from the topic of the three previous chapters to that of the present chapter. She was afflicted with a disease which commonly terminates fatally, though some cases are saved by a critical surgical operation, which often results disastrously. She writes:

"That you may the better realize my blessing, I must tell you, the honest truth, that I am a decided coward as to any inflicted pain, and when circumstances raised the question, in my mind occasionally—'could I ever consent to any operation?'—I never could answer, 'Yes.' No such thing seemed likely, and I put the thoughts away. But when disease was discovered, sure to be fatal, unless there should be escape by means of an operation, from the effects of which many sink, I was just enabled quietly to weigh the *pros* and *cons*, and *decide* that it should be done. For it was too critical a case for the doctors to prescribe such means; they simply suggest, and let the patient decide. Never before, I think, was I enabled to put the whole thing so completely into the hands of our loving Lord. I only remember two definite requests in my prayers about it: first, that I might not undergo the operation, unless it was to be successful; and secondly, that I might not dishonor him by fear. And emphatically were both petitions answered. During all the intervening months, *I had no fear whatever.* I talked of it as coolly as of any ordinary occurrence, with the full consciousness that there was something close by very dark, at which if I looked, for five minutes, I should be in perfect terror (I use the term advisedly); but if ever tempted so to do, there seemed a gentle whisper, that I was not to look at that, but at my loving Savior. My sleep was good. Some friends took leave of me, as they thought, for the last time; but I was kept calm and peaceful, up to the last moment; more even to my own astonishment, I think, than to that of my friends, because I alone knew my own cowardice. To show you that it was no natural calmness, I must add, that the supposed necessity for leaving my own home for medical treatment cost me some days of severe struggle, before my will could be brought to it. The will was subdued, and then I was graciously allowed to remain at home."

Here was a gift of grace, to overcome a natural infirmity—a special fear of suffering and danger. Prayer can equally bring divine aid to lift one above any other weakness, such as frailties of temper. Let the following instance illustrate the idea:

A Victory over Irritability. A certain lady, of whom the author heard, was in bondage to an impatient and irritable temper. Its sudden outbursts caused her much mortification and grief, for she felt that they were unworthy of a disciple of Christ. And yet she seemed powerless, when the disturbing occasions arose. She made solemn resolutions to restrain herself, and offered general prayers for divine aid, confessing her sin with humility and contrition. But the element of faith was lacking—the specific and assured faith warranted by the promises of the Bible. So she struggled, and resolved, and was continually defeated, so that she despaired of victory. But at a meeting of ladies for prayer, she was urged to make a more complete consecration of herself to God, and in connection with that to put a specific faith into her prayer, that she would be accepted and kept. She did so, and on her way to her house inwardly prayed for victory, as she knew that her temptations were most common and severe amid domestic scenes, and that she had declared these to be irresistible. But now she trusted her Savior, and believed, with Paul, that "the power of Christ" would "rest upon" her. Reaching home, and opening the front door, she saw a domestic violating one of her most explicit rules, by carrying a slop-pail down the front stairs. This was hard for her to endure with patience, when the act was so suddenly revealed; but to make the matter worse, and as trying as it well could be, the domestic was so terrified at the unexpected sight of her mistress, that she dropped the pail from her hand, and the contents flowed down the stairs and over the carpet to the hall below! The lady uttered not a word, but whispering to herself, over and over, "Jesus, help me! Jesus, help me!" gained the victory. With unruffled temper she went in and met the emergency. Learning thus the value of believing and ejaculatory prayer, she found thereafter no difficulty in curbing what she had supposed to be her uncontrollable irritability.

It will be remembered that, in Dorothea Trudel's prayer-institution the spiritual healing was made the prime thing, and the physical cure was the adjunct, and in a measure the consequence. Her biographer says: "She used to enter into conversation with the patient as to the state of his mind, and to seek out those inward enemies, which, like the Jebusites, wished to share the land with the Lord. She did not wish to bring Christians under the law again, but she was anxious to see God's freed children like coins, bearing on the one side the image of Jesus in his love, gentleness, patience, forbearance and humanity, and on the other side, the inscription, 'Let every one that nameth the name of Christ depart from iniquity.'"

This leads to the remark, that prayer holds the key to that precious experience which of late years has been often denominated the Higher Christian Life. The author has uttered his views of this experience, in his little book, entitled, "Spiritual Victory," (published by the Congregational Publishing Society,) to which he would refer the reader for many things which cannot be said here. The present object is, to draw attention to the relation which the "Higher Life" sustains to prayer, as illustrated by various personal experiences. No controversy need here be raised over the precise nature of that higher life, nor as to the most appropriate name by which to distinguish it. Suffice it to say, that it is a condition of entire consecration, of soul-liberty, of filial confidence, of assured hope, of conscious acceptance with God, of intimate union with him in all that respects one's purposes and expectations in life, and of victory over temptation and besetting sin. It is thus a great advance beyond that doubting, vacillating, fearful, conscience-stricken experience, which is so common, and in which there is much condemnation and little peace, occasional reviving and long declension, earnest revolving and small performance. It is a state of abiding light and love, in which the soul has entered into rest, and does God's will with a sense of freedom and blessedness.

It usually is not apprehended, until one has had

considerable experience, after conversion, in trying to maintain a spiritual life by dint of resolutions and will-work and legal struggles, and has been brought to a self-despair; when, under proper religious instruction, or through study of the divine word and illumination of the Spirit, the soul learns with surprise the simplicity and power of faith. Then prayer takes on new meaning, and has a continual prevalence, as Jesus said: "If ye abide in me, and my words abide in you, ye shall ask what ye will, and it shall be done unto you." John xv: 7. There are those who quietly glide into this victorious life; but more often a struggle precedes, a new submission of the will takes place, earnest prayer is made for the fulfillment of Scriptural promises, and a kind of second conversion occurs, which brings one upon a higher grade of holy living, characterized by habitual consecration, faith and prayer.

A Student's Victory. The following narrative was published some years since, in the *Oberlin Evangelist.* It was written by a student in an Eastern college, and gives the result, in his case, of prayer and faith brought to bear upon personal religious experience. Many similar narratives were given, from time to time, in that paper:

"When I felt the peace resulting from closing in with the gospel-terms of salvation, I could not mistake it. I knew I was a Christian, and I never was without evidence of the fact. But soon the tempter came in power, and tried to turn me back, but prayer disarmed him, and drove him back from his prey.

* * * For the first few months, it seemed as if I could attend to nothing, but examine my own heart, and read and pray. And the more I examined, the more I could discover the snares of the tempter, and the more it seemed impossible that I should overcome; but the Savior was ever nigh, and one look from him was enough. My greatest difficulty I found in my own heart. I was continually prone to indulge sinful thoughts, and I felt I ought not to have any. In short, without distinctly knowing what I was seeking, I was striving for freedom from sin, for a pure heart. * * * With strong crying and tears, I prayed and pleaded with God. My prayer was, that I might be made as much like Christ as it was possible for mortal man to be. Thus I continued for weeks. Gradually the burden left me. In the spring, after a season of great conflict with the tempter, and various humiliating circumstances, I enjoyed uninterrupted peace, for about two weeks. Then I was again left to buffet with the adversary for a few weeks, though at times I was filled with love. Afterwards I had another season of about four weeks complete peace. Then I had another struggle with the tempter; but by the grace of God I triumphed. All the time I seemed unworthy of the least notice from God, and the thought of my infinite unworthiness filled my eyes with tears. The first week in June, there was another protracted meeting. I felt happy, though most unworthy. Our prayers were continually ascending, and all seemed blessed. On the Sabbath, we celebrated the dying love of the

Savior. At the close, while singing, there was a sudden burst of light poured into my heart, and so excessive was the brightness that I could not sing, and I could hardly refrain from shouting aloud. For some weeks, I hardly dared move, for fear I should grieve the Spirit and lose my enjoyment. But gradually I acquired strength, my peace flowed like a river, and joy unspeakable and full of glory took possession of me. I have never lost it, from that time to the present, now more than fourteen months. I find no check to the full flow of joy, but weakness of body. My whole joy is in doing God's will."

MRS. WHITNEY'S "RICHER EXPERIENCE." Mrs. Whitney's narrative of the power of prayer to secure relief of temporal want, and the bestowment of physical healing, has been already given. She has printed, in a little tract, published at the "Willard Tract Depository," Boston, Mass., an account of its power in the higher sphere, entitling it, "My Richer Experience," from which the following is extracted:

"I sought in various ways, such as fasting, consecration, pleading, and good works. And I received many rich blessings, even baptisms of power, but nothing lasting. I had not then learned the beautiful lesson Christ taught, when he prayed the Father to sanctify his disciples "through the truth." At length I cried out from the depths of an anguished soul, 'Dear Lord, give me purity of heart, let it cost what it may. Make the cleansing complete.' God answered that prayer, and it cost me a great price, even the passing through the fiery furnace of affliction.

"First, I was called to relinquish many things desirable and lovely — called to leave my pleasant home in the West, to suffer the reverses of fortune, bid farewell to the dear church and friends, and all the pleasant associations, and to break the tender ties so dear to me, and seek a place among strangers, far from my childhood-home. I was particularly fond of society, and loved human sympathy, ah, so well! and my grief and sorrow were by so much the greater. But this was not all. While *en route* to my new home, I stopped to spend the Sabbath with a friend in Fulton, N. Y.

"On Monday, as I was about leaving, there came into my soul such a deep feeling of my need of special strength, that I went alone before God, and poured out my supplications to him.

"He heard that prayer, and gave me such a sense of his sustaining presence as satisfied me entirely. Oh, how timely! But for this I should have been crushed by the heart-rending scene that awaited me. Our eldest boy, of thirteen summers, asked and received permission to make a farewell visit to a favorite resort of his by the canal. With all the buoyancy of youth and beauty he left me; but scarcely had the sound of his light footsteps died away ere the word came, 'He is drowning!' I rushed to the spot. Oh, what a sight for a fond mother to see! Did it not require more than human strength, to witness such a scene —

my bright and beautiful boy struggling in death, and I without power to save! Ah, yes; and divine power did sustain me and enable me to say, 'Thy will be done.' The Lord in that moment brought home to my heart these beautiful words:

'Other refuge have I none,
Hangs my helpless soul on Thee;
Leave, oh leave me not alone,
Still support and comfort me.'

He did support and keep me calmly.

"The united efforts of kind and loving friends failed to save him. They bore his form above the waters,—that form which but a moment before was so bright and beautiful in life and health,—but it was now cold in death. The sight was too much for poor humanity. I sank unconscious of earthly surroundings. But Jesus, the dear, loving Jesus, lingered closely by me, whispering to my sorrowful heart, 'I will not leave you comfortless.' Oh, how precious were his words! how they strengthened me! Then and there he prepared me for coming scenes: to meet my companion from whom I had been separated six weeks; to perform the last sad offices for all that remained of our precious child; to take the last lingering look of the dear features, now so still and cold. Oh, what a moment of unutterable anguish, as we gazed for the last time upon our beautiful dead, our darling Willie—then to close the casket that contained that precious body, and commit it to the grave, there to leave him until the morning of the resurrection!

"How sad then to leave the place, and pursue my journey! Yet I was kept by divine love and power through weeks and months of extreme loneliness of heart, among strangers, bereft of all human sympathy.

"Last of all, I had to give up human sympathy, the very treasure I coveted most, and thought my nature demanded. But oh, how trifling it now appeared in comparison with the divine sympathy that the dear Lord was pleased to pour into my lacerated, bleeding heart!

"When my heart was emptied of all, and so purified to God, he entered the open door, and took the vacated throne within, and gave me perfect peace.

"The change seemed greater than my conversion, which had been clear and satisfactory. Even the Bible seemed like a now book, filled with so many precious promises; and as the 'Blessed Remembrancer' revealed the truths to me, verifying that promise, that he would 'take the things of Christ and show them unto us,' my spiritual vision became so clear that I could see light in his light, and build on that sure foundation, 'Christ being the chief corner-stone.' I realized that Christ had power to 'sanctify me wholly,' 'keep me from sin,' 'and preserve me blameless unto his coming.'"

A Physician's Experience. The reader has probably read in the papers of R. Pearsall Smith, an American Christian, of the denomination of "Friends," who has had much success in Germany and in England, in rousing the people of God to increased interest in divine things. He is the author of a little book, called "Holiness through Faith," in which he has embodied occasional narratives. One of these is that of a physician, of which the following is an extract:

"More earnestly than ever, and many times a day, I prayed for strength to overcome, but found no rest to my soul, until I stopped praying for grace to overcome, and *gave myself wholly to God, to be kept.* At this time the Lord revealed to me, in a wonderful manner, in all its majesty, the power of the prayer which he taught us to use: 'Our Father, which art in heaven, * * * lead us not into temptation, but *deliver us from evil;* for thine is the kingdom and the power and the glory, forever, Amen.' Oh, how my soul was filled, as I realized, for the first time, that it was his power that was to keep me—for 'Thine *is* the power'! The work was all done then—no more striving, no more praying for *strength* to overcome, but simply, day by day, 'Jesus, *keep* me; for thine is the *power* and the glory;' and there I rest and am *kept.*"

TESTIMONY OF A PRESBYTERIAN MINISTER. The same little work adduces the testimony of a Presbyterian minister, which may be thus condensed: "I had been preaching with much joy one evening, on the text, 'The blood of Jesus Christ, his Son, cleanseth us from all sin,' and seeking to teach through it, to the sinners present, their privilege of immediate and full remission of sins through the blood of Christ. On returning to my lodgings with a Christian brother, he spoke to me of his enjoyment of the address, and then went on to make some remarks on teaching half-truths from half-texts. He related how, that, for ten years, he had constantly preached from the words, 'Who his own self bare our sins in his own body on the tree,' without ever teaching the complement, in the last half of the verse: 'that we, being *dead unto sins*, should live unto righteousness.' He had taught abiding in Christ, without its result of sinning not. He had often said, 'Who gave himself for us,' without adding, 'that he might redeem us from all iniquity.' * * * At a conference meeting of Presbytery, it was one evening proposed, to consecrate ourselves more definitely and fully to God; and the act was accompanied by a wonderful baptism of the Spirit, which opened to my soul the hope of the near consummation of my soul-longings. * * * I was led to see, as never before, the privilege of an *entire* soul-rest in Christ; and that it was to be entered into by faith. * * * I proposed to a Christian manufacturer, that a few Christians should meet together, the next day, to enter into rest. I did not say to seek rest, but, so confident was my faith, '*to enter in.*' Ten earnest, godly men, mostly from his workshops, on the following day, knelt down in my friend's warehouse, among the boxes. We remained on our knees an hour and a quarter, in prayer, praise, and consecration. Of us too, it might be said: 'And when they had prayed, the place was shaken where they were assembled together, and they were all filled with the Holy Ghost.' I have been conscious, ever since, that it was then and there that, in a definite transaction with God, I entered into a complete soul-rest in Christ; a rest through the cleansing blood, which my soul has never lost for one hour since. It was attended by the satisfying certainty, that whatever spiritual blessings I thenceforth claimed, in simple faith, should be mine. * * * I can now see no limit to the possibilities of the life of Christ in my soul, since I have accepted the atonement in its full purposes, both of pardon and holiness."

Paul wrote to the Galatians (v : 16): "Walk in the Spirit, and ye shall not fulfill the lusts of the flesh." The relations which prayer sustain to this breadth and depth of experience, he thus sets forth to the Ephesians (iii : 14–21): "For this cause I bow my knees unto the Father of our Lord Jesus Christ — of whom the whole family in heaven and earth is named — that he would grant you, according to the wishes of his glory, to be strengthened with might by his spirit in the inner man; that Christ may dwell in your hearts by faith, that ye being rooted and grounded in love, may be able to comprehend, with all saints, what is the breadth and length and depth and height; and to know the love of Christ, which passeth knowledge, that ye might be filled with all the fullness of God. Now unto him that is able to do exceeding abundantly above all that we ask or think, according to the power that worketh in us, unto him be glory in the church, by Christ Jesus throughout all ages, world without end. Amen."

It was intended to insert several additional narratives, to the same effect as the foregoing; but space fails, and there is the less need so to do, as within a few years, many books have been published devoted specifically to this point. The attention of Christians of all denominations has been directed increasingly to the sanctifying power of a simple faith in God, to preserve the soul amid life's temptations. This faith, through prayer, draws at sight upon the divine treasury, for the needed influence of the Holy Ghost, and the draft is ever honored. There is more readiness, however, to admit a general grace of God adequate to general wants, than to believe in a spiritual power sufficient to give immediate and permanent victory over certain special temptations connected with physical habit. To these, therefore, our attention will next be turned.

"O thou, my God, my being's health and source,
Better than life, brighter than noon to me;
Stretch out thy loving hand, with gentle force,
Bend this still-struggling will, and draw it after thee.

"Return to me, my oft-forgotten God,
My spirit's true though long-forsaken rest;
Undo these bars, re-enter thine abode,
In thee and in thy love alone would I be blest.

"Re-mould this inner man in every part;
Re-knit these broken ties; resume thy sway;
Take, as thy throne, and altar, this poor heart;
Oh teach me how to love; oh, help me to obey!"

—*Horatius Bonar.*

CHAPTER XV.

PRAYER TO OVERCOME PHYSICAL HABIT.

In addition to the illustrations given in the previous chapter, of prayer as an instrument of sanctification in general, it is well to collect a few of the proofs which attest its power in a special field, and that one of peculiar difficulty. Most forms of evil indulgence produce permanent habits, which are well nigh ineradicable; because they have a double hold on the spiritual and on the physical nature. The will loses ability to resist, the desires are permanently excited, and become imperious, and the debauched imagination pictures delight in indulgence. Then a diseased condition of the nerves, the stomach, and other sensitive parts sets in, creating an intense craving for evil excitement, and a keen suffering when this excitement is denied. Hence the apparently hopeless condition of a confirmed drunkard, tobacco-user, opium-consumer, glutton, or debauchee. Soul and body are slaves to sensual indulgence, and who shall break the chains and pronounce the decree of emancipation?

Precisely here philosophy usually fails, and the gospel wins a divine victory. Therefore those make a capital mistake, who preach a religious philosophy, and think it is a gospel, because they connect a text and the word Christian with it. This is done, when the appeal made is only that of truth to the conscience, to arouse a sense of obligation, and to set the man upon a will-work of resolutions. Those resolutions are sure to be broken, and the man relapses into his habit with increased despair of ever being delivered. He alternates for a time, between reformations and relapses, and then ceases to struggle longer. His weakness is in the lack of the faith-element. Duty has been preached; but not power, hope, liberty, through the grace of Christ. He is only taught to await the slow result of a gradually forming good habit of body and mind. But there are many facts which go to show a special power in the gospel to cope with these foes—facts which point to prayer as the means of providing an effectual divine aid. These facts are not as yet widely known, and are likely not to be credited, except as unimpeachable testimony is brought to their support. But if such deliverance is possible, the truth should be proclaimed far and near, for the victims of these habits are many, and their friends have lost hope for them.

The chief reason for the discouragement is the failure of so many past efforts at reform. But was the prayer of faith offered continuously during the effort? Unless the spiritual law be followed in its conditions, there must be failure. These words express the conditions—consecration, prayer, faith. The breaking up of a sinful habit is not to be undertaken as an isolated thing. It must be part of a universal and thorough renovation, in which body and soul are yielded up to God in joyous and unconditional consecration, to be wholly and forever his. Then with this must be earnest prayer, and a corresponding expectation, based on the explicit divine promises. God says: "My grace is sufficient for thee; for my strength is made perfect in weakness." "God is faithful, who will not suffer you to be tempted above that ye are able; but will with the temptation also make a way to escape, that ye may be able to bear it." "Neither fornicators, nor idolators, nor adulterers, nor effeminate, nor abusers of themselves with mankind, nor thieves, nor covetous, nor drunkards, nor revilers, nor extortioners shall inherit the kingdom of God. And *such were some of you*, but *ye are washed*, but *ye are sanctified*, but ye are justified *in the name of the Lord Jesus*, and *by the spirit of our God*." Here is all the support which faith needs. Now for the corresponding facts.

Augustine's Defeat and Victory. The principle involved is well illustrated by the case of Augustine, who had been a slave to sensual habits, and who long had sought to overcome them, prior to his conversion, by resolutions and other legal struggles, after the impotent fashion described by Paul in the seventh chapter of Romans. His own account is: "Thus soul-sick was I, and tormented, accusing myself much more severely than my wont, rolling and turning me in my chain, till that were wholly broken, whereby I now was but just held. Thou, O Lord, didst press upon me inwardly, with severe mercy, redoubling the lashes of fear and shame, lest I should again give way, and that same slight remaining tie should recover strength and bind me faster. For I said within myself, 'Be it done now! Be it done now!' And as I spake, I all but enacted it, I all but did it, and did it not; yet sunk not back to my former state, but kept my stand hard by, and took breath. And I essayed again, and wanted somewhat less of it, and somewhat less, and all but touched and laid hold of it; and yet came not at it, nor touched, nor laid hold of it; hesitating to die to death, and to live to life; and the worse, where to I was inured, prevailed more with me than the better, where to I was unused. And the very moment wherein I was to become other than I was, the nearer it approached me, the greater horror did it strike into me; yet did it not strike me back, nor turn me away, but held me in suspense. The very toys of toys, and vanities of vanities, my ancient mistresses, still held me: they plucked my fleshly garment, and whispered softly: 'Dost thou cast us off? and from that moment, shall we no more be with thee forever? and from that moment shall not this or that be lawful for thee, forever?' And what was it, which they suggested, O my God? Let thy mercy turn it away from the soul of thy servant. What defilements they did suggest! what shame! But now I much less than half-heard them, not openly showing themselves and contradicting me, but muttering as it were behind my back, and privily plucking me, as I was departing, but to look back on them. Yet they did retard me, so that I hesitated to burst and to shake myself free from them, and to spring over whither I was called—a violent habit saying to me, 'Thinkest thou, thou canst live without them?'"

Then came up, he tells us, better thoughts, and "the chaste dignity of Continency" who seemed to say to him: "Canst thou not do what these youths, what these maidens can? or do they do it of themselves, and not rather by the Lord their God! The Lord, their God, gave me unto them. Why standest thou in thyself, and so art falling! Cast thyself upon him; fear not; he will not withdraw himself that thou shouldest fall. Cast thyself fearlessly upon him; he will receive, and will heal thee." * * * "I cast myself down, I know not how, under a certain fig tree, giving full vent to my tears, and the floods of mine eyes gushed out, an acceptable sacrifice to thee. And, not indeed in these words, yet to this purpose, spake I much unto thee. 'And thou, O Lord, how long? how long, Lord; wilt thou be angry forever? Remember not our former iniquities.' For I felt that I was held by them. I sent up these sorrowful words: How long? how long? To-morrow and to-morrow? why, is there not an end, this hour, to my uncleanness?" It was when he came to this point of prayer and faith, and rested, as related in a previous chapter, on the words, "Put ye on the Lord Jesus Christ, and make no provision for the flesh to fulfill the lusts thereof," that he gained the victory over all his habits.

VICTORY OVER TOBACCO AND OPIUM HABITS. Rev. W. H. Boole, in his missionary work in the city of New York, has paid much attention to this subject, and has published some of the facts which have come to his knowledge, in a tract called "The Wonders of Grace;" to the contents of which the author has made reference in his "Spiritual Victory," in these words:

"One is of an officer in a church in New York, who had used tobacco for forty years, making, during that time, many efforts to abandon the practice, but always failing because of the resultant inward gnawing. But he was brought to an act of specific faith in Jesus to save him from the appetite; and now, after several years, he testifies: 'From that hour all desire left me, and I have ever since hated, what I once so fondly loved.' Another is of a prominent church member in Brooklyn, N. Y., who had used tobacco for thirty years, and could not endure to be without a cigar in his mouth, and sometimes even rose and smoked in the night. After many failures to overcome the habit, one night when alone, he cast himself on his Savior for just this victory; and from that hour was delivered from the desire as well as from the outward act, and now wonders that he ever loved the filthy practice. A certain old lady, who lived near Westbrook, Ct., aged seventy, was a confirmed opium eater, and used daily an amount sufficient to kill twenty persons. She was led to see that the habit was a *sin;* and as such she abandoned it, with specific application to Christ to save her from it. She was heard, and lived for two years afterwards, free from any desire for that drug. A similar case was that of a carpenter in Brooklyn, N. Y., who, from taking morphine to allay the pain of a fractured leg, fell into its habitual use, till he almost lived upon it, for several years after his recovery. He once swallowed, in the presence of several physicians, a dose which it was calculated would destroy the lives of two hundred ordinary men! Not long since, he was made to look at this as sin, and tried to break off the habit, abstaining with an alarming reaction, till five physicians declared that death would ensue, if he did not resume it. This he did for a year; but, then, on a certain Sunday evening, broke off again, casting himself by faith on Christ, from which moment the desire left him, and has never returned, and he has experienced no reaction or other ill effect, but has greatly improved in health."

Cases Reported by Mrs. C. S. Whitney. In her letter to the author, on other relations of prayer, from which quotations have been made, Mrs. Whitney thus speaks on the point now in hand:

"My husband having used tobacco for twenty-five years, became convinced that the habit was sinful, and four years ago, he gave it up. Shortly after, he met a man on the street smoking a fine cigar, and the craving appetite that thereupon took possession of him was fearful. He was strongly tempted to yield; but the blessed Holy Spirit revealed Christ to him as able to save to the uttermost; and right there, on the street, he asked God to destroy the appetite. That prayer was answered immediately, and to this day he has never since had a desire for tobacco, but loathes it."

"A Christian brother, living near Boston, came to me recently, and asked me to pray for him, as that day he had been convinced that he could no longer indulge in the use of tobacco, and claim heirship with Christ. Having used it very freely for thirty years, he thought it would cost him a great struggle, to give it up; but he was resolved to do so, if it caused a separation of soul and body. He asked me to pray that he might be sustained during the conflict. I asked him if he could trust God to take away the appetite, that moment. After a brief hesitation he said: 'I believe he is able, and, I trust, willing.' In a very few words of prayer I asked the dear Lord to do this work — to break the bondage, the power of Satan, and set this man free. He responded: 'Amen: so let it be.' From that moment, he was so delivered from the appetite, that he has felt no temptation to indulge in it since."

PRAYER AND THE ALCOHOL APPETITE. Rev. Wm. L. Bray writes to the author, as follows: "Rev. Mr. H——, now of C——, is a converted drunkard. He was a drunkard for more than twenty-five years. When he was converted, his appetite was fearfully strong, and for years it clung to him and worried him. At one time he went to Grand Rapids for a load of lumber. It was a chilly day, and, on his way home, he would have to pass a rum-shop. As he neared that shop, his old appetite awoke in power, and it became more and more clamorous, until *he felt afraid* to go forward. He felt that he could not pass the rum-hole. He drove his team aside, went into the woods, fell down before God, and cried mightily for deliverance from this appetite. He said: 'The Lord heard me, and answered me, and I rose up a *free* man, and *have been free ever since!*' I had this statement from Mr. H——, himself, but I cannot give the date."

A Case in Ireland. Rev. William Gibson, in his account of the wonderful revival in Ireland, in 1859, gives an account of one David Cresswell, who had been a Romanist, and was afflicted with stammering to such a degree as almost incapacitated him for communicating his thoughts to others, yet who, as far as he could articulate, was a horrible blasphemer. He was, also, addicted to the most immoderate use of tobacco and of strong drink. But, passing a house, he heard the voice of prayer, went in, united in the devotions, and, on leaving, was soon overwhelmed with a sense of his sin, and fell prostrate to the earth. After a fortnight of distress of mind, he found peace in Christ, to whom he made believing application; and, singular to relate, he lost all taste for both liquor and tobacco, and was cured of his infirmity of speech! The particulars, at length, may be found on pages 369–371 of Mr. Gibson's book, "The Year of Grace."

Testimonies Collected by Rev. S. H. Platt. In a previous chapter an account has been given of the manner in which, through prayer and faith, Mr. Platt was cured of chronic lameness. He has given great attention to the subject of the present chapter, and has collected the evidence of the efficacy of prayer in this respect into a little treatise entitled, "The Power of Grace," to the careful perusal of which the unbelieving reader is recommended. A mere sketch of some of the cases detailed by him is all that can here be given. The accounts were received by him in reply to the following question, published in *The Christian Advocate and Journal*, of July 31st, 1873: "Can men be *instantaneously* delivered from the power of acquired habits, such as the use of tobacco, rum, etc., so that they shall thereafter have no craving for the indulgence?"

A minister testifies that, for more than thirty years, he had been a habitual smoker, and had at various times attempted to abandon the practice, but each time yielded to the craving of his appetite, and "became a more inveterate smoker than before." But more earnest endeavors to be wholly the Lord's, brought up the question afresh, and he laid the pipe aside, relying simply on his appeal to God to deliver him. He says: "I trusted in the Lord, and not one word of his precious promises has failed me. I have had no craving, no uneasiness, no desire." At the end of a year he writes: "I am filled with wonder, for I expected a terrible fight with an appetite strengthened by an indulgence of about thirty-five years; but the enemy has not showed his head. Not only has the desire for smoking been effectually squelched, but a perfect hatred of smoking has been developed, on account of the offensiveness of the odor of tobacco. Thanks be unto God, who giveth us the victory!"

Another minister states: "I had used tobacco from childhood, and the love and use thereof grew upon me. I became convicted of its sinfulness, went to God and said, 'Destroy the appetite, or give me power over it. Save me, that I may glorify thee as a God of power for our present sins, and I will glorify thee evermore.' I wrote out the contract, and signed it, and from that blessed afternoon until to-day have no recollection of ever desiring it even."

The President of a Young Men's Christian Association in Vermont, who had been greatly troubled by his tobacco habit, and "had tried a number of times to leave it off, but could not do so," says: "One night, as I was retiring to rest, I thought I would kneel by my bed, and ask him, who never refuses to answer prayer, to take from me the desire for tobacco; and from that moment it has been impossible for me to use it."

An editor in Tennessee, who was in this tobacco bondage, says: "I determined, time and again, to desist from it, sometimes abstaining for a few months, or weeks — once for twelve months — but *the desire for it never left me.* * * * One Sunday morning, the first day of December, 1850, I retired to a secluded place, got down upon my knees, and asked the Lord to help me quit it, determining, then and there, that I would, God being my helper, never touch the accursed thing again by any kind of use in the way of consumption; and from that day to this I have never had any desire to smoke or chew tobacco, or to use it in any way. But I did this, whenever I saw tobacco: I lifted my heart to God, imploring his assistance in abstaining from it. I have now been clear of the desire of it for nearly twenty-three years."

A man forty-two years old narrates how, from his youth up, he was addicted to tobacco and, also, to liquor, and became a confirmed drunkard. A minister held a prayer meeting at his house, and said that religion could cure all evil habits. He says: "The next morning I took out my tobacco, to take a chew, and thought of what the minister had said, the night before. It was a new idea to me. I put the tobacco in my pocket again, and said, 'I'll try it.' I was alone in my barn. I kneeled down and asked God to remove the appetite from me. It was done. Glory to God! I was cured. I felt it; I knew it then; I have never had a desire for it since; there has been no hankering for it, or for strong drink, since. My sins were all forgiven, and I was made a new man all over — inside and outside."

Another man, who had been under the same double bondage, says: "I felt my weakness, and called on my Heavenly Father, and told him the work was too great for me, and prayed that he would do the work for me, and take away the taste, or appetite. * * * He heard my prayer. I never have had a taste or desire for a glass of intoxicating drink, or a smoke or chew of tobacco, from that time until the present moment, which is nineteen years the seventh of last February, [1873]."

It is because these specific deliverances have been experienced, as well as those of a more general character, that the saint can sing with emphasis the familiar stanzas of Charles Wesley:

"Thou, O Christ, art all I want;
More than all in thee I find;
Raise the fallen, cheer the faint,
Heal the sick, and lead the blind.
Just and holy is thy name;
I am all unrighteousness;
Vile and full of sin I am,
Thou art full of truth and grace.

"Plenteous grace with thee is found,
Grace to pardon all my sin;
Let the healing streams abound;
Make and keep me pure within.
Thou of life the fountain art,
Freely let me take of thee;
Spring thou up within my heart;
Rise to all eternity."

CHAPTER XVI.

PRAYER FOR INDIVIDUAL CONVERSION.

THEOLOGICALLY it is a startling fact, that the Bible uses language which implies that one man may convert another. Thus James writes (v: 19–20): "Brethren, if any of you do err from the truth, and *one convert him*, let him know that *he who converteth the sinner* from the error of his way shall save a soul from death, and shall hide a multitude of sins." But if this language startles us, when we think of the thoroughness of human depravity, and the necessity of regeneration by the Holy Spirit, the case is wonderfully relieved, as we notice that the words just quoted from James immediately follows six verses which assure us of the efficacy of fervent prayer. This fact may warrant us in supposing, that the "converting" power is largely connected with the privilege which the Christian has of securing a divine co-operation with his labors. "For we are laborers together with God," said Paul, 1 Cor. iii: 9. And so the facts prove.

A BIBLE CLASS OF YOUNG LADIES. The author knows of a theological student, who in a Presbyterian church in New York city, took charge of a Bible class of about forty young ladies, with scarcely a professor of religion in it. He solemnly determined to seek the conversion of every member. His method was, in addition to a very faithful application of the lesson, on Sunday, and personal religious conversation, from time to time, with each at her home—to make every scholar a subject of special prayer, by name, in his closet. Usually he took up the cases, one or two at a time, and prayed and labored for their immediate conversion. Sometimes he was enabled, before going to the house, for conversation, to gain an assurance in prayer, that that soul would then submit; and such was the fact. The conversations were almost always closed with prayer, in which he previously urged the young lady silently to unite, and make her consecration to God. As the result of three or four years labor, nearly every member of that class was converted, and seldom did a communion-season occur, in that church, without additions from that class. There was but one of those who remained steadily in the class, who continued obdurate; and she set her will with great firmness against conversion, and seemed insensible to all appeals; though more labor was expended on her than on any two or three others. When the student finished his studies, and entered the ministry, Harriet J—— was apparently farther from God than ever. He went elsewhere to live and labor, as a minister of Christ, and had no further opportunity to speak with her about her soul's salvation. But occasionally she would occur to his thoughts, and he would pray God to touch her heart.

Time rolled on, and twenty-seven years had passed, when he chanced to preach, one Sunday, in Brooklyn, his own residence being a thousand miles distant. At the close of the services, a middle aged lady stood at the foot of the pulpit stairs, and as he came down, accosted him with the words: "Excuse me, but I used to be in your Bible class. Do you not remember Harriet J——? I am now Mrs. ——, and live in this city." Yes, indeed, he remembered her; how could he forget one for and with whom he had pleaded so often? He seized her hand, and said: "Harriet, do you love the Lord Jesus Christ?" And, to his unutterable joy, she replied, "Yes, I trust I do." His prayers, after all, had been heard, and the one notable exception had ceased to be such.

AN ILLUSTRATION BY PROFESSOR AUSTIN PHELPS, D. D. In a communication to *The Advance*, January 28, 1875, Prof. Phelps—whose charming little book on "The Still Hour," many lovers of prayer have read with spiritual profit and delight—gives account of an instance of success in prayer which is quite striking. This is the statement somewhat abridged:

A certain man was of Christian parentage, the son of an exceptionally devoted mother. He acquired an appetite for strong drink, from using it medically, became intemperate, abandoned his Christian hope and faith, and, to human judgment, was utterly abandoned of God. For twenty years, his few Christian friends prayed for him, against all probabilities, and hoped against all evidences. A heavy affliction having befallen him, in consequence of his intemperate life, these friends hoped that it might be made the occasion of his deliverance. They asked for him the prayers of a company of Christian ladies, entire strangers to him. To this day he is unknown to them, in name or person. He lived three hundred miles distant from them. His history was detailed to them, and they resolved to concentrate prayer upon him, for a time, and see what God would do. They prayed specifically for his moral reform, for the revival of his Christian faith, for his conversion as a child of the covenant. They persisted in prayer; agreeing that each one should bear him on her heart, in secret communion with God. Among these ladies were some who have had a remarkable experience of success in intercessory prayer.

The result is soon told. At about the time when his case was first named to that praying circle, with no knowledge on his part that they were interested in him, he suddenly dropped the use of intoxicating drink; and from that hour he has been absolutely free from the alcoholic craving. Within a week, the cavils at religious doctrines ceased. Then his prejudices against Christian usages and people gave way. The coat of mail, which he had worn for twenty years, dropped from him, and his heart lay bare to the power of truth and of the Holy Spirit. His childhood's faith returned to him, freighted with the teachings, the songs, and the prayers of a sainted mother. Then followed a period of profound despair. "No other sinner," said he, "can have sinned so damnably, as I have sinned. No hell can be worse than I endure. Oh, that I could sleep, and never wake again"! For ten days or more, this despair continued, prayer being made for him without ceasing. He seemed unable to pray for himself. He begged like a child to be taught how to pray. His locked lips were like a premonition of the retributive speechlessness of guilt at the day of judgment. At length a change occurred, which may be described in a letter which he wrote to the Christian who, unknown to him, had acquainted the praying circle with his case:

"I do not know that I can express intelligibly to you, the state of my mind; but most of the time, my soul is filled with what seems to me the joy of heaven. My room appears as if filled with angels. With reverence I say it, Christ seems to be with me. God seems to look upon me with a forgiving face. Last night, I could not sleep, but sat all night by the fire. My mind was full of the mercy of God, and the glorious goodness of Christ. I experienced such fullness of joy, as I never dreamed of before. When daylight came, I was astonished at the shortness of the night. I am not conscious of any excitement in it all. It is all peace, perfect peace. I am unable to feel any desire for prolonged life. I feel perfect trust in God. I would leave all that concerns me with him. * * * I feel that time alone can determine whether my heart is changed. My daily life must show it. Yet I feel like exclaiming: Father, I thank thee for this mercy to the worst of sinners! Then I ask myself, is it right for such a sinner as I to take so much delight in prayer?"

Prof. Phelps well asks, in conclusion: "Granting the fact of a diseased body, of a brain unnaturally excited by the sudden withdrawal of alcoholic stimulus [which, it seems to the author should depress, and not excite], and making large allowance for other peculiarities of physical constitution and condition, is this not, after all, a clear case of the saving mercy of God in *accenting* the physical conditions as they are, and using them in the conversion of the soul? And is it not as clear a case of answer to prayer, long deferred, and give at last to a *reinforcement* of the power of prayer, trustfully sought and importunately applied? Does it not confirm the faith of a believing spirit in the truth that concerted prayer is prayer intensified, as truly as any other form of concerted action.?"

EXPERIENCE OF CATHARINE ADORNA. We go back four centuries, to Genoa, in Italy, and there we find the pious Catharine Adorna, visiting and praying with the sick, in the Hospital and in private houses. A wife came to her, one day, and induced her to go to her house, and see her sick husband, who was likely to die, but had no interest in the subject of religion. She went, and talked with him, and left. On the way back, she and the wife stepped into a church, sought a retired place, and earnestly prayed for his conversion. When the wife returned home, she was astonished to find a great change in her husband's mind, and to hear him speak like a Christian. The next day, she hastened to carry the news to Catharine Adorna; but, says her biographer, Dr. Upham: "The news was not surprising to her. She had prayed earnestly for the sick man, and she had reason to believe that her prayer either had been or would be speedily answered. This belief was founded upon the fact, that, in offering up her supplications for him, she had found herself inwardly and specially drawn by the influences of the Holy Spirit. It seems to have been her practice, in what may be called her special supplications, not to move by her own choice, by the self-originated impulse of her own volition; but to keep her soul in the attitude of humble and quiet waiting, that it might first be moved by the Holy Ghost. And when she prayed to God, under the influence of this specific divine operation, her faith could generally see the result in the petition itself. And this was the case, in the present instance." It is interesting, as showing the far-reaching effect of the prayer thus offered, that the wife was so impressed by the result, that when her husband died, she attached herself to Catharine Adorna, in her labors of mercy, became her constant companion, and was with her at the hour of death.

THE CONVERSION OF AN INFIDEL. In the "Incidents in a Pastors' Life," Rev. William Wisner, D. D., gives an account of which the following is an abridgement:

A skeptical young man was induced, during a revival, to accompany a lady, with whom he boarded, to an evening lecture; but he purposely divested his thoughts from any attention to what was said. On their return, the lady and a pious young woman left him in the parlor, and retired to their own rooms, in a distant part of the house, to pray for his salvation. While on their knees, pleading in his behalf, they were alarmed by a cry from the parlor. Repairing thither, they found the family Bible open on the table, and the young man standing near, with marks of agony on his face. When they inquired what the matter was, he was about, in pride (as he afterwards said) to reply, "Nothing;" but before the words passed his lips, he was so overcome with anguish, that he exclaimed, "Oh, I am an infidel; pray for me," and fell prostrate on the floor. About midnight, he requested that some of his companions of the legal profession might be sent for, that seeing his remorse they might take warning. At two o'clock, in the morning, Dr. Wisner was called from his bed, to talk and pray with him; and found him on his knees, not praying, but giving vent to his anguish, and saying, "I am an infidel! I have denied my Savior, and am now given up of God, to eat of the fruit of my own doing." The next evening, there was a meeting for inquiry, and among others came the despairing young lawyer, supported by two friends. He received further gospel instruction, but only said: "These provisions were once for me, but I have rejected them. I have sinned away my day of grace." But after returning home, about eleven o'clock, he submitted himself unconditionally to God, which, he said, he had before been unwilling to do. Then his soul embraced Christ and he was filled with peace and joy. At the time Dr. Wisner wrote the narrative, he had been a pillar in the church for twenty-four years, and an officer of it for more than fifteen. Thus we may see that the most desperate cases yield to prayer.

A Prompt Answer. Dr. Wisner also makes this statement, with reference to his accepting an invitation from a neighboring pastor to come and assist in some special meetings: "I took one of my elders with me, and went to the house of my brother, agreeably to his request. He had made an appointment for me to preach that evening. The congregation was large and solemn, and there were some indications of the special presence of the Holy Spirit. That evening, my elder led our devotions in family prayer, and poured out his soul in great fervency for the conversion of sinners. He earnestly besought the Lord, that he would so trouble the impenitent that they would feel constrained to awaken us in the night, to inquire what they should do to be saved. After prayer we retired to rest; but about midnight the pastor came into our room, and awoke us, to tell us that a number of sinners had collected at the Academy, who were so distressed with a sense of their lost condition, that they had sent a request for us to visit them. On repairing to the place, the pastor and my elder (for I was not well enough to go out at that hour,) found the principal of the Academy, with a large number of the scholars and some other persons assembled to inquire what they must do to be saved. The next morning there were a number rejoicing in hope, and many more deeply bowed down under a sense of their sins. We remained there a few days, and had the pleasure of seeing many proud hearts apparently humbled at the foot of the cross. It was the Lord, who taught my brother thus to pray; and it was the Lord who answered that prayer by giving us the very thing prayed for. If Christians lived in habits of communion with God, would not his Spirit more frequently teach us what to pray for, and more frequently give us the very blessings which we ask?"

Conversion of a Husband. In that exquisite volume, entitled "My Mother; or Recollections of Maternal Influence," published anonymously, but ascribed to a well known pen, is a touching account of the manner in which the husband and father was brought to God. He had for years been the object of the religious solicitude of his wife, and finally as his case became more discouraging than ever, in a seeming moral apathy, the mother proposed to her children, at home and abroad, to meet with her at the throne of grace in his behalf, at a certain hour of the day. The account continues: "Whatever may have been the mental state of him who was the object of our concert, there was a growing feeling of intensity in our mother. Her spirit had no rest. After they had retired, one night, she said a few words expressive of her concern for him; he gave her an indifferent answer, and fell asleep. She arose, in the fullness of an anxious heart, and returned to the sitting-room, raked open a bed of coals, and spent the night in prayer. It was cold, being the latter part of February. Behold the difference between the believer and the unbeliever: the one sleeps over his own impending ruin; the other wakes, and wrestles for him, in agonizing prayer.

"As the day dawned, she fell into a train of reflections like the following: 'I have borne this burden forty years; I can carry it no further; it is too heavy for me; I must roll it off on God. I feel that I have done. *I* cannot convert his heart. I *can't* convert, however much I distress myself. Perhaps I have sinned in distressing myself as I have. God may have seen in me the want of a simple reliance on him; or the want of true and absolute submission to his will. He may have seen me unwilling, or afraid to commit the matter of my husband's salvation *entirely* to him. But I feel that I *must*, and *do* thus commit it to him now. I will afflict myself no more. I shall still pray for him, and use such means as may seem advisable, but — saved or lost — I leave the result with God.' * * * She was conscious of a simplicity of trust, now, and a relief of mind such as on that subject she had never felt before. So prayed and found relief, the wife of Elkanah. In the morning, after breakfast, finding him alone, she said a few words to him, to this effect. She remarked, that they had lived together above forty years; that their union had been an affectionate and happy one, and it was painful to think, that they were soon to be separated without any prospect of ever being reunited. * * * 'And now I have this one request to make: *devote this day to the concerns of the soul;* devote it to reflection and to prayer. If you cannot do it for your own sake, do it to oblige me!' Struck with her earnest manner, he said, decisively, '*I will.*' He was 'not able to resist the wisdom and the spirit by which she spake.'

"She saw no more of him till quite night, when he came in and sat down, sad and thoughtful, by the fire. She did not know the nature of his feelings; nor was any allusion made to the interview of the morning. It was evident that he was not happy. He had an eye more expressive of sorrow than any eye I ever saw. It glistened, but did not flow with tears, and its color seemed to deepen. Sorrow was in him a sealed fountain: it found no vent in words. The next day he again disappeared, and was gone till evening. His countenance and manner, when he returned, were still thoughtful; but there was a serenity in his look, which was not there before. 'I do not know,' said he to my mother, 'what has ailed me to-day; my feelings have been unusual, and, indeed very strange.' 'Why, how have you felt,' she asked. 'I can hardly tell you,' he replied: 'I have no reason to think myself a Christian, or, perhaps, that I ever shall be; but it has seemed to me, this afternoon, as if everything was changed. Everything appeared to speak of God. The trees, the hills, the skies — everything, seemed to praise him. And I felt that I loved everybody. If there is anyone that I have hated, it is Mr. G. (a certain revivalist, the particular type of whose zeal, or whose *tactics* had disgusted him); but I have felt to-day that I loved him like a brother.'

"It was afterwards known, that he spent the former of those two days in a retired valley on his farm, and the other in a wood. He had engaged to spend *one* day in retirement. That he might have appeared to do, merely to fulfill a promise. The second day was eminently probationary and eminently critical. * * * On the following morning, the minister of the place happened to call. He knew nothing of my father's state of mind. * * * They had a long conversation, and, on leaving the house, the minister said to the first Christian he met, 'I have great news to tell you; Mr.—— has become a new man. I have just come from conversing with him, and have no doubt of the reality of his conversion to Christ. The change in him is surprising; he is indeed a perfect child in religion.' * * * After suitable delay and self-examination, he made a public profession of his faith, receiving baptism in connection with that act. * * * My father lived ten years, to test the genuineness of his faith. He died at the age of seventy-five."

THE EFFECT OF HABITUAL PRAYER. The steady occurrence of conversions in connection with habitual labor and prayer is well illustrated by the facts mentioned in the biography of Normand Smith, Jr., of Hartford, Ct., in which we read:

"The means he used to impress the minds of those

who from time to time came into his family were various: sometimes he would converse with them separately; at others, he would address them together; but depended most of all upon the presentation of truth in family worship, and the daily exhibition of a Christian example, together with a manifest tender concern for their salvation. He has been known to sit up half the night in prayer for a member of his family, whose mind he knew was impressed on the subject of religion. On his dying bed, nearly the last words he said to his brother, engaged with him in business, were, *Take good care of the boys!* He felt the same benevolent concern for the domestics of the family; and it is an interesting fact, that all who resided in the family, in this capacity, during the last four years of his life, hopefully became Christians. One of the number thus converted, heard him one morning very early, before the family had risen, earnestly at prayer. She listened, and found it was for herself. Her mind was impressed, and she sought and found the one thing needful.

AN UNPROMISING CASE SELECTED. A ministerial brother tells of a highly-cultivated lady, the principal and founder of an important ladies' seminary, who, for some cause, began to doubt whether the Lord accepted her services in that institution. Feeling that her intent was simply to please him, and to build up a seminary that should combine learning with religion, and should send forth Christian and educated women to benefit the world, she laid the matter before the

Lord in prayer. Feeling a desire to test the thing practically, and to see if the Lord would use her to secure the results upon which she had set her heart, she selected from among her pupils a most unpromising person, upon whom to bring to bear any religious influence — perhaps the most difficult and trying case in the school — and she asked the Lord to give her that soul. It was an earnest asking, a pleading which felt that everything was at stake, and the prayer went up night and day. The young lady concerned knew nothing of this struggle, at the mercy seat, in her behalf; yet, in less than a week, she came of her own accord to the principal, inquiring the way of salvation, and soon was rejoicing in the Savior. Not only so, but, after a little, her mind became interested in the lost condition of her sisters in the heathen world, and she devoted herself to a missionary life. It is not amiss to add, that this auspicious result was not only a source of new hope to the self-denying principal, in her depressing labors, but was actually a fore-token of the kind of work which her institution was successfully to do through the coming years. It has ever been a fountain-head of piety and missionary interest.

Mr. Finney's Praying Acquaintance. In his lecture on "The Spirit of Prayer" Rev. Charles G. Finney says: "I was acquainted with an individual who used to keep a list of persons that he was especially concerned for, and I have had the opportunity to know a multitude of persons for whom he became thus interested, who were immediately converted. I have seen him pray for persons on his list when he was literally in an agony for them; and have sometimes known him call on some other person to help him pray for such-a-one. I have known his mind to fasten thus on an individual of hardened, abandoned character, and who could not be reached in any ordinary way. In a town in a north part of the State of New York, where there was a revival, there was a certain individual who was a most violent and outrageous opposer. He kept a tavern, and used to delight in swearing, at a desperate rate, whenever there were Christians within hearing, on purpose to hurt their feelings. He was so bad, that one man said he believed he should have to sell his place, or give it away, and move out of town, for he could not live near a man that swore so. This good man, that I was speaking of, was passing through the town, and heard of the case, and was very much grieved and distressed for the individual. He took him on his praying list. The case weighed on his mind, when he was asleep and when he was awake. He kept thinking about him, and praying for him, for days. And the first we knew of it, this ungodly man came into a meeting, and got up and confessed his sins, and poured out his soul. His bar-room immediately became the place where they held prayer-meetings." Probably this man of prayer was "Father Nash," of whom mention was made in the chapter on the "Prayer of Faith," and whose success in supplication was noted throughout Central and Western New York.

FACT COMMUNICATED BY DR. POND. In a letter from the venerable Enoch Pond, D. D., he speaks of "a young man, a member of Amherst College, some thirty years ago. He was bright, social, amiable, not vicious, but pretty likely to be led astray. It was a time of special revival in the college, and the mother of this young man (who was a pious Christian woman) received a letter from one of her son's classmates, saying that several of the class had set apart the next week to unite in prayer for the conversion of her son. They asked that she would unite with them. She did so, I doubt not, with all her heart, and in about two weeks she had another letter, from the same hand which wrote the first, saying that her son was among the converts. He became an earnest Christian, and was a very successful teacher in Connecticut for many years. He is dead now, but died in hope of the glory of God. I was well acquainted with all the facts in this case, and with all the individuals concerned."

TESTIMONY FROM REV. P. HAGLER. Mr. Hagler is a Baptist minister at Duquoin, Ill., and he writes to the author, as follows: "Last fall we commenced a protracted meeting, which lasted seventeen days. When the meeting commenced, there were three or four of us covenanted that we would pray for the conversion of a certain skeptical man and his family. The result was, that, about the third day of the meeting, he came to church, but sat very near the door. But he soon became interested, and, the second time, he asked for the prayers of the church, and it was not long before all the family were enlisted. Before the meeting closed, himself, wife, and four of the children, were converted, baptized, and added to the church. He was a major in the army, in the late war, had been strongly inclined to infidelity, and, according to his own statement, had not been inside of a meeting-house for fifteen years. We all believe it was in answer to prayer."

A TRIPLE SUCCESS. A letter from Rev. James Aiken, D. D., of Haverhill, N. H. says: "I send you the following statement made to me by the late Rev. Walter Harris, D. D., of Dunbarton, N. H. He said, that at a weekly prayer-meeting, held at his house and attended by three brethren, members of his church, it was suggested and agreed, that they should pray especially for *three prominent men* of the parish, that they might be converted to God. In accordance with this agreement, earnest prayer was offered for many weeks. Now for the result. These three men, thus prayed for, came successively, the same evening, to the parsonage, to inquire what they must do to be saved. They found their minister at home, and the brethren with him assembled for prayer. These anxious inquirers soon found peace in believing in Jesus. Of each of them it could be said, 'Behold, he prayeth!'"

A FATHER CONVERTED. An aged widow, whose husband was a clergyman noted for his broad plans and useful efforts, but whose name is here omitted from deference to her modesty, writes as follows to the author: "I was conscious that my father, although a very moral man, did not understand the new birth, and I often made him a subject of prayer. When he was about sixty years old, I was residing about six hundred miles from home, and one Monday evening, I felt a strong desire to attend a "Monthly Concert" of prayer; but my children were small, and I found it inconvenient to leave them. I decided to spend what time I could, in my room, praying for the conversion of the world. The moment I entered my room, my father came before my mind, and I lost all sight of the rest of the world. With groans and tears I agonized on his behalf, till at length I cast him over upon Christ, and felt a perfect peace. The next day, I thought I must continue my effort, and I tried to pray again for my father; but, to my great surprise, I had nothing to say. I could not frame a prayer; a rebuke came over me, which greatly humbled me, that I should be teasing the Lord, after he had already answered my request. From this time I began to look for a letter announcing the conversion of my father. A letter came, and in my haste, I concluded not to read the introduction, but to look about the middle of the first page, where they would speak of father's conversion: and there it was, precisely as it lay in my mind! After communicating with my friends, I found that he had submitted the same evening upon which I had prayed for him."

Men of the world may call this a mere coincidence; but surely it bears marks of being something more; especially in the light of Scriptural doctrine. Can we not see in it the work of the Holy Spirit, who inspires the very prayers which he is about to answer?

On Missionary Ground. In the *Congregationalist*, (August, 1875,) Rev. Allen Hazen gives an account of the conversion of a learned Brahman for whose case prayer had been specially offered by the missionaries for many years; as he had been employed as an assistant in translation, and had been led to a high respect for the Christian religion. But he did not forsake his native faith, though he became eclectic in his views, and, while he worshiped at the heathen temples, would also, on passing a church building, raise his hands and say "Glory to Christ." He led of late years an ascetic life, ate but once a day, and spent much time in meditation, with his body in a painful position. Early in 1875, he was living far from his missionary acquaintances, was old, feeble, nearly blind, and suffering intensely from rheumatism. Thinking that there could be no relief from the pain, he determined to kill himself, and was going up into the third story of the house to throw himself down, when the thought came to him: "I must not imitate Judas, in killing myself?" He thought the suggestion came from Jesus, and he prayed to him for relief from the pain he was suffering, and vowed, that if the relief came, he would at once confess Christ, and profess his faith by baptism. His prayer was heard, and the relief came. True to his word, he went to the nearest missionary station, and was baptized. All who know him express confidence in the reality of the change. Here was a double answer to prayer. The Brahman was cured in body and saved in soul, and not only his prayer was heard, but the prayers were answered which had been offered for him by name, for many years, by the missionaries, who had watched his career with so much interest. Prayers are never lost, even when, as in this case, some of the petitioners have passed from earth, without seeing the desired event. In God's time and way the blessing is sure to come.

A Female Skeptic Converted. Miss Lucy R. Drake has communicated to the author this striking illustration of the effect of prayer in leading a soul out of utter unbelief. She writes as follows:

"While spending a few days in a seminary, among the young ladies who came to me for religious conversation was one of the senior class, who frankly stated her condition to be that of a skeptic, particularly as regarded Christ's divinity. She remarked that this had been growing with her, even through all the Bible lessons attended by her in the seminary. Still she told me, with much evident interest, that she had seen persons in whom she was convinced there was something—a power to be kept from sin—that she had not. 'They say it is a divine work; but I am skeptical; yet this one thing I know, I would be willing to do anything, to have what they possess.' 'Would you, indeed, be willing to do anything?' I asked. 'Yes.' 'Will you stand by this assertion?' 'Yes.' Then I quietly but firmly said, 'There can be no difficulty; you will obtain; skepticism cannot prevent it.'

She looked up surprised, and yet with hope; for previously she had evidently regarded her skepticism as an insurpassable obstacle. I then remarked that God had said, 'Ye shall seek for me and find me, when ye shall search for me with all your heart.' It is his work to manifest himself to you; but it is yours to seek him with all your heart. You have a heart, and can put your interest fully into seeking him with all your heart. Will you?' 'Yes,' she replied. I then said: 'We will kneel; I will pray first, and then you follow, and *seek him.*' 'Oh, I cannot; I never prayed before any one, and then I do not believe.' 'You said you would do anything; tell God all that is in your heart, your unbelief, and just what you want.' 'I will,' she firmly said. After praying myself, she commenced, and having told the Lord, that she did then seek him with her whole heart, she exclaimed, 'I've found him! Christ is divine! HE IS DIVINE! He is revealing himself to me. How could I have doubted him!' and tears of penitence and joy rolled over her face. From the testimony of others I have since learned that she has been, from that moment, a cheerful, devoted Christian, a possessor of that which she sought.

"In religious work I have never known it fail, that God's promises have been fulfilled, no matter how great the difficulties, if the conditions he has laid down so plainly are complied with by the suppliant. Personally, I have found that 'if ye have faith as a grain of mustard seed, ye shall say unto this mountain, Remove hence to yonder place, and it shall remove, and nothing shall be impossible unto you.'"

MR. D. L. MOODY AND THE INFIDEL. After the return of Mr. Moody from his labors in Great Britain, he went to Northfield, Mass., his native place, and in a meeting, there, gave this illustration of the power of prayer to reach the most unlikely cases of sin and unbelief. He is thus reported: "There is not a heart so hard that God cannot touch it. While we were gone, this time, an incident occurred that interested me very much. While in Edinburgh, a man was pointed out to me by a friend, who said; 'Moody, that man is chairman of the Edinburgh infidel club.' So I went and sat down beside him, and said: 'Well, my friend, I am glad to see you at this meeting. Are you not concerned about your welfare?' He said that he didn't believe in a hereafter. I said, 'Will you just get down on your knees and let me pray for you.' 'I don't believe in prayer.' I tried unsuccessfully to get the man down on his knees, and finally knelt down beside him and prayed for him. Well he made a good deal of sport over it, and I met him again many times in Edinburgh after that. A year ago, last month, while in the north of Scotland, I met the man again. Placing my hand on his shoulder, I asked, 'Hasn't God answered the prayer?' He replied: 'There is no God. I am just the same as I always have been. If you believe in a God, and in answers to prayer, do as I told you—try your hand on me.' 'Well,' I said, 'God's time will come; there are a great many praying for you, and I have faith to believe you are going to be blessed.' Six months ago, I was in Liverpool, and there I got a letter from the leading barrister of Edinburgh, telling me that my friend, the infidel, had come to Christ, and that of his club of thirty men, seventeen had followed his example. How it happened, he could not say, but whereas he was once blind, now he could see. God had answered the prayer. I didn't know how it was to be answered, but I believed it would be, and it was done. What we want to do is, to come boldly to God."

PRAYER OPENS A HOUSE. Rev. J. Boyes relates this incident in the *Wesleyan*, on the authority of the missionary concerned. There was a town-missionary who greatly desired to gain access to a lodging-house, which was of such a low and dangerous character as to make it hazardous to life to enter. He prayed over the matter, and finally concluded to risk the consequences. He knocked, and after some rough language addressed to him, was allowed to enter. He found a villainous-looking man within, who, learning his character and religious object, said: "I will ask you a question out of the Bible. If you answer me right, you may call at this house, and read and pray with us or our lodgers, as often as you like: if you do not answer me right, we will tear your clothes from your back, and tumble you neck and heels into the street." The missionary quietly said, "I will take you." "Well then: is the word *girl* in the Bible; if so where, and how often?" The missionary replied: "The word *girl* is in the Bible; but only once, and may be found in the prophecy of Joel, chapter iii., verse 3: 'And sold a girl for wine, that they might drink.'" "Well," said the man, "I am dead beat; I durst bet five pounds, you could not have told." "And I could not have told, yesterday. For several days I have been praying that the Lord would open me a way into this house; and this very morning, when reading the Scripture to my family, I was surprised to find the word *girl*, and got the Concordance, to see if it occurred again, and found that it did not. God knows what will come to pass, and his hand is in this for my protection and your good." The result was, that the inmates came under religious influences, and the man, his wife and two of the lodgers were converted.

How an Emperor was Converted. The following facts are taken from the journal of Stephen Grellet, a member of the Society of Friends, who, with William Allen, visited Russia on a spiritual mission, and received the account from Prince Galatzin himself. When Napoleon's army entered Moscow, a panic seized St. Petersburg. But amid the universal alarm Prince Galatzin remained so calm, that the Emperor, Alexander I., inquired the reason. The Prince drew from his pocket a Bible, a book of which the Emperor was quite ignorant, and was handing it to the Emperor, when it dropped open on the floor. Raising it, and glancing at the open page, he said, "Permit me to read this very passage, from the ninety-first Psalm: 'He that dwelleth in the secret place of the Most

High shall abide under the shadow of the Almighty.' Oh, that your Majesty would seek this retreat!" The Emperor stood astonished, and then went to the great church for public worship, as was customary, whenever he left the city for some time. Strange to say, the officiating priest read the same psalm. When sent for, after the service, and asked if Galatzin had told of the interview, the priest said he knew nothing of it; but that he had desired in prayer that the Lord would direct him to the particular portion of the inspired volume he should read, to encourage the Emperor; and that he judged that that psalm was the word of the Lord to him. The Emperor proceeded on his way, for some distance, and late in the evening, sent for his chaplain to read the Bible to him, in his tent, as he felt great seriousness of mind. The chaplain came, and began to read: "He that dwelleth in the secret place of the Most High shall abide under the shadow of the Almighty." "Hold," said the Emperor; "who told you to read that?" Has Galatzin told you?" "No; but surprised at your sending for me, I fell upon my knees before God, and besought him to teach my weak lips what to speak. I felt that part of the holy word to be clearly pointed out to me. Why has your majesty interrupted me?" The Emperor was astonished, listened attentively, and from that time concluded to read privately a chapter in the Bible, morning and evening. He took Prince Galatzin's Bible, and, to use his own language, "I devoured it, finding in it words so suitable to and descriptive of the state of my mind. The Lord, by his divine Spirit, was also pleased to give me an understanding of what I read therein. It is to this inward teacher alone that I am indebted." Messrs. Grellet and Allen found him ready to converse on spiritual subjects, and in repeated interviews he knelt with those two simple-hearted Friends, and joined in their fervent prayers.

THE CONVERSION OF SEVERAL CHILDREN. Mrs. C. S. Whitney, whose interesting experience of healing, in answer to prayer, has been given in a previous chapter, says further: "In regard to the conversion of souls, many times prayer has been answered immediately. At one time, in a little prayer meeting, a desire was given me for the speedy conversion of several children present. After some conversation and prayer, we agreed that, each in our own home, the next morning, at nine o'clock, should ask God to bless and save. At our next meeting, ten of the children gave evidence of a change of heart; which had occurred at that very hour."

A SISTER'S PRAYERS AND WAITING. Miss Shipton, from whose "Secret of the Lord" a fact was quoted in a previous chapter, gives, also, this item of her experience: "One day, I was in great sorrow over the backsliding of a dear brother. I felt as if Satan stood by, to resist every effort I made to help this wanderer. During a night of special prayer, and many tears, the word came to my mind, 'If thou wouldst believe, thou shouldst see the glory of God.'

I took my Bible, to comfort my heart with God's blessed promises, and I opened at John xi: 23: 'Thy brother shall rise again.' 'Said I not unto thee, if thou wouldst *believe?*' Blessed promise! I did believe; but it was not an abiding belief. I looked on the waves of circumstance, and not on him who ruled them. All without was dark, and I, more sad-hearted and dispirited, listened to the tempter's voice, 'Hath God said?' I sat in the garden, praying to the gracious Comforter to comfort me, and to deliver his wandering child. As I prayed, I received strength to take God at his word. My eye was attracted to a spider's web, on a rose tree near me, in the sunlight. A poor fly was caught in the mesh; the more it struggled, the deeper it was entangled. I felt fascinated, so that I could not withdraw my eyes. The great black spider, in ambush, was ready to destroy his victim. All hope seemed over, when a blast of wind rent the prison in twain, and the bright-winged captive flew by me in freedom. Then I praised the Lord. Six long years of waiting, with the promise given me often conned, and the picture of the broken web often before me, when, lo! the stone was rolled away, and he that was dead came forth. My Father! I thank thee that thou hast heard me. A day or two after this blessed assurance of life was given me, I received a letter from a Christian friend, and she gave me for my portion—'Said I not unto thee, that, if thou wouldst believe, thou shouldst see the glory of God?' I did not apply it at once, yet the words deeply impressed my heart.

But, in the night-watch, the words came again, and I was led back, step by step, through my hopeless unbelief, my cruel doubt of God's faithfulness, my ready ear to the tempter's voice, the night of weeping, and the morning of hope, when, in a parable, the Lord wrought out his loving promise; and, in tears of joy and mingled shame at my own unfaithfulness, I again exclaimed, 'This God is my God, forever and ever. He shall be my guide even unto death.'"

A Dreaded Duty and Saving Results. Normand Smith, Jr., of Hartford, Ct., was accustomed to take part of the apprentices, whom he had in his business, into his family, that he might watch over their moral and religious welfare. They were always present at family worship. He had occasion to leave home, for a week or ten days, and his wife, who had been searching her heart of late, and endeavoring to make a perfect consecration of herself to the Lord, suddenly found this question raised in her mind: "Are you willing to pray in your family during the absence of your husband?" She shrank from such a trial, for she was young, her disposition was retiring and timid, and the apprentices were from sixteen to twenty years of age. Her mental distress was great, but she wisely carried the matter before the Lord. Leaving all her household matters with her widowed mother, who resided with her, she gave up the day to prayer, from the morning hour, and it was not till late in the afternoon that, alone in her room with God, she felt that she had gained the victory, and was prepared for the dreaded duty.

Then great peace came at once into her soul, and she realized the privilege of presenting those young men to God in prayer. To use her own words, in a letter to the author: "In the morning worship, I only had to open my mouth, and God filled it. The room, and even the house, seemed so full of God, that it was impressed on my mind that God was willing to do a work in the family. So I invited Mr. Barrows (now Rev. Prof. E. P. Barrows, D. D.,) to call, at tea-time, and converse with the young men. He did so, and one of them gave his heart to God during the conversation; and, before the week was out, two others did the same, as did three of their companions in the next house. One of them soon began to prepare for the ministry, and is now a settled pastor." When her husband returned to the city, he did not follow his usual custom, of going first to the store, but came directly to the house. Mrs. S. said to him: "I am afraid you will not believe what has taken place in the family, during your absence, if I tell you." He replied: "I am prepared to believe anything; for my mental exercises were such, while I was away, that I knew that something had taken place, and I came directly to the house, without going to the store, that I might learn what had occurred." And this was the beginning of a precious revival of religion.

It is needless to multiply these illustrations, as the

experience of earnest Christians given to labor and to prayer, abounds in them.

Christ stood in the light, which my eye could not see,
But a bright ray passed down from his spirit to me;
Wherever I wandered, 'twas with me, and when
I prayed for a soul, it shed light on it then.
Though I did not see it, and went on in pain,
Though the soul did not feel it, and knew not its gain,
Still it never departed, 'twas fixed to the spot;
I moved from the place, but it changed not.
"I touch through thy hand," said the Savior to me,
"And that which I touch shall never get free.
My hold, though it be but impalpable ray,
Shall enlighten that soul till I usher in day.
The day of salvation must come to the heart,
Which has ever been touched; the lowliest part—
E'en the hem of my garment—the humblest thing
That belongs unto me, this great virtue doth bring.
Art thou, then, a member, and dost thou not know
That wherever thou goest, I surely there go;
That the work that thou doest is not solely thine own?
It is mine, and I never will leave it undone.
Go, touch, then, the sinner—go whisper my word,
Though thou canst not see me, I'm there," saith the Lord.

—*Extracted from "The Two Dreams."*

CHAPTER XVII.

PARENTAL PRAYERS.

In every age the power of parental prayer has been signally illustrated. One might well expect this to be the fact, in view of the nature of the family-institution, its basal relation to church and state, the special covenants and promises made in the Bible to parental faithfulness, and the design of prayer as part of God's moral system. But faith is strengthened by particular historical instances, as well as by general considerations. Let us note some of them.

Augustine and his Mother, Monnica. The famous church-father, Augustine, has immortalized the piety and faith of his mother Monnica. He grew up, in Carthage, a young man of genius and of strong passions. The latter led him into sensual excesses, and intellectual pride carried him into the heresy of the Manicheans. His mother, a devoted Christian, mourned with deepest grief over the sins and errors of her gifted son, and ceased not to pray for his conversion, day and night. Augustine affectingly sets forth the facts in his penitential "Confessions," where he says: "And thou sentest thy hand from above, and drewest my soul out of that profound darkness; my mother, thy faithful one, weeping to thee for me, more than mothers weep the bodily deaths of their children. For she, by that faith and spirit which she had from thee, discerned the death wherein I lay, and thou heardest her, O Lord; thou heardest her, and didst not despise her tears, which streaming down watered the ground under her eyes in every place where she prayed. Yea, thou heardest her; for whence was that dream whereby thou comfortedst her?" The dream was a vision of her son symbolically represented as coming to the same position of faith and life as herself.

Years passed, however, during which his case seemed to be desperate; for he writes: "Almost nine years passed, in which I wallowed in the mire of that deep pit and the darkness of falsehood, oft essaying to rise, but dashed down the more grievously. All which time, that chaste, godly and sober widow (such as thou lovest), now cheered with hope, yet no whit relaxing in her weeping and mourning, ceased not at all hours of her devotion to bewail my case unto thee." His mother besought a bishop to argue with him; but the bishop saw that he was too opinionated and puffed up, to be won in that way, and therefore said to Monnica: "Let him alone awhile; only pray God for him; he will of himself, by reading, find out what that error is, and how great its impiety." And when she still urged her point, he said: "Go thy ways, and God bless thee; for it is not possible that the son of these tears should perish." Which answer, Augustine says, she took as if it had sounded from heaven.

But now came a trial of her faith, and also an illustration of the unexpected ways in which God answers prayer. For Augustine announced his intention to remove to Rome; of which he thus writes: "So why I went hence, and went thither, thou knowest, O God, yet showedst it neither to me, nor to my mother who grievously bewailed my journey, and followed me as far as the sea. * * * And yet refusing to return without me, I scarcely persuaded her to stay that night in a place hard by our ship, where was an Oratory (a place of prayer) in memory of the blessed Cyprian. That night, I privily departed; but she remained in weeping and prayer, with so many tears, but asking of thee that thou wouldst not suffer me to sail. * * * For she loved to have me with her, as all mothers do, but much more than most; and she knew not how great joy thou wast about to work for her out of my absence."

At Rome, he taught rhetoric, and soon passed to Milan in the same profession, where he came into personal friendship with the celebrated Ambrose, under whose preaching he was converted from Manichean error, after many internal struggles to overcome his evil habits. He was, with his friend Alypius, when the final decision was made, and they both joined in it. "Then," writes Augustine, "we went in to my mother [she had followed him to Milan] and told her, relating in order how it took place. Then did she leap for joy, and triumph, and bless thee, who art able to do more than we ask or think." May it not be well said, that

Monnica had travailed in birth for her son, spiritually as well as physically? And what mother may not draw encouragement from her example to pray with faith for the conversion of children? And who can tell what honor God will put upon parental importunity and perseverance? Monnica's prayers saved Augustine, and Augustine's influence on the Christian church has been scarcely second to that of any uninspired man; for not only has he been (with some errors) authority for much that has been good in the Romish church, but he impressed the minds of Luther, Melanchthon, Calvin, Knox and other Protestant reformers more than did any other author.

THE SOURCE OF PARENTAL FAITH. Many, who are content with a superficial piety, and have no deep earnestness for the salvation of their children, cannot understand how it is that some parents have assured faith and put forth prevailing prayer. It is through the indwelling of the Holy Spirit in truly consecrated souls, by reason of which they realize the necessity of conversion, are filled with intense longings for the salvation of their children, and are enabled to plead with broad intelligence God's covenant and promises. Rev. C. G. Finney in his lecture on "The Spirit of Prayer" well remarks: "Thus it often happens, when professors of religion are praying for their children. Sometimes they pray, and are in darkness and doubt, feeling as if there were no foundation for faith, and no special promises for the children of believers. But while they have been pleading, God has shown them the full meaning of some promise, and their soul has rested on it, as on the mighty arm of God. I once heard of a widow who was greatly exercised about her children, till this passage was brought powerfully to her mind: 'Leave thy fatherless children with me, and I will preserve them alive.' She saw it had an extended meaning, and she was enabled to lay hold on it, as it were, with her hands, and then she prevailed in prayer, and her children were converted. The Holy Spirit was sent into the world by the Savior, to guide *his people*, and instruct them, and bring things to their remembrance, as well as to convince the world of sin."

View of Rev. Howard Crosby, D. D., LL.D. A lady in New York City, who attended the "Annual Maternal Meeting," in February, 1864, made these notes of the remarks of Rev. Dr. Crosby, who addressed the mothers present. "He said he believed the conversion of children rested in the hands of parents, and it was according to their faith. In dedicating our children to God, we were required to believe that God accepted them and would honor his covenant. Faith honored God, and if we clung to the covenant, even though we failed in many particulars in training, our children would be saved. He knew two families in this city; was on intimate terms with them both. Each had brought up a large number of children, surrounding them with similar religious influences. In one family not a child was as yet converted; in the other, every child had grown up to be strong in Christ.

In conversing with the mother of the first-named family, a few months since, on the subject of her children's salvation, he referred her to God's promises. She replied: 'Oh yes; I know he has given these promises; *but there are so many exceptions!*' 'Ah Madam,' said he, 'here is the secret of your children's condition out of Christ.' The father of the other family was once met in the street, walking with four little boys, by a friend, who said to him, 'When you look at those little ones, and think of their future, don't you feel anxious?' 'No,' replied the father, 'I *know* they will all be saved, and, besides this, I know they will all be converted in childhood.' And they were."

Two Mothers. Harlan Page, writing to his parents of revival-incidents in 1831, said: "A case occurred last week of special encouragement to praying parents. At the close of the afternoon exercises, a meeting for religious inquirers was held in the lecture room, and a few professors, who lived at a distance, stayed in the church, till the evening service. Among them were two mothers who, though strangers to each other, agreed to go to a retired pew, and spend the season in prayer. As the question arose, what they should pray for, one said, 'I have a daughter, who has no hope.' The other replied, 'So have I an only daughter, and she is now in the inquiry-meeting, and we will pray for them.' They kneeled, and while they were still praying, one of the daughters came, found her mother, and, as soon as she could do it, without interrupting her, took her by the hand, saying, 'O my mother, I hope I have found Christ to be precious.' They all knelt again in prayer, and offered their united thanksgiving to God. The other daughter was hopefully converted on the following day."

A Son's Account. From Rev. C. B. Crane, D. D., pastor of the South Baptist Church, of Hartford, Ct., the author has received the following interesting account of the answer given to his father's prayers and faith:

"In the spring of 1835, I entered Hamilton College, New York, full of worldly ambition, but a stranger to the grace of God. On a certain Sunday, near the end of the term, though there was no special religious interest in the college, I was impressed so profoundly, by the love of Christ for sinners, that I at once devoted myself to his service. I promised not only to be his disciple, but, also, to give myself to the ministry of his word. Yet I had entered Hamilton College solely for the reason that, under Theodore Dwight, then at the head of its law school, I might qualify myself for the legal profession. And it was to me the wonder of wonders, that I could so readily surrender what had been the purpose of my life, and consecrate myself to a work which I had well nigh abhorred. In thus readily changing the plan of my life, I was conscious of no struggle. I was borne onward as a vessel is impelled by the tide.

"My father, a calm, well-balanced, and thoughtful man, was then pastor of the church in the neighboring village of Cassville. In reply to my letter announcing my purpose to live the Christian life, and to enter upon the Christian ministry, and my desire to unite myself with his church, on a baptismal profession of my faith, to my very great surprise, he expressed no surprise at all. For, as he afterwards related to me, a day or two before the eventful Sunday above mentioned, as he was riding, alone, in the round of his pastoral calls, his whole soul was drawn out in prayer to God, that I might become a Christian man and a Christian minister. As he prayed, his desire rose to almost an agony of earnestness; when suddenly he gained the assurance that his prayer was granted. And he awaited my next letter in confident expectation that its contents would be what they were.

"Here is a case which, I am sure, will allow no rationalistic explanation. The 'nervous excitement' theory of revivals and conversion is not apposite. One man, so little given to fanaticism as to be almost cold-blooded, is praying, at a distance, for another man of a like temper. And the second man, in a college where the state of religion is unusually unpromising, obtains an experience which is the exact answer to the prayer."

A Family Experience. Rev. A. S. Kedzie, of Dowagiac, Mich., furnishes a narrative of the steady influence of parental prayer through a series of years. Having described his father's prayerful character and household piety, as exhibited in the commencement of a new settlement in Michigan, he continues thus:

"Two years after our settlement in Deerfield, my father died. His children then were all under sixteen years of age. For my mother to take his place, as the religious instructor of the family, was a great trial; but her husband's faith was in her, and she would not stand in the way of answers to her husband's prayers. Her timidity could not do this in the presence of the hired men; so she detained the children after breakfast, and called them in before tea, and had family worship, in the absence of the hired men. So mother went on for a year. Then a 'four days' meeting' was held at Ypsilanti. Mother took my oldest brother to the meeting, and the confident expectation of the family was, that he was to be converted. The case was stated, that a widow had brought her eldest son forty miles, to be converted. Prayer was offered in his and her behalf. When they returned, we did not dare ask James if he was a Christian; but we knew the question would be answered when the time came for family worship. After tea, mother brought out the old family Bible, and asked James to take his father's place, in conducting family worship, which he promptly did. We younger boys preserved our gravity till the close, when we scud to the barn, and screamed with delight, chiefly from sympathy with our mother.

"Other 'four days' meetings' were held at Monroe and elsewhere, and to these, one after another of the children went, with the same expectation on the part of the family, and with the same result. And our mother was spared in life, till she found answer to her own and her husband's prayers, and to see her five sons and two daughters members of evangelical churches; three of the sons sustaining official relations, one as a ruling elder in a Presbyterian Church, one as a pastor in a Congregational Church, and one as a class-leader in a Methodist Church."

To this narrative Mr. Kedzie appends this true remark: "Here is illustration of the commonest office and the largest work of prayer. Little provision is made to justify prayer to the skeptic, by frequent, startling, visible, and undeniable issue of prayer in answers, which, in silencing the skeptic, would foster fanaticism in our weak nature. Instead, in millions of hearts it keeps alive the sense of spiritual things lying back of sense. In prayer, these hearts seek right adjustmont to those spiritual forces, and so it serves vaster interests than skepticism can comprehend."

Two Mothers. A quiet, steady faith, leading in the family to persistent and united prayer for spiritual results, receives a sure reward, as the following brief narative by Rev. Burdett Hart, of Fair Haven, Ct., proves:

"Two mothers, the only Christians in their households, most excellent ladies of strong faith and of efficient works, *agreed to pray*, on a certain hour of each day, for their husbands and children, *till they should be converted*. They did so pray, and their lives harmonized ever with their prayers. One by one, their husbands and children were *all* converted. Those husbands became efficient and esteemed officers (deacons) in their respective churches. One of the children became a minister of the gospel, and others were active and benevolent supporters of the cause of Christ. The mothers deemed that their prayers were answered."

A Praying Father in Scotland. "*The* (London) *Christian*" newspaper gives, on the authority of Rev. J. H. Wilson, of Edinburgh, an interesting account to the following purport: A pious girl in Edinburgh observed in the street, another girl, in charge of some children, who seemed sad; and she ventured to ask whether she was a Christian. "Who bade you ask that?" was the reply. "The Lord bade me." "The Lord?" she said: "I have been praying that, if there is a God in heaven, he would send some one to speak to me about my soul." She explained that she was from Aberdeen, had accompanied her mistress to Edinburgh on a visit, and had been deeply impressed by a sermon she had heard from Dr. Bonar. Maggie, who had spoken to her, not being very competent to instruct, gave her at parting these words of Jesus: "Him that cometh unto me, I will in no wise cast out." Two days later she came to Maggie, to announce that she had "found Jesus;" and not long after brought her sister, when the three had a little prayer meeting, and the sister, too, went away rejoicing in hope."

And what lay back of all this? *A father's prayers!* For Maggie soon received this letter: "*Dear Miss*

M——: You will perhaps think me rather forward in writing to you, but I feel as if my heart would burst with gratitude for the kindness you have shown to my daughters, in being the means of leading them to the Savior. I have long prayed for them both, and when they left here to go to Edinburgh, I prayed that the good Lord would save them both, before they came back. He has heard my prayer. On the same day that you spoke to Mary, I was ill in bed; and as I prayed for them, I felt the preciousness of the text: 'Him that cometh unto me, I will in no wise cast out.' You can, perhaps, fancy my joy, when by the next post, came a letter to tell me that Mary had found Jesus from that very text. Dear Miss M——, I cannot thank you enough, but the Lord will reward you for the joy you have brought to an old father's heart. You will excuse the writing; I am well nigh seventy years old. I have only one thing to ask you; if you get a holiday in summer, come and see poor old Davie; you will be made as welcome as the angels in heaven. Mary says you are an orphan, but you will never want a friend, lass, as long as Davie Ferguson breathes the breath of life. And at the judgment you can take my Mary and Jane up to Jesus, and say, 'Here are two that, by the Spirit's help, I led to thee.' We all send our greatest love to you."

Here was an instance of secret causation. To human view, the events, in Edinburgh afforded by their connection a satisfactory explanation of the result reached. But a hidden cause lay back of them, known to God, though unsuspected by others. A sick father's earnest prayer was ascending in Aberdeen, while the child was being reached savingly in Edinburgh.

A Mother's Confidence. An instance of that assured expectation which sometimes supervenes upon long-continued, importunate supplication—which is not the fruit of our volition, or of our voluntary faith, but is an impression born of the Spirit, apparently, as a prophecy of the coming blessing—was mentioned in the daily prayer meeting at Cincinnati, during the revival season of 1857–8. Mr. Shipley, the leader of the meeting, related the case of a mother who had prayed for her son, for many years. He grew up to maturity, went abroad, and had lately come back from an eastern city, where there had been a great revival, but without having been himself a subject of it. He told his mother of a number of persons who had been converted, but said nothing to her of himself. After he had retired, her soul being burdened with intense desire for his salvation, she took the Bible, approached his bedside, told him her feelings and the assurance she had that he would be converted that night, read a chapter suited to the circumstances, offered a prayer of intense earnestness in his behalf, and bade him good night, saying that she would greet him a happy Christian in the morning. No sooner had she left the room, than he was overwhelmed with conviction, and his bed seemed as if on fire. He arose and knelt down to pray, and his eye fell on the open Bible, and the chapter which his mother had been reading. He read it again, and spent the night in a mental struggle, which resulted in his submission to God, with joyful hope in Christ, so that in the morning he met his mother as a changed man. The time had come, when prayer was to prevail, and God gave a premonition of the fact.

A North American Indian Mother. Rev. E. P. Hammond, the well known evangelist, in a conversation with the author, stated the following instance of success in a mother's prayers, of which he had learned just before, in a visit to the British Possessions, on the Pacific coast. In an Indian Sunday School, at Victoria, he found a chiefess, or queen, whose people lived about six hundred miles further north. Seven years before, she had come to Victoria, and had attended an Episcopal church since that time, without any one inviting her to Christ. Passing by a Sunday School, one day, she went in, heard of Jesus as having died for sinners, and ere long put her trust in him. Her joy was such, that she invited her Indian acquaintances to go there, and numbers of them were converted. And now a great burden came upon her heart for her son, the chief, who lived with his tribe, near Fort Simpson. She longed for his conversion, but knew that nothing was likely to affect him up there, with all the tribe about him. So she spent whole nights in prayer, asking that the Lord would send him down to Victoria to be converted. This son was a very hard character, and had even acted the cannibal. She had not seen him for years. How was he to be induced to journey six hundred miles? It seemed hopeless praying; but she persevered. And what was the result? The son took a fancy to go to Victoria, and have a time of carousing; and he made the voyage in a canoe with his wife and his uncle. As soon as his mother saw him, she told him of Jesus, whom she was now loving and serving, and urged him to go to the Indian Sunday School. He disliked it at first, but she brought him there again, still praying for his conversion. He was greatly impressed, when he heard a converted Indian, named Amos, pray. Having learned to read, when he was a boy, his mother had him read to her the fourteenth chapter of John's gospel, and explained to him the way of salvation through Christ. His heart was at last touched and melted, and the cannibal warrior accepted the Savior. Then he begged for a missionary for his tribe, and went home to tell his people of the Lord Jesus. It is said that several hundred were induced to follow his example, and they gave Mr. Pollard, the missionary, a wagon load of idols which they had worshiped. Such were the results following the importunate prayer of a once heathen mother for a still heathen son! Her prevailing faith reminds one strongly of the similar faith and success of the Syro-Phenician mother, when Jesus was upon the earth.

A Burden Rolled off. Mrs. Normand Smith, Jr., of whose happy experience in conducting family worship, at one time, during the absence of her husband, mention has been made in the previous chapter, not many years after that was left a widow, with three young daughters. She says: "I had an uncommon burden for the early conversion of my children. I retired, every evening, to my room, for special prayer on this subject. One night, while I was pleading for covenant blessings upon them, a voice seemed to speak to me: 'If you have evidence that you are a child of God, then you have a right to the blessings of the covenant for your children.' I said: 'Yes, Lord, I am thine,' and then I pleaded for my children. I did not expect an immediate answer, yet it was but a short time, before they were all converted by the quiet leading of the Spirit." And that mother's prayer continued to be answered in the use to which God put these daughters. One became the wife of a minister of Christ; a second was the widely known Mrs. Marshall O. Roberts, of New York city, whose spiritual character and extended Christian influence in a high social position were of such value, in addition to her connection with benevolent institutions and the Ladies' Union Prayer Meeting; and the third has pursued quiet walks of usefulness amid the churches and Christian enterprises of her native city.

HEARD AT LAST. A correspondent of the *Christian at Work*, in the number for August 26, 1875, gives an account of a touching scene of which he was an eye-witness in the army, during the late war. It was after the battle of Gettysburg, and a white-haired old man, in one of the temporary hospitals for the wounded, was seen to speak to a young man of twenty, who was lying in a critical condition on one of the beds. He drew out a small Bible to present to him, when the young man pushed it back with scorn, saying he did not wish to be troubled with it, and had learned, while in the army, that its claims were false; he did not believe a word of it. The old man bowed his head in silent sorrow and prayed, for a moment. Then calling the youth by his name, "John," he reminded him that, after the battle of Bull Run, when the call was made for more troops, he had come home to his mother, (the old man's only sister,) and announced the fact that he had enlisted; and that, after sitting stunned for a few minutes, she broke out into an agonizing prayer that her son's life might be preserved, if possible, and at all events that he might be converted, and his soul be saved. He told him, also, what he had before intended to conceal, that two weeks before that mother had been laid in the grave, leaving, as a dying injunction to her brother, to go to the army, find her boy, and tell him to remember all her words; to say that she had prayed for his salvation seven times a day, since he had left home; and to give him that little Bible, in which she had marked passages for him to read. When the young man heard this, he cried out in anguish, and after a severe struggle of will, gave up his opposition to Christ, and accepted his mother's Savior. Three days after, he died, blessing God for the prayers of a pious mother.

A Son at School. A mother writes how the earnest, parental prayers were answered for her son, when reinforced by those of other pleading saints. The parents sent the son to the educational institution which was established for a time on Lookout Mountain, Tenn., hoping for spiritual as well as intellectual benefit. The mother's narrative says: "One Sabbath, it was agreed by the teachers and some Christian pupils, that he be made the subject of special prayer for his speedy conversion. When the afternoon service was over, this little company retired to a large, flat rock, with the canopy of God's blue heaven over head, and sheltered by the trees his own hand had reared. There they prayed for this one specific object. The ear of him who never slumbereth, when his children cry, had received the request. The evening service came; the student, entirely unconscious of the interest in his behalf, was present as usual. But a power, such as he had never felt before, attended that sermon; and when the service was ended, he was compelled, by the pressure on his spirit, to seek the counsel of one of his religious class-mates, that he might learn what he must do to be saved. The Spirit *that night* answered the prayer of the *afternoon*, and that soul was born into his kingdom. He is now studying for the ministry."

This is a pleasant illustration of the intermingling of the labors and prayers of parents and teachers. In thousands of instances, pious parents have sent their children to school and college, following them with continued supplications to God in their behalf; and then, under the faithful influence of Christian teachers, a religious interest has sprung up in the institution, and the children have written home to gladden the parental heart with the tidings of salvation found!

A Warning; Unsubmissive Prayers. The importance of submission to the superior wisdom of God, when we pray, should be especially heeded by parents, whose natural desires are strong with reference to their children. Rev. Mr. Kilpin, of Exeter, England, once gave this testimony: "I knew a case, in which the minister, praying over a child apparently dying, said: 'If it be thy will, spare this child.' The poor mother's soul yearning, for her beloved, exclaimed: 'It *must* be his will? I cannot bear *ifs*.' The minister stopped. To the surprise of many the child recovered, and the mother, after almost suffering martyrdom by him while a stripling, lived to see him hanged before he was two-and-twenty."

A very striking case is narrated by Dr. Edmund Calamy, in his life, as occurring in a family by the name of Mart. A young son was exceedingly ill, and the parents were so vehement in their prayers, and so unconditional, that a pious woman expostulated; when the father exclaimed: "Let him prove what he will, so he is but spared, I shall be satisfied." He grew up, manifested a most abandoned disposition, consorted with villains, committed gross crime, and was condemned to die. His excesses had previously driven his mother to derangement and suicide. Dr. Calamy went to see him, a few days before his execution, and found him in a most hardened state of mind. He railed at his father, who was present, and scoffed at all religious appeals. In this state of mind he died, and on the day of his execution, his father told Dr. Calamy of the unsubmissive prayer offered so many years before, and said: "This I now see to have been my folly. * * * I read my sin very distinctly in my punishment; but must own that God is righteous in all his ways and holy in all his works."

Other such instances might be given, but these will suffice as a warning against unsubmissive prayers, such as parents are tempted to offer in behalf of children whose lives are in danger. It is a happy fact, that we are always safe in pleading importunately for spiritual blessings in their behalf.

Dear Savior! if these lambs should stray
  Beyond thy blest inclosure's bound,
And lured by worldly joys away,
  Among the thoughtless crowd be found;

Remember still that they are thine;
  That thy dear, sacred name they bear;
Think that the seal of love divine,
  The sign of covenant grace, they wear.

In all their erring, sinful years,
  Oh let them ne'er forgotten be!
Remember all the prayers and tears
  Which made them consecrate to thee.

And when these lips no more can pray,
  These eyes can weep for them no more,
Turn thou their feet from folly's way;
  The wanderers to thy fold restore.

—*Mrs. Hyde.*

CHAPTER XVIII.

PRAYER FOR MINISTERS, CHURCHES AND REVIVALS.

The prayers of Christians naturally sweep a wider circle than that of individual conversions, in which one may have special reason for feeling an interest. Beyond the single soul, beyond the family circle, go out the longing and the petition of the Christian heart, and fasten on the local church with its pastor and other officers, on the universal church with its ministry and membership, and on a world ruined by sin, and needing the application of atoning blood. A blessing must be brought down, and so the anxious Jacobs of the church begin their wrestling, and ere long become prevailing Israels. Sometimes prayer is directed to God, first of all, in behalf of a minister. It may be to obtain one for a vacant church, which greatly needs a spiritual pastor. Then we have a class of cases like that described in the following statement, by Rev. Samuel Wolcott, D. D., of Cleveland, O.

Praying to Obtain a Pastor. Dr. Wolcott writes: "In a church of which I was formerly the pastor, there were three or four ladies, somewhat advanced in years —one of them a widow, whose life had been eventfully associated with the progress of Christ's kingdom in another community — who seemed to have special power in prayer. For years they had kept up a weekly prayer meeting, open to others, though seldom attended by any but themselves. They were sedate and serious, but cheerful; calm, not impulsive; and their evident spirituality was accompanied with a beautiful simplicity of character and transparency of feeling, without the slightest morbid development. They met for prayer during the two weeks I was supplying the vacant pulpit, at the residence of the lady with whom I was staying. I had made up my mind not to encourage any movement toward a call, or to listen to any overture. They knew this, and spread the case before the Lord. They continued in prayer until the assurance came into their hearts, that I should be their pastor. Had I given a negative answer to a call, I should not have been more confident that I was not coming. Had they received an affirmative, their confidence that I would come, would not have been stronger. Had this been a solitary experience, I should lay less stress upon it. But during a ministry of twelve years which succeeded, in which 350 persons were received to the church, and of which the prayers of these godly women were to the last the principal support, I had repeated occasions to notice answers to prayers which were prophetic. I became convinced, that the Most High was in gracious communication with them, and heard and answered their prayers — occasionally revealing to them his purpose, through his Spirit, as clearly as your note before me discloses to me a purpose of your own. * * * I thus came to understand, during my last ministry more fully than before, the meaning of this prayer of faith, as set forth in the New Testament. When the soul comes into perfect accord and sympathy with the Lord Jesus Christ, its affections, desires and petitions fasten upon the same objects, and no other, which engage his own infinite approval and love. The intense longings imparted by the Holy Spirit are accompanied by the Spirit's discernment. Filled with the Spirit, the believer's desires are concentrated upon the objects which are dear to the indwelling Spirit. Thus he asks in Christ's name, and receives; for God is waiting to bestow."

Praying for the Spiritual Baptism of the Pastor. Many a revival in a church has commenced in the earnest prayers of a few brethren or sisters for a new spiritual baptism of the pastor. Sometimes a defect has been noticed in his ministrations; in other instances, there has only been a desire that he might be still further instructed by God himself in the deep things of the Spirit, and that he might be specially prepared for carrying forward a work of power in the community. A case in point has come within the knowledge of the author.

There was in one of our Eastern cities a minister of rare genius, whose discourses had such literary excellence as to attract large and admiring audiences. He was not sensational, in conscious aim and general spirit, but was pure and simple in character and preached the gospel, as he understood it. But he had unusual talent, was of an emotional and poetic temperament, and chiefly interested the people by discussing themes which are on the outskirts of religion, and belong to its morality and esthetics rather than to its central heart and life. The consequence was, that while applauding crowds came, there were few conversions, and there was no deepening of the spiritual life of the church. Thinking sorrowfully over this fact, a few brethren agreed to make the pastor a subject of special private prayer, that the Lord himself would be his teacher. This united prayer was continued for some time, when, one Sunday, the pastor went into his pulpit, and prayed and preached in a manner which astonished his audience, by its gospel-simplicity, its spiritual fervor, its moving pathos and its earnest endeavor to bring men to an instant and full acceptance of an atoning Savior. He told the wondering people, that he had recently experienced so total a change of view and feeling, that it seemed like a second conversion. The old Bible truths had opened to him with a new meaning, and especially the fact that Christ had made an atoning sacrifice for human sin, and that the vilest sinner might be "justified" before God, on repenting of his wickedness, by faith in this finished work and prevailing intercession of the Son of God. All hearts were melted, as they listened, and all eyes filled with tears, and especially did those praying brethren overflow with thanksgiving, as they saw the answer which God had mercifully granted. After that, there was no more feeling that only the intellect was fed. A succession of discourses came, filled with the very marrow of the gospel, and from that day to the present, this minister has been as noted for the spirituality as for the intellectual richness of his preaching. When he subsequently learned of the prayers of that pleading band of brethren, he understood the way in which the Lord had led him, and that the secret of a pulpit of power is a praying church.

Incidentally it is well to notice how much wiser was this conduct of the brethren in question, than if they had begun publicly to criticise the pastor and form a dissatisfied party in the church; or to make him in the church conference meeting the subject of prayers which reflected on his piety and preaching; or to annoy him by sanctimonious exhortations in private, to be repeated afterward to a coterie of self-righteous malcontents. Had they so acted, they might easily have soured their own minds, repelled him from the truth, and split the church into discordant factions. As it was, they brought a blessing upon the pastor, upon themselves, and upon the entire church.

Another Case. Rev. C. G. Finney mentions, in one of his Revival Lectures, a somewhat similar instance. He says: "I knew a case of a minister in ill health, who became depressed and sunk down in his mind, and was very much in darkness, so that he did not feel as if he could preach any longer. An individual of the church was waked up to feel for the minister's situation, and to pray that he might have the

Holy Ghost to attend his preaching. One Sabbath morning, this person's mind was very much exercised, and he began to pray as soon as it was light, and he prayed again and again, for a blessing *that day.* And the Lord, in some way, directed the minister within hearing of his prayer. The person was telling the Lord just what he thought of the minister's situation and state of mind, and pleading, as if he would not be denied, for a blessing. The minister went into the pulpit and preached, and the light broke in upon him, and the word was with power, and a revival commenced that very day.

The connection of prayer with the usual revivals in churches is too familiar to call for evidence. The rule, with scarcely a known exception, is, that prayer of an earnest and importunate character always precedes. It may have been on the part of the church in general; or it may have proceeded from a single persevering suppliant, as in the following instance, communicated by one long in the Christian ministry and of large experience in revivals.

THE RED SCHOOL-HOUSE. Religion was at a very low ebb in a town in Vermont. The discouraged pastor gave notice that the usual weekly prayer meeting in the red school-house would be discontinued, as so few attended. It was in the winter, and a deep snow lay on the ground. There was a praying old lady in the church, who, undismayed by the pastor's notice, and in fact, inspired by it with a new earnestness, took her lantern on the usual evening, plodded her way to the school-house, and there spent an hour in wrestling prayer for a revival. On her way home, being exhausted, she stopped at a good deacon's to rest. Astonished to find her out alone, in such weather and at such an hour, he asked, "Where have you been, mother?" "Why, to the prayer meeting," she replied. "I thought that was given up," said the deacon. "Not at all." "Indeed! Who was there?" "Why, God, the Father, was there; God, the Son, was there; God, the Holy Spirit was there; and unworthy I was permitted to be there! We had a most blessed time, and next week we are to have another meeting." Next week came, the word had been passed around, and the red school-house was crowded with penitent professors of religion, who confessed their past coldness, and renewed their consecration. A revival of great interest followed. Nearly every church has had experience of the more usual relation of united prayer, and perhaps a single instance will suffice as an illustration, condensed from Dr. Wm. Wisner's "Incidents in a Pastor's Life." There had been some special interest in the church of which Dr. Wisner was pastor, but it had soon abated:

"The enemies of religion began to rejoice aloud, that the excitement, as they called it, was over, and only a few young people and children had been affected by it. * * * On the next Sabbath I preached, with an aching heart, from the text, 'The triumphing of the wicked is short.' * * * At the close of the exercises, Monday was appointed as a day of humiliation and prayer; and when it came, it found the whole church with one accord in one place. Christians were deeply humbled under a sense of their sins, and with many tears poured out their agonizing prayer to God, that for his holy name's sake; he would hear the voice of our supplications and revive us again. Tuesday and Wednesday, the little church continued instant in prayer. On Wednesday afternoon, as we were all on our knees, in the parlor of a private house, one of our elders, an old man full of the Holy Ghost, while pleading with sobs and tears for the return of the Blessed Comforter, said in a tone of humble confidence: 'O Lord, open our eyes, that we may see, as thy servants did of old, that there are horses and chariots of fire between us and our enemies, and that they that be for us are more than they that be against us.' * * * * *

"That evening, two or three individuals requested the prayers of God's people; and that night one of the leading physicians in the place obtained comfort from the Lord. The next morning, as we were, a few of us, met at his house for prayer, his wife requested us to pray for a sister of his, who was up stairs, in deep distress of mind. While we were on our knees, praying for her, she came down so full of joy and peace, that she wished us to return thanks to the Lord, for snatching her as a brand from the burning. A new impulse was given to the work. Friday and Saturday were days of much fervency of prayer, and several were brought to submit themselves unto God.

The Sabbath was a solemn day, and, I trust, a day of salvation. On Monday evening, at my meeting of inquiry, the room was crowded with anxious sinners, and two precious souls, we had reason to hope, were in that meeting delivered, from their bondage to Satan.

"The next morning, as I was going into a house, where the man and his wife were the night before convicted of sin, a young man came running across the street, and in great distress threw his arms around me, and besought me to pray for him. I told him, I could not do so there, but I would meet him, in thirty minutes, at Mr. Herricks — a merchant who had recently been converted to Christ. I went into the house where I had intended to visit, and told them they might meet me in half an hour at the place I had appointed for the young man. I went immediately to Mr. H.'s, and told him we would, a few of us, be at his house at nine o'clock, to spend an hour in prayer. I then notified two or three Christians of the meeting thus unexpectedly appointed, and, at nine, we commenced praying with perhaps half a dozen Christians, and four anxious persons. As soon as we began to pray, the Spirit of God seemed to come down with great power, and three of the four anxious persons soon began to rejoice in the Lord. When these things were noised abroad, the multitude came together, and in a short time two good-sized rooms, which opened into each other, were crowded to overflowing; and many who came to see what was doing, went away rejoicing in Christ. At noon, I endeavored to send the people away; but they would not be persuaded to disperse, and the whole day was spent in prayer and religious conversation. That evening, we had a prayer meeting in the court room, which was much crowded, and several there indulged a hope of pardon and eternal life. At nine o'clock, the congregation was dismissed, and we returned home with more of a disposition to pray than sleep.

"Wednesday morning, at nine, the assembly at brother H.'s was so large, that we were obliged to remove to the court house, which was filled to its utmost capacity with Christians and anxious sinners. We remained here, with an hour's intermission, until nine at night, when the congregation was again reluctantly sent away. The next morning, we met at the sanctuary, to observe our annual State Thanksgiving. The house was so greatly crowded at an early hour, that, though it was large, and the aisle supplied with benches, all could not be seated. An awful solemnity pervaded the whole assembly, and for a time the only noise that was heard was the half-suppressed sobs, which now and then escaped from an overburdened soul. Never before had I beheld so solemn an assembly, and never before or since have I felt so deeply the awfulness of the divine presence. I preached from the words: 'Rejoice with trembling,' and never have I felt so much like a dying man preaching to dying men. Through the remainder of the week the court room was crowded from nine in the morning until nine at night, with praying and inquiring souls, and very many of our leading citizens were brought to put their trust in the Lamb of God. The next Sabbath was our communion, and eighty-six persons were received into the church. A pleasing work of grace continued through the winter."

It will be noticed that this revival was born of prayer, and that the special prayer was occasioned by the scoffs of the wicked. This inspired God's people with zeal for his glory, and led to earnest and believing supplication for the outpouring of the Holy Spirit. A multitude of revivals have had a similar origin.

REVIVALS UNDER REV. CHARLES G. FINNEY. Mr. Finney was the most powerful and successful of the revival-preachers during the period from 1825 to 1835. His labors extended, at times, into New England, but were chiefly confined to the state of New York. The work was remarkably thorough, as his preaching was searching, and often destroyed the hopes of those who had been professors of religion for many years. The conviction of sin in the revivals of that period was deep, and the process of conversion sharp-cut and decisive. A distinguishing feature was the prominence given to prayer. Mr. Finney insisted on greater importunity and faith, and almost made Christians feel, that they had never before prayed at all. He assured them that one of the chief stumbling-blocks in the way of the wicked was, that they heard so many prayers, and saw so few answers. Plainly the professed people of God had very little power in prayer, and did not expect to receive the things for which they asked. Some of Mr. Finney's most valuable and influential sermons were on this point. Let the reader turn to his "Lectures on Revivals," and he will find that Lecture IV., is on "Prevailing Prayer"; Lecture V., is on the "Prayer of Faith"; Lecture VI. is on the "Spirit of Prayer," and Lecture VIII. on "Meetings for Prayer." In the first of these he remarks: "Prayer is an essential link in the chain of causes that lead to a revival; as much so as truth is. Some have zealously used truth to convert men, and laid very little stress on prayer. They have preached, and talked, and distributed tracts with great zeal, and then wondered that they had so little success. And the reason was, that they forgot to use the other branch of the means, effectual prayer. They overlook the fact, that truth *by itself* will never produce the effect, because it will not be believed, without the Spirit of God." The sixth lecture he concludes thus: "Now will you give yourselves up to prayer, and live so as to have the spirit of prayer, and have the Spirit with you all the time? Oh for a praying church! I once knew a minister, who had a revival fourteen winters in succession. I did not know how to account for it, till I saw one of his members get up in a prayer meeting, and make a confession. 'Brethren,' said he, 'I have been long in the habit of praying every Saturday night, till after midnight, for the descent of the Holy Ghost among us. And now, brethren,' and he began to weep, 'I confess that I have neglected it for two or three weeks.' The secret was out. That minister had a praying church." In the other lectures he constantly reverts to this topic. Thus in the thirteenth, on "How Churches can Help Ministers," his fifth point is, that they should pray for them, and he says: "I have seen Christians who would be in an agony, when the minister was going into the pulpit for fear his mind should be in a cloud, or his heart cold, or he should have no unction, and so a blessing should not come. I have labored with a man of this sort. He would pray till he got an assurance in his mind that God would be with me in preaching, and some times he would pray himself sick. I have known the time, when he has been in darkness, for a season, while the people were gathering, and his mind was full of anxiety, and he would go again and again to pray, till finally he would come into the room with a placid face, and say, 'The Lord has come, and he will be with us.' And I do not know that I ever found him mistaken." Probably this was "Father Nash."

A Praying Soul and a Succession of Revivals. In his seventh lecture, on "Being Filled with the Spirit," Mr. Finney states these singular facts: "A pious man in the western part of the state of New York was sick with the consumption. He was a poor man, and sick for years. An unconverted merchant in the place had a kind heart, and used to send him, now and then, some things for his comfort, or for his family. He felt grateful for the kindness, but could make no return, as he wanted to do. At length he determined that the best return he could make would be to pray for his salvation. He began to pray, and his soul kindled, and he got hold on God. There was no revival there, but, by-and-by, to the astonishment of everybody, this merchant came out on the Lord's side. The fire kindled all over the place, and a powerful revival followed, and multitudes were converted. This poor man lingered in this way, for several years, and died. After his death, I visited the place, and his widow put into my hands his diary. Among other things, he says in his diary: 'I am acquainted with about thirty ministers and churches,' and he then goes on to set apart certain hours in the day and week, to pray for each of these ministers and churches, and also certain seasons for praying for the different missionary stations. Then followed, under different dates, such facts as these: 'To-day, (naming the date,) I have been enabled to offer what I call the prayer of faith for the outpouring of the Spirit on —— church, and I trust in God there will soon be a revival there.' Under another date: 'I have, to-day, been able to offer what I call the prayer of faith for such a church, and trust there will soon be a revival there.' Thus he had gone over a great number of churches, recording the fact that he had prayed for them in faith, that a revival might soon prevail among them. Of the missionary stations, if I recollect aright, he mentions in particular the mission in Ceylon. I believe the last place mentioned in his diary, for which he offered the prayer of faith, was the place in which he lived. Not long after noticing these facts in his diary, the revival commenced, and went over the region of country, nearly, I believe, if not quite, in the order in which they had been mentioned in his diary; and in due time news came from Ceylon, that there was a revival of religion there. The revival in his own town did not commence till after his death. Its commencement was at the time when his widow put into my hands the document to which I have referred. She told me he was so exercised in prayer during his sickness, that she often feared he would pray himself to death. The revival was exceedingly great and powerful in all the region, and the fact that it was about to prevail had not been hidden from this servant of the Lord."

This last remark gives the true explanation of the series of facts. "The secret of the Lord is with them that fear him," and the Holy Spirit, having a work of salvation to perform, inspires his people to pray for the very blessing which he is about to bestow. All things concur and co-operate in the wise and comprehensive plans of God.

A Scotch Revival two and a half Centuries Since. This connection of remarkable outpourings of the Holy Spirit with specially earnest prayer is no new experience of the church. From the day of Pentecost onward, this has been God's method. Let us take an illustration from Scotland. Fleming, in his work entitled, "The Fulfilling of Scriptures," remarks: "I must also mention that solemn communion at the Kirk-of-Schotts, June 30, 1630; at which time, there was so convincing an appearance of God, and down-pouring of the Spirit—even in an extraordinary way, that did follow the ordinances, especially that sermon on Monday, June 21, with a strange, unusual motion on the hearers, when a great multitude were convened of divers ranks—that it was known, which I can speak on sure ground, near five hundred had at that time a discernible change wrought on them, of whom most proved lively Christians, afterwards. It was the sowing of the seed through Clyddisdale, so as many of the most eminent Christians in that country could date, either their conversion, or some remarkable confirmation in their case, from that day. And truly this was the more remarkable, that one, after much reluctance, by special and unexpected providence, was called to preach that sermon on the Monday, which then was not usually practiced; and *that night before, by most of the Christians there, was spent in prayer;* so that the Monday's work might be discerned as a convincing return of prayer." "Ask, and ye shall receive," has always been the law of God's kingdom, and the privilege of Christ's household.

Recent Revivals. The revivals of the last twenty years have been numerous, and have pervaded the United States, Ireland, Scotland, and England. They have followed the usual law of divine providence in the furtherance of good causes, to-wit: a development of new methods and fresh sources of influence. Thus the revivals of a generation since were chiefly the result of God's blessing on the preaching of ministers — pastors and evangelists. But now, an impetus has been given to lay agency, and to conference meetings, instead of preaching services. This was a signal characteristic of the great refreshing which began after the financial crisis of 1857. The establishment of the Fulton Street Noon Prayer Meeting, in New York, in September of that year, and its marked success, led to the establishment of a multitude of similar meetings in all parts of the land. Those in the principal cities soon overflowed the largest churches and halls. Besides these central and union noon-day services, thousands of churches commenced special meetings for prayer in their own sanctuaries; which were continued for weeks and months, and resulted in thousands of conversions. The value of this experience lay in the fact, that it brought out the lay-element, in prayer and exohrtation, and showed that revivals needed no elaborate machinery, or learned pulpit effort; but that God would bless earnest and prayerful endeavor, by whomsoever put forth. From that time to the present, prayer has been more largely relied on, and the meetings have assumed a primitive simplicity of type, which, properly guarded, augurs well for the purity of our religion, theologically and experimentally. The grand test is working power. No system of doctrine, preaching and worship which fails to develop prayer, faith, spiritual labor, and success in converting souls from sin, can long have the face to claim to be the religion of Jesus Christ. And with such lack of result, the greater the exclusiveness, the more preposterous the claim will be pronounced. There can not fail to be a deep impression upon the church, and upon the world, in favor of prayer as an instrument of power, when it is seen what marked results come from the simplest means.

Prayer and the Irish Revival of 1859. There is not space to reproduce the facts which occupy a volume of nearly 500 pages, from the pen of Rev. William Gibson, who, being Professor in Queen's College, Belfast, and Moderator of the Presbyterian General Assembly, and having previously visited this country to ascertain the character of the revival here, was specially qualified to treat of the subject. He makes the part which prayer bore in the introduction of those spiritual triumphs duly prominent. Thus, of the General Assembly of 1858, he says: "It devolved on the convener, the Rev. Dr. Kirkpatrick, of Dublin, to advert to the extraordinary display of divine grace with which the American churches had been visited during the preceding winter, and the accounts of which had been already widely circulated throughout the community. On the reception of his report, the Assembly resolved to devote a portion of its sittings to special conference and prayer, with reference to this great spiritual movement. The season thus set apart was one of peculiar solemnity and sacredness; and when one after another of the fathers rose up in his place, to tender his paternal counsels, and when the voice of praise and supplication ascended afterwards to heaven, all hearts were touched as by a common sympathy, while from the reigning harmony and fervor many fondly cherished the expectation of a time of more abundant blessing." The acknowledged birth-place of the revival was in the prayer meeting established in a Sabbath school at Tannybrake, County of Antrim. Among others who were associated in the Sabbath school prayer meeting, were the four young men whose names have been much before the public in connection with the subsequent revival. As they were some miles apart, they resolved to meet at a central place, and, for this purpose, chose an old school-house, where were conducted the exercises which have been generally regarded as the origin of the revival. "For a few months," says Mr. Gibson, "they had to walk by faith. * * * They wrestled on. They prevailed. Surely, when God's set time is come—when he intends signally to answer prayer—he disposes the supplicant to plead, and with growing anxiety to plead on, till the blessing is secured." One of the ministers, in whose congregation a powerful revival-work was enjoyed, had, a few weeks before, recorded this in his diary: "I am beginning to have more hope in prayer than I had. What I have heard of the Lord's wonderful doings in America, and in this land, and all, apparently, in answer to believing prayer, causes me to hope that God will answer my earnest prayers for the outpouring of his Spirit here." And when one comes to read an account of the details of the wide-spread work, he finds prayer interlaced with everything. The leading exercises in many of the places were prayer meetings, and the single cases of answer to prayer were many and marked. The coming of the revival to each place, or district, seems to have been preceded by earnest pleading on the part of certain souls, whom God inspired with the spirit of supplication. In the concluding chapter, Mr. Gibson says: "From first to last, the work has been, to a great extent, a record of answered prayer." During 1859, about 10,000 communicants were added to 306 Presbyterian churches, in Ireland, as the first fruits of the revival.

THE SCOTCH REVIVAL OF 1859–61. The same tidal wave of religious interest passed from Ireland to Scotland. Its history cannot here be written. A good summary of events will be found in Rev. Dr. S. Irenæus Prime's "Five Years of Prayer." What is now in point is, to notice the distinct connection of the revival with special prayer offered by God's people. In reference to the beginning of the work at Glasgow, the *Scottish Guardian* said: "Our readers are aware that ever since the news of the great revival in America reached Scotland, prayer meetings for the special purpose of imploring a similar blessing have been held in Glasgow, as well as in other places. The intelligence which has reached us recently leaves no room to doubt that these prayers have been heard. * * * God has been pleased, from the very beginning of these prayer meetings, to use them as the means of convert-

16*

ing souls and quickening his own people. * * * Christian men and women appear to be attaining to greater faith in the power of prayer." Of the work at Port Glasgow, it was said: "We have been visited here with blessed times of refreshing. We had long been praying much for the gracious manifestation of God's presence and power among us, and when the intelligence of the revival in Ireland reached us, this gave a new impulse to our faith and prayer. * * * One feature of this work is a deep conviction of sin. * * * Another feature of the work is exceeding earnestness in prayer." We are further told that "in Annan the Week of Prayer (the first week in January, 1861,) was observed with great solemnity, and earnest supplications went up to the throne of grace for the outpouring of the Spirit. The answer was very speedy." Of the parish of Kirkmahoc we read: "Every word that was said to them seemed to have no effect, and we felt it high time to invoke God's blessing. After engaging in prayer, we recommenced the inquiry-meeting: we were doing something, but not what ought to be done. A second and a third time we engaged in prayer, and after this, every word seemed to be winged with the power of the Spirit of God." Rev. H. H. MacGill, Secretary of the United Presbyterian church, in a published statement declared: "The invariable testimony of the brethren is, that a spirit of prayerfulness preceded the revival. In Burghead, one of the fishing villages in the North, the first special fact noticed as preceding the revival was the following: that at a prayer meeting held in the house of a Christian woman laid for the last thirty years on a bed of affliction, the burden of the prayers, at her request, was for the outpouring of the Spirit for the quickening of God's people and the conversion of sinners. Ere long, the careless fishing people were awakened, and many of them converted to the Lord." In the report on the revival made to the Free Church Assembly, Rev. Dr. Woods said: "I scarcely know of any instance where the awakening has not been preceded by the spirit of prayer and expectation. * * * There was increased attendance at prayer meetings, and an increase in the exercise of prayer in our social circles, in our families, and in secret. And when the Lord had thus prepared us for receiving the blessing, it pleased him to pour it out very remarkably, and very abundantly."

THE REVIVAL IN WALES. At the same time, a similarly mighty work, involving most thrilling incidents, was going on in Wales, as the result of which, in a single year, there were accessions to the churches of about thirty-five thousand members. All agree that the grand instrumentality was prayer. Rev. John Venn, the historian of the revival, says: "Without disparaging the pulpit, or in any way degrading the offices instituted by Christ in his church, it must strike all, that prayer, oral, united prayer, has been greatly honored of God, as a means of commencing and extending the present movement. The exact place of prayer, in the great machinery of moral means, has been better understood, and the belief in its efficacy has been more fully acted upon now than at any former time." Another writer says: "We expected that the great outpouring of the Spirit would come by means of preaching. It was so in former days — it may be so again — and it is so now to some extent, * * * but still it is quite clear that the Holy Spirit's influence, at the present time, is communicated by means of prayer." Still another says: "I am persuaded that the means blessed of God to create and carry on the revival in most places, if not in all, is PRAYER. You can trace its origin and progress in every locality to prayer." Yet another thus testifies: "Prayer meetings have been the principal means with us of awakening the churches. In many places union prayer meetings have been very useful in drawing the public mind toward the great question of salvation." And so the universal statement goes. God is plainly teaching his people a partly forgotten lesson as to the power of prayer for spiritual blessings on churches and communities.

THE WEEK OF PRAYER. Reference was made in one of the Scotch accounts to the fact that in one place the revival followed speedily upon the Week of Prayer. No sign of the times is more marked than the establishment of this custom, first suggested by a company of missionaries in India, of observing the opening week of each year as a season of special prayer for the progress of religion in the world. The request was very gradually assented to; but now the custom is well-nigh universal among evangelical denominations, and the effect has been every way note-worthy. In proportion to its earnest observance there has been awakened increased desire and faith, and revivals have been more frequent and prevalent, commencing very commonly with the exercises of that week.

Day of Prayer for Colleges. About fifty years since, Christian men were led to think of the great number of students in the colleges of this country, of the vast influence which they would soon exert upon the character of the land, of the peculiar facilities offered by their isolated condition for religious awakenings, and of the readiness of God to hear united prayer for specific objects. So they first selected each Sunday morning, and then agreed to observe the last Thursday of February, as an annual concert of prayer for the reviving of religion in colleges and kindred institutions. From that time, began a series of more or less powerful revivals in our American colleges. Prayer increased more and more, and with prayer came earnest desire and appropriate labor. Faith and works wrought together, and the blessing came. The Secretary of the College Society, Rev. Theron Baldwin, D. D., thus speaks of the results, after a series of years: "From 1820 to 1823 inclusive, there were revivals in fourteen different institutions; in 1824 and 1825, in five different colleges; in 1826, in six; in 1827, in four; in 1828, in five; and in 1831, in nineteen colleges, resulting in the hopeful conversion of between three hundred and fifty and four hundred students. In one of the colleges the revival commenced on the very day of the concert. In 1832, some few institutions were blessed with the effusions of the Spirit, and also in 1833. A larger number were blessed with revivals in 1834, and no less than eighteen in 1835, and between one and two hundred students were hopefully brought into the kingdom of Christ. It has been estimated that fifteen hundred students were made the hopeful subjects of grace in thirty-six different colleges, from 1820 to 1835 inclusive." It may be added, that the experience of the succeeding forty years has been similar to that just given, though the statistics are not at hand.

THE LABORS OF MR. MOODY ABROAD. There is not space left to describe such an extensive work as that recently wrought in connection with the preaching of Mr. D. L. Moody and the singing of Mr. I. D. Sankey. But from beginning to end, it has been a signal reward of faith, and an answer to prayer. Before his departure for England, Mr. Moody earnestly sought divine guidance, and received an assurance that he was called to labor for a time in that distant field. Hence his famous reply, when asked why he was going thither: "Ten thousand souls for Jesus!" And God has given him these, apparently, many times over. And the minute history of his labors,—especially in the disappointing circumstances of their beginning, as to the expected human helpers, and the consequent necessity to fall back on God, in earnest prayer—reveals the same subsequent spirit. So also does the manner in which the exercises were conducted in all the places where he labored, in Scotland, Ireland and England—prayer being everywhere put forward as the chief reliance. Indeed, pages might be occupied with the striking incidents, in response to prayer, which occurred in preparation for the meetings and in connection with the exercises, by which God removed serious obstacles, and converted hundreds and thousands of souls to himself.

PROF. THOMAS C. UPHAM'S VIEW. An excellent summing up of these facts, as illustrative of Bible-truth, is furnished by the following extract from Professor Upham's "Divine Union": "The soul which is fully in the experience of divine union will harmonize perfectly with the desires and emotions of the divine mind. If, for instance, there are soon to be especial operations of the Holy Spirit, and if souls are to be enlightened and restored to God, the preparations for such events will always exist first in the mind of God himself. It is not possible that such things should exist accidentally. They are the developments, coming in their appropriate order and under appropriate circumstances, of the divine thought, of the divine feeling. But if it be true that the heaving of the billows, whether gently or more powerfully, will first show themselves in the great ocean of thought and feeling, it will also be true that they will excite a corresponding movement in all smaller streams and fountains which are in alliance with them. In other words, God, in all good works, moves first; and the minds of his people (all those who come within the particular sphere of the movement) move in harmony with him. If God desires a particular thing to take place within their particular sphere of feeling and action, the desire of the Infinite mind sympathetically takes shape and develops itself in the finite mind; and the unspoken desire of the Father shows itself in the uttered prayer of the children. As in nature a small moaning sound of the winds often precedes a wide and powerful movement, so the sighing in the bosoms of the finite denotes an approaching movement of far greater power in the Infinite."

When Jehovah turned again,
  Zion's sore captivity,
Like the dreamers of a dream,
  Seemed one in that day to be;
Filled with laughter was our mouth,
  And our tongue with melody.

Spake our heathen lords: Great things
  Hath Jehovah for them done;
Great things hath he done for us,
  We will joy in him alone.
Turn our bondage, Lord, like streams
  Dried up by the southern sun.

They shall reap their fields in joy,
  Who in sowing weep and mourn;
He that goeth forth in tears
  With his seed, shall yet return,
In the gladness of his heart,
  With his sheaves of harvest corn.

—*Bonar's Version of Psalm cxxxi.*

CHAPTER XIX.

PRAYER FOR CHARITABLE INSTITUTIONS.

THE spread of Christianity has everywhere been accompanied by the establishment of hospitals, asylums, and other charitable institutions for the relief of human distress. As nothing could be more harmonious than this result with the spirit of the gospel, and as nothing also could more favorably impress the world with its divine origin, so it might be expected to give occasion to special and successful prayer. And such has been the fact.

FRANKE AND THE ORPHAN HOUSE AT HALLE. Augustus Herman Franke was a minister in Halle, Germany, on a small salary, and with no property but his books. He conceived the project of an orphan asylum for the children of the poor. In due time it was opened, and he had several hundred children depending on him for food, clothing and education, and no other resources, but the voluntary gifts of the benevolent. When his treasury was utterly exhausted, he was in the habit of reporting the fact to the Lord, and asking for the needed aid. This was sure to be given, and it will aid faith to hear a part of his testimony:

"In the month of April, 1696, our funds were exhausted, and I knew not where to look for the necessary supplies for the next week. This caused me great distress; when some person, who is yet unknown to me, put into my hands a thousand dollars, for the orphans. At another time, when our stores were exhausted, we laid our case before the Lord, and had scarcely finished our prayer, when there was a knock at my door, and a letter was handed in, with fifty dollars in gold. Twenty dollars soon after came, which fully supplied our wants, and we were taught that God will often hear prayer almost before it is offered. In the month of October, 1698, I sent a ducat to a poor and afflicted woman, who wrote me that it came to hand at a time when she greatly needed it, and she prayed God to give my poor orphans a heap of ducats for it. Soon after, I received from one friend two ducats; from another, twenty-five; from two others, forty-three; and from Prince Paul, of Wurtemberg, five hundred. When I saw all this money on the table before me, I could not but think of the prayer of the poor woman, and how literally it had been fulfilled.

"In February, 1699, I was almost entirely without funds, though much was needed for the daily wants of the children and other poor. In this state of difficulty, I comforted myself with the promise of the Lord Jesus: 'Seek ye first the kingdom,' etc. When I had given out the last of our money, I prayed to the Lord. As I left my room, to go into the college, I found a student waiting for me, who put seventy dollars into my hands. Soon afterwards, we were in the greatest want, but I trusted in the Lord, and determined to go to my closet and spread my wants before him. I arose to go to my closet, and, while on my way, a letter was put into my hands from a merchant, informing me that he had received a check for a thousand dollars, to be paid me for the orphan house. How forcibly did I feel the truth of the promise: 'Before they call, I will answer, and, while they are yet speaking, I will hear.' I had now no reason to ask for assistance, but I went to my closet and praised the Lord for his goodness. At another time, the superintendent of the building came to me, and asked if I had received any money for the payment of the laborers. 'No,' said I; 'but I have faith in God.' Scarcely had I uttered these words, when some one was announced at the door. On going to him, I found that he had brought me thirty dollars. I returned to the study, and asked the superintendent how much money he needed. He replied: 'Thirty dollars.' 'There they are,' said I. At another time of great need, I prayed particularly, 'Give us, this day, our daily bread.' I dwelt upon the words, 'this day,' for we needed immediate aid. While I was yet praying, a friend came to my door, and brought me four hundred dollars.

"At one time, I was recounting to a Christian friend some of our remarkable deliverances from want, by which he was so much affected that he even wept. While I was speaking, as if to confirm my statements, I received a letter containing a check for five hundred dollars. At another time, I was in need of a large sum, but did not know where to obtain even ten dollars. The steward came, but, having no money for him, I asked him to come again after dinner, and, in the mean time, gave myself to prayer. When he came, in the afternoon, all I could do was to ask him to come again in the evening. In the afternoon I was visited by a friend, with whom I united in prayer to God. As I accompanied my friend to the door, on his departure, I found the steward standing on one side, and on the other a person, who put into my hands a hundred and fifty dollars. On another occasion, the superintendent began to pay the laborers with only fourteen dollars, but, before he got through, he received enough to complete the payments."

The steward became so accustomed to this experience, that when new straits came, he would remark: "Now we shall have reason, again, to admire the manner in which God will come to our aid." The institution was firmly established, and exists at this day on a grand scale, having sometimes three thousand pupils. As Professor Stowe pertinently remarks, in review of this narrative, "If any one can believe that such a long series of answers to prayer can be accounted for on the ground of accidental coincidences, such a man would scarcely be persuaded though one should rise from the dead."

Louis Harms and His Missions. About the year 1850, Louis Harms became the pastor of the humble

Lutheran church at Hermansburg, Germany, a rural village on the Lüneburger Heath. From spiritual deadness he stirred the whole region into life. He also established a training mission-house, built and sustained a mission-ship, sent out and supported a large number of missionaries, set up a printing press to issue religious books and tracts, published a monthly missionary magazine, and founded local reformatories. In six years, the expenses thus incurred were 115,676 crowns, (a crown being little more than a dollar,) while the receipts were 118,694 crowns. Whence this income? He started with nothing, putting all his reliance on prayer. "I prayed," said he, "fervently to the Lord, laid the matter in his hand, and as I rose up at midnight from my knees, I said in a voice that almost startled me in the quiet room, *Forward now, in God's name!* From that moment there never came a thought of doubt into my mind." The result may be learned by this abridged extract from his own account: "It is wonderful, when one has nothing, and 10,000 crowns are laid in his hand by the dear Lord. I know from whom it all comes. I went to my God, and prayed diligently to him, and received what I needed. To the question, Shall we print? we did not answer, Certainly we can; but we cried to the Lord, Grant it to us. And he granted it; for we immediately received 2,000 crowns, although the thought had not been known to any one; we had only to take and be thankful. A short time ago, I had to pay a merchant, in behalf of the missions 550 crowns, and when the day was near I had only 400. Then I prayed to the Lord Jesus, that he would provide me with the deficiency. On the day before, three letters were brought; one from Schweim with 20, one from Bücksburg with 25, and one from Berlin with 100 crowns. The donors were anonymous. On the evening of the same day, a laborer brought me 10 crowns; so that I had not only enough, but five over. I must tell you what brought tears into my eyes, and confirmed me anew in that word. 'Before they call, I will answer.' A medicine-chest was urgently wanted for the mission. I reckoned up, to see if there was enough left to supply it. Before I had finished, and when I had not yet well begun to commend this matter to the Lord, a letter was brought, in which the anonymous writer stated, that for some time he had been collecting for the mission and had determined to purchase a medicine-chest. The chest accompanied the letter; he only begged it might soon be sent out to the heathen." In 1858 he wrote: "I needed for the mission 15,000 crowns, and the Lord gave me that, and 60 over. This year I needed double, and the Lord has given me double, and 140 over."

George Müller and the Bristol Orphan Houses. Mr. Müller has been having a similar experience, on a still larger scale, at Bristol, England, where he has established an immense asylum for orphans, which is sustained wholly by contributions. Mr. Müller's own account of his aim, in starting, states: "I remembered what a great blessing my own soul had received, through the Lord's dealings with his servant, A. H. Franke, who, in dependence upon the living God alone, established an immense orphan house, which I had seen many times with my own eyes. I, therefore, judged myself bound to be the servant of the Church of Christ in the particular point on which I had obtained mercy, namely: *in being able to take God by his word, and to rely upon it.* * * * Now, if I, a poor man, simply by prayer and faith, obtained, *without asking any individual*, the means for establishing and carrying on an orphan house, there would be something which, with the Lord's blessing, might be instrumental in strengthening the faith of the children of God, besides being a testimony to the consciences of the unconverted of the reality of the things of God. This, then, was the primary reason for establishing the orphan house. * * * The first and primary object of the work was, and still is, that God might be magnified by the fact that the orphans under my care are provided with all they need, only by *prayer and faith*, without any one being asked by me, or my fellow-laborers; whereby it may be seen that God is FAITHFUL STILL, and HEARS PRAYER STILL."

From Mr. Müller's Thirty-sixth Annual Report, which brings the account of the institution down to May 26, 1875, we learn that his faith was put to trial during the last year. This commenced with about $20,000 in the orphan-treasury; which sum, in the course of three months, was reduced one-half, or to only enough to meet the expenses of a single month. So low the treasury had not been for twelve years, although, in that time, the orphans had doubled in number! Yet, one month later, after that sum had been expended, such receipts had come in as to leave a balance of $48,000! Mr. Müller adds: "What cannot God do, in answer to believing, expecting prayer? Dear Christian reader, seek to rely upon God increasingly, and you will see how blessed it is to do so under all circumstances. I have walked, by God's grace, in this happy road for forty-five years and six months, out of the forty-nine years and eight months during which I have been a believer; and on these principles, 'Trust in the living God and prayer,' this institution has been carried on for forty-one years, during which time, without applying to any one, I have received, simply in answer to believing prayer, the sum of £665,000 ($3,325,000)." He then gives, as the results of the use of this money, the following: 46,400 persons taught in schools wholly sustained, besides tens of thousands in other schools assisted; 96,000 Bibles, above 247,000 Testaments, and 180,000 smaller portions of the Scriptures, circulated; above 53,500,000 tracts and books, in various languages, distributed; many missionaries, of late years over 170 annually, assisted; 4,677 orphans cared for; and five large houses built, at a cost of $575,000, able to accommodate 2,050 orphans. "As to the spiritual results," says Mr. M., "I will here say nothing; indeed, eternity alone can unfold them; yet, even in so far as God has been pleased to allow us to see already the results of our service, we have reaped most abundantly, and do so more and more, every year, whilst going on in the work."

THE CONSUMPTIVES' HOME. This is an institution at Boston, Mass., which was established by Charles Cullis, M. D., eleven years since, to provide a place for consumptives who were in poverty, and who, as incurable, were not admitted to the hospitals. He determined to follow Mr. Müller's plan, and solicit no aid from man, but build up an institution by prayer and faith alone. His tenth annual report, the latest published, at the time of writing this account, says: "During the past year the Lord has sent us in cash $22,262.48. For the ten years that the work has been established, without any solicitation from man, but in answer to prayer, God has sent the amount of $238,061.69. Also in answer to prayer, towards building the Cancer House, $4,269.54." The various annual reports are filled with interesting details from the diary of Dr. Cullis, showing how the gifts dropped in voluntarily from all parts of the land and the world, as the benevolent learned of the nature of the work, and how they came as they were needed, from day to day, in answer to prayer for the supply of specific wants.

THE CHICAGO FOUNDLINGS' HOME. This was established on the same principle, by George E. Shipman, M. D., whom the author has known from boyhood, in school, college and active life. In a pamphlet of great interest, which gives an account of the first four years of the Home, Dr. Shipman says of its origin: "Then as to the needful funds, where were they to come from? This was made equally clear. God gave me the work to do, and he would provide the means. It seemed to be his will, not only that a Home should be opened, but that it should be maintained in a manner that should demonstrate that he was the hearer of prayer, and that he was ever mindful of his promises. This would not be so apparent, if I depended upon begging, for the support of the home. * * * I have never asked anything for the Home, directly or indirectly, and have never authorized any one to solicit for it. Those who have given entertainments for the Home, of one kind or another, have done it of their own accord, and, in most instances, in fact, I did not know that they had been given till I received the money." Dr. Shipman's journal is filled with details of self-denying labor, of great straits, of earnest prayer, and of ultimate deliverance. The institution has now a large and convenient building, and during these four years, notwithstanding the great fire and the financial panic two years later, the Home has received $23,951.06 for current expenses, and $29,820.21 for the building; making a total of $53,771.27. At the close, Dr. Shipman says: "Can the candid reader peruse these pages, and deny the efficacy of prayer? Is there not evidence adduced sufficient to satisfy any one willing to be convinced? Repeated instances are given — and many more might have been furnished — when help has come just at a moment of need, known to none outside of the Home, but the Lord himself, who sent the supply. These have occurred too often to allow the supposition of an accidental concurrence of need and supply; if, indeed, there is any such thing as accident."

It would not be proper to dismiss the case of these Charitable Institutions without comment upon a theory which has sought to establish itself upon their experience. The theory is, that we ought not to solicit benefactions, to aid a religious or charitable cause; but should allow the work to make its silent appeal to men, while we utter its wants in the ear of God, and trust to his providence alone to send the supply. This is considered the true method of faith; and there is a disposition to claim for it a superiority over other methods, and even to demand that it should be adopted as the only really Christian method. On what possible ground of reason, or Scripture, is such a doctrine based? Let us see.

1. There would appear to be nothing in the reason of the case to warrant it. Solicitation is a natural act, in case of want. The poor solicit aid of the rich, the child of the parent, man of God. Why should there be less reason, or more harm, in soliciting for another, or for a cause which represents the wants of many, than for oneself? Moreover, if all should be influenced by love, and if it is really a privilege to share our blessings with the less favored, and especially with the suffering, then others may be said to have a moral claim on us to let them know of the necessities of the

poor. How are they to act, if left in ignorance of the facts? Can the benevolent do good, without knowing of the opportunity? Solicitation, rightly performed, is simply diffusing a knowledge of human need, and providing an opportunity for its supply. If it were not God's plan, to use men to bless men, that the benefactor might have a benefit as well as the beneficiary, there might be reason in the idea, that our appeal should be made only to God. But as he uses others to aid us, so he uses us to furnish them with the opportunity to do good. Why should not his Holy Spirit inspire an appeal to them, in behalf of his poor, or of his cause, as well as inspire their readiness to contribute needed aid? The mistaken theory puts singular limitations on the action of the Holy Spirit, as if he could move men to give, but not to solicit!

And if men are reluctant to perform the duty of giving, if they have never awaked to the privilege of using money for the promotion of the happiness and well being of others, we owe it to their souls, to cultivate in them the grace of liberality. And this is to be done by public and private instruction; by the presentment of motives; by personal example and influence; by an array of convincing and persuasive facts. Nothing could be a better means of grace to such souls, than to be solicited to take part in a work of beneficence, by those who will press the subject upon the conscience and heart on truly Christian grounds. To refuse to solicit from them, is to let them alone in their sin!

And how does reason sanction making a distinction between obtaining money for God's cause, and aiding it in other ways? What is there so peculiar in the nature and relations of money, that we must only pray for it, in behalf of a good object, but must never solicit it from those to whom God has, in his providence entrusted it; while in all other matters, no one thinks it right to pray, without also putting forth the appropriate effort? If we pray for the conversion of a man, we feel bound to labor for it, also, if that be possible. We consider it an inconsistency to neglect the action, and rely only on the prayer, in such a case. We tell the farmer to pray for a harvest, and to feel his dependence on God for it; but we likewise insist that he must use the legitimate means, and plough, and sow, and cultivate his land, expecting God's blessing to come in connection with these wise efforts. What authorizes us to take the matter of benefactions out from under the rule, that prayer and human effort must co-operate?

2. There would seem to be nothing in Scripture to uphold the theory in question. It bids us pray in faith; but it also tells us to labor in faith, and assures us, that "faith without works is dead." When Jesus needed an ass-colt on which to ride, as he came to Jerusalem, he sent two of his disciples to obtain it, charging them to say to the owners: "The Lord hath need of it." It is really performing the same deed, if, in this day we go to a man for five dollars, or ten dollars, or a hundred dollars, in behalf of a good object,

telling him, in like manner, "The Lord hath need of it!" When Paul wrote to the Galatians, of the way in which James, Cephas and John gave the right hand of fellowship to him and to Barnabas, when about to go on a mission to the Gentiles, he says: "Only they would that we should remember the poor; the same which I also was forward to do." That is, they requested Paul, to present the wants of the poor saints at Jerusalem to the Gentile churches, and to secure collections on their behalf; and he tells the Galatians that he was "forward to do" this work of solicitation. And from his appeals on the subject in his various epistles (Rom. xv: 26, 1 Cor. xvi: 1–3, 2 Cor. viii: 1–15, ix: 1–9) we learn how true this was. He considered himself the agent of the Jerusalem-poor, and earnestly pleaded their cause. Why should we fear to imitate the apostle, in behalf of the poor of our day?

3. There would seem to be nothing in the history of Christian beneficence, to support this theory of non-solicitation. It is true, that large institutions have been established by gifts voluntarily sent in; as we have seen in the case of the orphan-houses of Müller, the Consumptives' Home at Boston, and the Foundlings Home at Chicago. But then thousands of charitable institutions have also been established through Christian solicitation, in which good men have carried their object before God, in their closets, beseeching him to open men's hearts, and to prepare the way for the application that was to be made, and to aid them in pleading his cause against the prejudices and

the avarice of men. And these prayers were signally answered. God enabled them to speak for him and for his poor, and he led men to respond with unexpected and unwonted generosity to their appeals. They thus did a work of faith and prayer.

Moreover, it can hardly be claimed with accuracy, that the institutions so often referred to, as established and supported by prayer and faith only, were not indebted to *any* soliciting agency. There may be the thing without the name. It may be by printed statements, when there are no verbal appeals. One institution may send out an agent, to relate the story of its necessities and invite charitable people to contribute; and another may rely on an annual or monthly printed report, which tells of its work, its need and its receipts, and that it depends wholly upon what the charitable may be inclined to send to it. It is difficult to see the radical difference between the two methods; especially if, in the latter case, the friends of the institution solicit in its behalf, as individuals, among their acquaintances, and remit the amount collected. The sensible thing, on any plan, is, to get the facts clearly and fully before the benevolent, that there may be a chance for sympathy and for charitable aid. This is accomplished in both classes of institutions; and the delusion is a mild and harmless one, if one class supposes itself to be indebted *only* to prayer.

But do not the so-called faith-institutions teach us some important lessons? Yes; they impress, clearly, certain truths, which, though connected with other methods also, need to be specially emphasized. Their success shows the readiness of God to respond to prayer, and to put honor on faith. Straits often come for which human wisdom cannot provide, and then prayer brings divine aid. Effort is to be used, when possible; but if circumstance forbid it, the appeal may be made to God. Mr. Müller, Dr. Cullis, and others, feel that their whole time and strength are needed to conduct the internal affairs of their institutions; and that being so, God will provide the external help through the agency of others. Their success also demonstrates the needlessness of relying on any but Christian motives and instrumentalities, and is a proper protest against the use of dubious and evil methods of inducing men to contribute to charitable causes. A genuine work is its own best recommendation, and God will use the simple statement of the facts, to draw forth the needed pecuniary aid, without a recourse to motives of pride, ambition, ostentation, sectarian zeal, or other selfish principle. We may be thankful that an example has been set in favor of a gospel simplicity of method and motive, even if some distinctions are made without a difference.

My God! is any hour so sweet,
From blush of morn to evening star,
As that which calls me to my feet—
The hour of prayer?

Lord! till I reach that blissful shore,
No privilege so dear shall be,
As thus my inmost soul to pour
In prayer to Thee!

—*Charlotte Elliott.*

CHAPTER XX.

REVIEW OF THE FACTS—CONCLUSION.

THAT it may not be supposed that the author is ignorant of the objections that may be urged to such a collection of facts as has been presented, or that he fears to face them, he will here insert a letter received from a ministerial brother in answer to a circular note sent to him, among a number of others, asking for facts of interest which might illustrate the power of prayer.

"In all soberness, I want to suggest to you whether the very tenor of your circular-note to me, and the object you have in preparing your book on prayer, does not contain its own refutation. It appears that, although there are thousands close round about you who are praying every day, yet the answers are so scarce, that you have need to cover a great area to get your evidence. To make my meaning plain, the Bible says seed-time and harvest shall not fail. Suppose, now, that, in order to prove that seed-time and harvest do not fail, you found it necessary to write to intelligent farmers, all over the land, to get statements of here and there a successful harvest, while ten thousand farmers in the adjacent counties of Illinois were mourning short crops—subtantial failures. The twenty, or two hundred, or two thousand, rich harvests, gathered up from a continental area, would be no evidence that seed-time and harvest, as a general rule, do not fail. I am a little out, dear brother, with this prayer-controversy, on both sides. For, wherever I go, I find that the Christian world is always sticking that man, Müller, in my face, as a proof that God does answer prayer. Millions of saints praying, all over the world, and when I ask, 'Are your prayers answered?' they say, 'There's Müller, at Bristol; see how his prayers are answered!' My dear brother, in your church, and in my church, and in every church in the land, Christian women are praying for their sons and husbands, and their prayers are not answered. If you want to make your book perfectly fair, you ought, it seems to me, to take a given area, say three churches in Chicago, and get a statement: first, as to the total amount of praying; second, the total amount of failure; and, third, the total amount of answering."

Neither the inquiry made for illustrative facts, nor the object of this book, implies any scarcity of answers to true prayer. The author holds, on the contrary, that *all* true prayer is answered. But the ordinary use of prayer is so blended with every other part of the life and action of a Christian, while the answers are so varied in form, and received in a way so closely connected with human agency, that no one can draw the line between the influence of prayer and that of other instrumentalities. If one were required to define exactly what proportion of strength was due to respiration of pure air, in distinction from the effect of food and exercise, of light and warmth, it would puzzle him to answer, though he might have no doubt of the necessity of such respiration. It might help him, however, were certain striking cases presented, in which persons previously ailing had received decided and speedy benefit by changing from the atmosphere of a low, malarious district to that of a mountainous region. And so, while prayer is daily and hourly bringing ten thousand answers, as every spiritual Christian knows, it is not easy to distinguish, for the benefit of an unbeliever, its effect from the coincident influence of other temporal and spiritual causes. Yet, while this is the common rule of divine procedure, there occur partial exceptions, meeting peculiar exigencies in life, which are sufficiently numerous and striking, to indicate clearly a divine agency in response to human petition. These serve an important purpose in encouraging doubting saints, and in inducing thought in skeptics and scoffers.

The writer of the letter apparently falls (at least his objection does) into the same error with the skeptical physicists, exposed in the seventh chapter; in that he assumes that the answers to prayer are capable of being ascertained and tested in a tangible and mechanical way, as are the effects of physical forces. Otherwise, why should he suppose, or think that the author of this book supposes, that the vast proportion of the prayers offered are not answered? Why make the absurd suggestion of taking three churches, and ascertaining the number of prayers offered, and the proportion of the answered to the non-answered? Who could possibly number the petitions of the members of three churches? Who could tell how many of them complied with the spiritual conditions of success, so as to be true prayers, in the sense of the Biblical declarations and promises? Who could understand the forms in which God might see fit to send the answers? Prayer deals with subtle, spiritual forces, as to its moral conditions, and largely also as to its immediate and ultimate effects. And these cannot be seen and handled, weighed and measured, like the crops of a farmer. Hence the agricultural illustration need not stumble the thoughtful reader.

Indeed, it may be put to use on the other side. Let it be supposed that a new territory has been opened to settlement. An experienced scientific agriculturist states that abundant harvests can be secured by attention to deep ploughing, steady cultivation of the growing crops, and a proper system of irrigation. Soon a hundred thousand settlers have made their homes there, and begun to till their farms. At the end of the year, a complaint arises that no crops can be relied upon in that territory, and the scientific agriculturist is accused of making false statements. What does he, to disprove the charge? Finding that the mass of the immigrants have paid little or no attention to his carefully stated directions, and therefore have raised small crops, and in some cases have failed to secure any, he does not trouble himself to publish *their* experience; for it really has no bearing on the question. He sends to a hundred farmers, of whose diligence and care he has knowledge, and requests them to testify what *their* experience has been. They state that they followed with exactness the rules which he laid down — they ploughed the land as deeply as they could turn a furrow; they put in their choice seed; they kept down the weeds; they resorted to timely and abundant irrigation — and they secured rich harvests. Would the publication of such testimony be worthless? Could the alleged barrenness of the lands of other farmers avail as a contradiction, until it should first be proved as a fact, and should then be shown to have followed a faithful compliance with the directions originally given?

Now the truth is, that there are prayers and prayers. Multitudes "say a prayer," who yet do no praying. Many Christians and churches also pray so defectively, as to strength of desire, importunity, faith, consecration and other required conditions, that they do not come within the scope of the Scriptural promises. What is their experience worth then, in the matter before us? It should not be said that their prayers are not answered; but that they do not pray — in the Bible-sense. Yet their apparent failure fills their minds with doubt as to the real power of prayer. Skeptics, likewise, stumble over the seemingly vain petitions. Thus there comes to be a pervading unbelief on the subject, outside of the church, and a paralyzing uncertainty, inside of it. This grieves the Holy Spirit of God; this dishonors the name of Christ; this reflects upon the love and faithfulness of our Heavenly Father. The result is spiritual barrenness, as to character and influence. Worldliness prevails, backsliding is common, and revivals are few and feeble.

In such circumstances, it is well, to aid a weak faith, first by clearly defining the meaning and operation of prayer, and secondly by citing such marked instances of its value, as will illustrate its methods, and vindicate the fidelity of God to his promises. This has been the author's aim in these pages, and he must believe, that no one can read what has been here declared, without finding his faith quickened, and his closet made more attractive. It is not possible to transfer to print the daily experience of the man who lives by prayer, and receives perpetual answers amid life's multitudinous events. Another cannot see with his eyes, any more than to love and trust with his heart. But occasionally a crisis occurs; a particular want, or danger, or trial stands out with great distinctness, and human help is unavailing. Then an appeal is made to God, in the name of Christ, under the inspiration of the Holy Ghost, and in the use of the divinely appointed instrumentality of prayer. The relief comes so adequately, as to time and measure and means, that even a mere spectator can see that the hand of God is in it.

Daniel had prayed, for years, and yet his enemies were not convinced that there was any power in his supplications. God suffered them to put his prayers to the test in the den of lions; and there came such a signal deliverance that, "King Darius wrote unto all people, nations and languages, that dwelt in all the earth: Peace be multiplied unto you! I make a decree, that in every dominion of my kingdom men tremble and fear before the God of Daniel; for he is the living God, and steadfast forever, and his kingdom that which shall not be destroyed, and his dominion shall be even unto the end: he delivereth and rescueth, and he worketh signs and wonders in heaven and in earth, who hath delivered Daniel from the power of the lions."

It probably never occurred to any one, that to put this striking fact on record, was to imply that ordinarily prayer was not heard. It remained for a modern minister to fall into so strange a misinterpretation of a narrative of marked answers to prayer! Others, blessed with a better vision, behold the illustration of divine power and love, and the encouragement of human faith. To those who still imagine a multitude of seemingly unanswered prayers to be among the unaccountable phenomena, we commend the significant words of James: "Ye ask, and receive not, because ye ask amiss;" and the suggestive lines of one of the quaint and godly poets of the olden time:

Poor heart lament;
For since thy God refuseth still,
There is some rub, some discontent,
Which cools his will.

Thy Father *could*
Quickly effect, what thou dost move;
For he is *Power;* and sure he *would;*
For he is *Love.*

Go search this thing;
Humble thy breast, and turn thy book;
If thou hadst lost a glove or ring,
Wouldst thou not look?

What do I see
Written above there? *Yesterday,*
I did behave me carelessly,
When I did pray.

And should God's ear
To such indifferents chained be,
Who do not their own motions hear?
Is God less free?

But stay! what's there?
Late, when I would have something done,
I had a motion to forbear!
Yet I went on.

And should God's care,
Which needs not man, be tied to those
Who hear not him, but quickly hear
His utter foes?

Then once more pray:
Down with thy knees; up with thy voice;
Seek pardon first; and God, will say;
Glad heart rejoice!

—*George Herbert.*

THE END.

www.ingramcontent.com/pod-product-compliance
Lightning Source LLC
LaVergne TN
LVHW020100110826
845151LV00001B/34

* 9 7 8 1 4 2 5 5 4 4 7 6 8 *